Canadian history dull? Not the way Gordon Donaldson tells it. In this series of bright and lively biographies of Canada's prime ministers, he sheds new light on the lives of these unusual and unpredictable men. We see the leaders growing up in such different circumstances as the poverty of Mackenzie and the easy wealth of St. Laurent. We follow their public and private lives, discovering the personal tragedies that almost drove Sir John A. out of politics, the agony of Laurier, torn between his French-Canadian roots and his mission to unite Canada, and the bitter loathing that Mackenzie King and Meighen felt for each other.

This is a newly revised and expanded edition of *Fifteen Men,* first published in 1969 and updated in 1975. Now Pierre Trudeau's remarkable career, and equally remarkable comeback, is examined in full. And the short, unhappy reign of Joe Clark is dissected with humor and insight.

Here is Canadian history in its most readable and entertaining form, seen through the personalities of sixteen fascinating men and told with wry wit and an irreverent pen. It is the story of those "who built a nation in defiance of history, geography and climate" and whose country is always threatening to fall apart. This threat was as real in Macdonald's 1860s as it is in Trudeau's 1980s.

ALSO BY GORDON DONALDSON

*Niagara! The Eternal Circus*
*Battle for a Continent*

# Sixteen Men
## The Prime Ministers of Canada

## by Gordon Donaldson

Doubleday Canada Limited, Toronto, Ontario
Doubleday & Company, Inc., Garden City, New York
1980

Library of Congress Catalog Card Number 80-1805
ISBN 0-385-17267-2 (hardcover)
        0-385-17268-0 (paperback)

First edition of *Fifteen Men* published 1969
Second printing 1970
Third printing 1971
Fourth printing 1971
Fifth printing 1975
First printing of *Sixteen Men* 1980


Printed and bound in Canada by
T. H. Best Printing Company Limited

PHOTOGRAPH CREDITS

The photograph of Lester Pearson is courtesy Ashley
and Crippen. The photograph of Joe Clark is courtesy
the Canadian Press. All other photos are courtesy the
Public Archives of Canada.

*To*
Jeremy, Peter and Susan

# Contents

## Preface to *Sixteen Men*

This is a revised and extended version of *Fifteen Men,* which first appeared in 1969 and was updated in 1975. One prime minister, Joe Clark, has been added to the original total, although he was rapidly subtracted from the office.

The Americans have a different way of numbering their leaders. The current President (Carter) is the thirty-ninth, although only 38 men have held the job. That's because one, Grover Cleveland, left office but later returned with a new number. Hope springs eternal under the Canadian system, which does not limit the number of terms a prime minister can stay in power. Four of the 16 have been kicked out, then welcomed back in. So we stick to a simple body count.

And they don't *have* to be men. I'd be happy to write *Seventeen Persons.*

There is a temptation to dwell on recent events because one has lived through them, but I have tried to set the later prime ministers in the context of the whole story. It is obviously too soon to assess Pierre Trudeau's place in history and I do not believe Joe Clark can be written off as an asterisk to a footnote. I have tried to give them equal time with the leaders of the past.

This is a crucial period in the history of the prime ministership, sure. But, looking back, *all* periods have been crucial. The fascinating story goes on; the faces change, but the basic problems remain the same.

G.D.
May, 1980

# One Nation, Divisible

In the year that man landed on the moon, planted a national flag and began his colonization of infinity, his native world was breaking up into ever smaller political pieces.

Viewed from 240,000 miles away, the globe was the same shape as the schoolroom model — you could see Canada on it — but it was free of the red splotches that used to mark the British Empire, the green ones covering the U.S.A. and the U.S.S.R. and the yellow mass that was China. It was all bluish-green and silvery white. Yet it bubbled with more national and tribal emotions than ever.

The old empires were gone, leaving 126 independent and argumentative members of the United Nations. The post-war empires of the United States and the Soviet Union were disintegrating politically. China was alone once more; the Communist bloc in Eastern Europe was no longer solid; and the various regional cadet corps organized by the United States under the banner of One Big Bomb were marching to different drummers. In the Americas, practically every nation not frozen in the grip of a dictatorship was being torn by internal strife. In the United States, riots were giving way to guerilla action as militant blacks fought against the whites, and young anarchists sabotaged the system.

In Canada, the ill-fitting jigsaw pieces that linked the half-continent were coming loose. Tribalism was rampant in French Canada, regional self-interest in the rest. Piece by piece, the nation's assets were being sold to the Americans.

Canadians had always been too embarrassed to chant slogans such as "One Nation, Under God, Indivisible" because they always knew that their nation was extremely divisible. And, as Pierre Trudeau pointed out, there was no God-made law that said any country had to hold together. The two basic threats to Canada's unity, and therefore to its very existence, had been present since Confederation — the racial and religious differences between Quebec and the other provinces, and the possibility of a takeover by the United States. There have always been some Canadians who asked not only "*can* Canada exist?" but "why should it?" There have always been some, and there are plenty today, who would welcome complete economic union with the United States, with all its political consequences.

Canada did develop into and remain an independent *political* unit because Canadians were more fortunate than many in their leaders, their prime ministers. There were poor prime ministers and stupid prime ministers, but not one of them was venal or mad; which is a good record for sixteen men raised through conceit, ambition or force of circumstance into an office that transcended their normal fields of competence. They shaped Canada to a much greater extent than most U.S. Presidents shaped America or than British Prime Ministers shaped the United Kingdom. In Canada they had so much more and rawer material to shape.

Sir John A. Macdonald was a giant in the guise of a tippling old procrastinator, Mackenzie King a muddler of almost supernatural skill, Laurier a noble figure and Borden a noble man. The rest, even the minor ones like the terrible Sir Mackenzie Bowell, illuminated either the path ahead or the path back; both views were needed. At any stage one completely irresponsible demagogue could have wrecked Confederation; but none reached the office of Prime Minister.

On the other hand, neither the three French nor the thirteen English-speaking prime ministers seriously tried to settle the French-English problem. Each bore that burden, manfully or otherwise, preparing to hand it over to his successor intact, and a little heavier than before. And once independence from Britain had been achieved, the later prime ministers connived at the new state of economic dependence upon the United States. None was prepared to buy back economic sovereignty. As Lester Pearson said, this would cost a reduction of twenty-five to thirty percent in Canada's standard of living, and he didn't think many Canadians would or should pay that price.

Once the tremendous task of creating a nation from sea to sea was accomplished, very little was done towards expanding northward towards Canada's third sea — the Arctic Ocean. John Diefenbaker had a vision about that but nothing much happened, and Canadian sovereignty in the far north is now being challenged because there are so few Canadians there.

These failures are condoned by the voters who, by and large, don't want to aggravate the problem of race and blood by drawing attention to it, who won't relinquish their near-American standard of living, and who don't want to live in the Arctic because it's cold.

But a leader's function is not to follow. Because King, the most skilled of prime ministers, led without appearing to do so and once said that his greatest contribution lay in avoiding unwise decisions, his less able successors have sometimes taken his precepts as an excuse for dodging both leadership and decision. In doing so, they abdicate the responsibility painfully won for them and their nation by the great prime ministers of the past. The leader may moonlight as teacher, preacher, visionary, advocate or back-slapper, but his real job is to steer the country, with the wind where possible, against it if necessary.

Canadians are not given to hero-worship, least of all the worship of Canadian heroes. This deprives them of some of the trappings of national identity and gives the totally false impression that Canadian history is dull. This book is not an attempt to set up graven images, but to survey the adventures of the fifteen lively men who built a nation in defiance of history, geography and climate.

When the Canadian federation was launched there was grave doubt that it would last. That doubt persists. But the rest of the world, so solid and secure in 1867, is now even less certain of its continued existence than is Canada.

Canada's relative position has improved enormously. It is not a super-power. If its people have loud self-doubts, they are happily free of insufferable conceit or the awful bloodthirsty certainty of crusading zeal. They and their leaders try to offer to the world the uninspiring but invaluable gift of common sense.

Often they fail, but sometimes they succeed.

**MACDONALD**

1867-73
1878-91

# I. *Young Tomorrow*

The cowcatcher stuck out in front of the train, sweeping the newly-laid track as the iron engine clawed and clattered its way through Craigellachie. Just above it, clutching a narrow rail beneath the smokestack, sat an old man and his wife, sensibly bundled up against the tearing winds of the mountain passes. The ties skimmed below them and the freshly-scarred rock face sliced past, shimmering pink, green and purple. Never before had they seen such sights. Never before had they been west of Ontario.

At 71, Sir John Alexander Macdonald, first Prime Minister of Canada was rumbling forth with his lady to view the nation which he, more than any other, had sewn and patched together from a jumble of inappropriate pieces. His leg ached from sciatica and his big whiskey-veined nose glowed with the promise of troubles to come. But John A. had survived his winter illness and recovered the jaunty air with which (in public at least) he faced good times and bad. This was a good time — July, 1886, a month after the first Canadian transcontinental train had clumped from Montreal to Port Moody, British Columbia. Eight months before, the last spike had been hammered home at the spot called Craigellachie in Eagle Pass, British Columbia to complete the railway that had cost Macdonald much of his strength, one government, and much of his reputation. The CPR had gone broke so often that neither his friends nor his foes expected him to live to see it built. His friends pictured him smiling down from Heaven on the finished job; the others said if the day ever came he would be grimacing up from below. John A. announced happily: "I am taking the horizontal view."

And there he was on the cowcatcher, a still-raffish figure, the epitome of Canadian style in late-Victorian politics, taking the kind of dangerous, romantic ride that future charmers like Robert Kennedy and Pierre Trudeau would essay. Hurtling down the Fraser canyon near Yale, British Columbia, the cowcatcher struck a pig and threw it up within inches of Macdonald and his stately wife, Agnes — a narrow escape.

Few men have seen their life's work spread out before them as he did on that tremendous train journey. He had bullied Nova Scotia, bribed British Columbia, snatched the Prairies, beaten back the ever-rapacious Americans and created an office different from anything previously seen within the British Empire or without — the Prime Ministership of Canada. Every succeeding prime minister has to be matched against John A. and only a few stand the comparison. His creation had great faults and so did he. He left to his successors the vast problem of achieving a balance between the demands of French-Canadians and the rest — a problem poisoned and inflamed by the one notably vindictive act of his career, the hanging of rebel Louis Riel. None has managed to solve it. Several of them have been *better* men than Macdonald, none has been greater.

He accepted human frailty. Indeed he worked as a master

craftsman in manipulating it. He recognized his own, and laughed. Although born in Glasgow, he had Highland parents. He was a Celt, thin, gangling, crowned by curly black hair. Within him passions flashed and flamed and died, rather than smouldering with the awful righteousness of the Lowlander. It is necessary to distinguish between the two basic types of Scot, because throughout Macdonald's career Scots dominated the politics of Upper Canada.

He retained as his Scottish birthright a healthy distrust of the English — particularly the chinless aristocrats who ran the North American colonies before the colonies achieved a measure of popular representation and responsible government. There was, he declared, no place in the government of Canada for "overwashed Englishmen, utterly ignorant of the country and full of crotchets as all Englishmen are."

Even when full of years and honors, Macdonald never looked overwashed. He carried a gay, disreputable air about him, a breath of smoky back rooms and a sniff of whiskey. He needed earthy politics as an antidote to the loneliness of leadership and the torments of his tragic private life.

His first wife was constantly, desperately ill. For a dozen years he watched her dying. His first son died a baby and to the end of his days Macdonald kept a box of the child's toys. His daughter was born retarded. Late in life, the Prime Minister would go home from the Commons to read fairy-tales to her, although she was a grown woman. At times his grief drove him to the bottle. At other times he just happened to be there, arm on the saloon bar, eyes twinkling and big nose blazing, entertaining his cronies with coarse jokes and fine-cut political jibes. The public, he said correctly, preferred John A. drunk to his enemies sober. Yet he was not a man of the people. He was a townsman, a sophisticated lawyer, at a time when "the people" were farmers. If John Diefenbaker, the prairie visionary who tried so hard to identify with Macdonald, had lived in the same times he would have been much closer to his beloved average Canadian. In 1958 when he finally set the country afire, the average Canadian lived in cities or the split-level sprawl around them.

When the Macdonalds emigrated from Glasgow to Kingston, Ontario in 1820, that city was the size of a modern village. But it fancied itself as a center of trade and culture and it was to become for a time the seat of government of the Canadas. It was a well-established Scottish community, close, clannish and canny. The Scots tribal password: "We're all Jock Tamson's bairns" applied. This meant each Scot would help the other up to a certain point — at which he either stood on his own feet or got out from under foot. So father Hugh Macdonald got a warm welcome from his clansmen who had left Scotland before him. But they didn't buy enough to keep his general store going. Within four years he was bankrupt. Another store and a grist mill failed and he had to take a job as a clerk in the Commercial Bank.

Managing money was never to become a Macdonald family talent. While smiling Scots bankers with hearts of flint were multiplying across the land, John A., even in the robes of a Privy Councillor, was to feel the hot breath of creditors on his neck.

"I had no boyhood," he wrote later. "From the age of fifteen I had to earn my own living." True — his brother James died and he had to help support the family. But he enjoyed himself. He took early to the taverns. He laughed too much for a lad just articled to a dusty law firm. There was nothing in his awkward figure to indicate ambition, drive or dreams. He read a lot — but he wore foppish suits and outrageous waistcoats, like another young man called Benjamin Disraeli beginning his career in London about the same time.

Fancy waistcoats on a young swinger did not sit well with the solid burghers of Kingston. Young John was permitted to perform small chores for the Tory party. His pub experience was useful, since votes were bought with whiskey, but he was not considered likely to go far. Tales were told of his first trip to the United States when he played the concertina and collected pennies while a companion danced, dressed up as a bear. At twenty-one, he took cursory law examinations in Toronto and became a barrister-at-law. A cloth robe, later to be replaced by the silk of a Queen's Counsel, draped the angular shoulders, and a new white wig perched on the unruly hair. A year later, in 1837, he took up a musket to repel William Lyon Mackenzie's revolutionaries.

Mackenzie had mobilized a ragged troop of farmers on the outskirts of Toronto to overthrow the "Family Compact" which ruled Upper Canada. The Kingston Scots had no time for the Anglican snobs in Toronto. But the town was loyal to the Crown in a way that only a town threatened by repeated Yankee raids from across Lake Ontario could be. The Crown kept the Americans out and subdued the raging papists in Lower Canada a few miles to the north-east. Kingston was not ripe for revolution.

Macdonald never had to fire his musket as the Mackenzie rebellion collapsed after a skirmish on Yonge Street, but the Kingston people began to realize that he might be more than a shallow roisterer. Soon he was leading the St. Andrew's Society, marching in his kilt behind the pipes and drums.

His career at his new Bar began with two spectacular cases. In both he defended the most unpopular causes imaginable; yet the Kingstonians respected him for it.

First he took on the imposing Colonel Dundas, commandant of Fort Henry. He represented the fort's jailer, John Ashley, who had been arrested and accused by the commandant of helping fifteen prisoners to escape. Ashley sued Dundas for wrongful arrest. Despite public outcry over the escape, Macdonald persuaded a jury to award the wronged jailer £200 in damages.

Then he undertook to advise, in a military court, the most despised of all underdogs, captured American invaders. They had been caught, with their weapons, after an abortive border raid near Prescott in which sixteen Canadian militiamen died and one Canadian body was mutilated. John A. represented their leader, the Polish aristocrat Nils Szoltecky von Schoultz.

The handsome raider's guilt was plain and he refused to beg for mercy. His lawyer could only stand by him, refuse his fee and escort him to the gallows. Their brief meeting did Macdonald more good than von Schoultz, for it impressed upon him forever the determination of land-hungry Americans to swallow the rest of the continent. Six raids like von Schoultz's were launched during 1838 by the Hunters' Lodges and Patriot societies of the border States. Hundreds of Americans and Canadian refugees from the 1837 rebellions were openly recruited and drilled on U.S. soil for the purpose of invading Canada. Although the government in Washington tried to avoid unfriendly acts, the raiders had the sympathy, if not the active support, of state militia units along the border. American courts refused to convict them for breaking neutrality laws.

A poem published in the Cobourg *Star*, February, 1838, gives a Canadian Tory view of the American attitude:

> Neutrality it was their law,
> But that they never minded,
> They sympathized with rebels so
> It quite their reason blinded.

> Their papers, too, were filled with stuff
> With nonsense and with lies;
> So fast they told them that you'd think
> They lied but for some prize.

This "stuff and nonsense" built up into the doctrine, first spelled out in 1845, that it was the "manifest destiny" of the American republic to occupy the entire continent "for the free development of (its) yearly multiplying millions."

Canada could lay no claim to multiplying millions — even at Confederation it could muster fewer than four. And young John A. had no dreams of expansion. In 1840, Upper and Lower Canada (soon to become Ontario and Quebec) set up a joint legislative assembly. For years Macdonald opposed even the extension of this union to include the Maritime provinces. His realization that the nation must stretch from coast to coast if it were to survive came much later. When he entered the joint parliament in 1843, he simply wanted to preserve the Canada he knew — the Kingston clansmen, the Toronto snobs, the St. Andrew's Society and the Orange Lodge. If it took an alliance with the French-Canadians to accomplish this, good and well. He was a conservative, but a moderate.

Politics in the mid-nineteenth century was a mess of short-lived coalitions that tried to bridge the gap between French and English, Catholic and Protestant, bigot and bigot. There were High Tories, remnants of the Family Compact; Clear Grits, self-righteous and anti-Catholic; and Robert Baldwin Reformers, a moderate type of liberal. French-Canada provided the Parti Rouge, radicals who dallied with the Grits, and the Parti Bleu, the conservatives led by Georges Etienne Cartier.

Macdonald recognized that only a moderate coalition with fuzzy middle-of-the-road views could hope to govern. It must blur over sharp differences and cool passions. And it must have a strong Quebec wing with an identifiable French-Canadian leader. Compromise must be its battle-cry and vagueness its creed. So he put together his Liberal-Conservative party and set the pattern for all successful leaders of Canada. Cartier would manage Quebec for him, but as a partner not an underling.

All this took years. Macdonald was to be called "Old Tomorrow." He did not jump into the Tory leadership; he drifted along casually with the moderate mainstream until more and more Tories jumped in to follow him. He was a good administrator — as Receiver and, later, as Attorney-General for Canada West (Ontario). He was honest by the political standards of the times. He bought votes, but votes did not buy him. He displayed no burning ambition. For much of the time his mind was not on his job or his future.

It was at home, at the bedside of his first wife, Isabella. She had been a gay Highland girl when he met her on a trip to Scotland. Brought to Canada she drooped and lived in pain for most of their thirteen years of marriage. With terrible effort, she produced two sons — John Alexander and Hugh John. John Alexander died just after his first birthday, leaving a hollowness in his parents' hearts that was never filled. Macdonald disappeared from his office and law-practice for months at a time, moving Isabella from one health resort to another until she died in 1856.

His drinking bouts became famous, thanks largely to editorial comments in the Toronto *Globe*, which was edited by his great enemy George Brown. Brown was a red-haired, lantern-jawed Lowland Scot — six feet four of backbone and Presbyterian prejudice. He lead the Clear Grits (who described themselves as "all sand and no dirt, clear grit all the way through"). He saw the need for Confederation long before Macdonald. But he lacked patience. "The great reason why I have always been able to beat Brown," Old Tomorrow wrote, "is that I have been able to look a little ahead while he could on no occasion forego the temptation of a temporary triumph." There was another reason. Brown, the militant anti-papist, could never handle French-Canadians.

Macdonald revealed his attitude toward them in a letter to a Montreal journalist, written in 1856. "No man in his senses," he wrote, "can suppose that this country can for a century to come be governed by a totally unfrenchified government. If a Lower Canadian British desires to conquer he must 'stoop to conquer.' He must make friends with the French without sacrificing the status of his race or language, he must respect their nationality. Treat them as a faction and they become factious. Treat them as a nation and they will act as a free people generally do — generously."

For views like this and for sticking by his Quebec ally Cartier, Macdonald was cursed in Ontario as a traitor to his race and religion. The same abuse would be heaped upon every subsequent prime minister, French- or English-speaking, who tried to maintain a more or less equal partnership with the other side. Those not called traitors were to be judged failures.

By 1864 the move toward a wider Canadian partnership had begun. Below the border "manifest destiny" was on the rampage. There was no longer any doubt that the North would win the Civil War, and once that was done its enormous military machine would be available for other tasks. Battle-hardened and confident, the Grand Army of the Republic could roll over Canada in a few weeks. Angry Northern newspapers demanded it do so.

The Yankees were furious at Britain for her tacit support of the South, for her fumbled attempts at mediation and for the launching of Confederate raiding ships like the *Alabama* from British yards. There had been a war scare four years earlier when a U.S. warship stopped a British mail steamer at sea and seized two Confederate envoys. Britain rushed 14,000 troops to Canada and 40,000 members of the Canadian Sedentary Militia grabbed shotguns and pitchforks to defend their colony. Nothing happened, because Lincoln's Grand Army was busy in the South. But by 1864 the story was different. No sedentary farmers could save British North America and Britain did not seem disposed to try. The British government was eager to propitiate Washington at the expense of Canada or anyone else.

The dreary partisan wrangling in the Canadian Assembly over how, if, or in what order a federal union of the provinces could be achieved ended with a generous gesture by George Brown. Macdonald's Conservative government had been defeated in the House. The Governor, Lord Monck, had given permission for the dissolution of the Assembly. Brown, as Grit leader, was handed another "temporary triumph." He didn't take it. Rising to his full stature, political and physical, he told the House he would negotiate with John A. about forming a coalition government.

It was a joyous moment. The snarling pack of parliamentarians had been through two general elections and seen three governments fall in the past two years. They couldn't face the thought of returning once again to their bored constituents.

A member described seeing "an excitable elderly little French member rush across the floor, climb up on Mr. Brown . . . fling his arms about his neck and hang several seconds there suspended to the visible consternation of Mr. Brown and to the infinite joy of all beholders."

The big dour Lowlander joined a new government under the titular leadership of Sir Etienne Taché, sitting down beside John A., the man he had called a drunkard and a scoundrel. The Fathers of Confederation were assembling.

Rapidly they agreed to try to unite all the Eastern provinces in one federation. Letters were sent to Nova Scotia, New Brunswick and Prince Edward Island suggesting a conference. The approach was low-keyed and indirect. The Maritimers were staging a meeting of their own to discuss union of their three units. The Canadas merely asked if they might attend.

So began in Charlottetown, P.E.I. in September, 1864, the movable feast of the Fathers. It perambulated rummily onward to Halifax, Quebec City, Montreal, Ottawa, Toronto, Hamilton, and ended, like a blown-out windstorm, in St. Catharines.

It began in comedy. Only one man in a rowboat came to greet the steamer *Queen Victoria* as she sailed into Charlottetown bearing Macdonald, Cartier, Brown, and the hopes of Canadian nationhood. The emissaries from Nova Scotia and New Brunswick were asleep or drunk and the Prince Edward Islanders were in a state of high excitement — not over the conference, but because a real circus had come to town, the first in 21 years. So the hotels were full up and the Canadians had to stay on their ship. But the meeting was a success. It was soon obvious that Maritime union was getting nowhere and the delegates listened to the notion of a bigger federation. By the time they had soused and gobbled their way through the banqueting halls of Charlottetown and Halifax, Confederation was woozily on its way.

At Quebec, the heady ideals had to be distilled into a Constitution. Here John A. established his true claim to be father of the country. The Quebec Resolutions, the basis of the British North America Act, were largely his work, drafted in his devious mind and scratched out in his handwriting. He was a late convert to federalism but truer than many born to the faith. Not ideals, but practical necessity, brought him to it. He had tried to govern within the existing system and failed. So the system must be changed because, by this time, Macdonald knew he *had* to govern. That remarkable brain, which could weigh its own faults and virtues along with those of his contemporaries, told him so. It now seems that it was right.

The Constitution of the United States is revered by every American schoolboy, who salutes it, hand on heart, each weekday, and praised by politicians and thinkers (whether they agree with it or not) as a marvel of the Western world. The greatest military force the world has seen stands ready to defend it to the death and the U.S. Supreme Court labors daily to determine exactly what it means.

No such honors are accorded the constitution of Canada as worked out by John A., presumably in his sober moments. Yet it, too, is a powerful document.

It created a federal system suitable for governing a vast continent, only a tiny fraction of which was populated or even controlled at the time. (The same conditions applied in the United States 90 years earlier when its constitution was written.) Macdonald strove for a British nation which would have room in it for a proud and, he hoped, contented French minority. He would set no melting pots aboiling; that way disaster lay. He and most of his friends and foes at Quebec used the American way as a prime example of how not to do things.

There was no written British constitution to work from, only a set of ideas applicable to the government of a small island where every subject knew his place and had been in it for umpteen generations. It came supplied with an ancient aristocracy which served a purpose, in the House of Lords, by overseeing the work of the people's elected representatives.

Canada, too, would have an Upper House, filled with senators appointed for life. Since native Canadian aristocrats were in short supply, loyal old party men would do. Thus the Senate was an anachronism from the day it began because the Senators were anachronisms — politicians who had outlived their usefulness in day-to-day affairs. It had and still has a political wisdom of its own. It accurately reflects the thinking of the period ten or fifteen years ago when the bulk of its members were appointed.

The American system of choosing a President every four years and a Congress every two was considered barbaric. Parliament should be free to respond to the will of the people, as interpreted by their elected members, to overturn governments and require elections to be called when needed — though, please God, not too often. The Americans might need a chieftain assured of four years in office to maintain the continuity of their system — which at that moment was being butchered by the Civil War. But Canada had the Queen and was blessed by the ultimate authority of the Mother of Parliaments at Westminster.

Under the U.S. Constitution, the federal government took certain powers and left the rest to the states. Canada's federal government gave certain powers to the provinces and kept everything else. It retained the right to overrule provincial legislation. Ottawa, in theory, is a much stronger central government that Washington. Yet Washington has repeatedly sent troops to enforce its laws in "sovereign" southern states while the government of Canada hardly dares to complain when the provincial authority in Quebec usurps its most precious, hard-won right — that of dealing with foreign countries.

In the late fall of 1864, the last of seventy-two Quebec City resolutions was passed and the Fathers of Confederation junketed by special train through southern Ontario. Vast were the meals and mighty the flagons consumed, but the Fathers had earned the right to sleep through each other's speeches.

They sailed for London the following spring. Macdonald

and Brown played euchre on the ship's deck, first as a grim contest, then as a cheerful game. By the time they reached England they were enjoying each other's company, though not, of course, admitting it. They were presented to the Queen. And they went to the Derby in their toppers and tails with eight other Canadians, lunch baskets from Fortnum and Mason and several dozen bottles of champagne. One of the party, Alexander Tilloch Galt, described the carriage ride back to London — the Fathers, armed with peashooters standing on their seats to fire at the crowds along the road. Brown, he said, became a good shot.

Negotiations for British approval of Confederation went smoothly. Britain was waking up to the value of what Disraeli had once called " those wretched colonies." There was money to be made in the empty lands that had fallen almost haphazardly under the Union Jack. If they were not given a more workable form of government, the Americans would seize them. The mighty days of Empire were beginning.

Back in Canada, Confederation ran into trouble. Joseph Howe, the great Nova Scotian who had dreamed of a nation from sea to sea when Macdonald still confined his thoughts to Kingston, turned against his own concept because he felt left out of things. Macdonald's ally, Dr. Charles Tupper, was getting the glory as Confederation's man in Nova Scotia. "If you had a circus," Howe grumbled, "how would you like it if that fellow Tupper stood by the door and collected the shillings?"

Confederation's man in New Brunswick, Premier Lemuel Tilley, was routed at the polls. The Prince Edward Islanders turned insular once more. And as the parliamentarians in Quebec City prepared to move to Ottawa, the chosen capital of a federated British North America, it seemed unlikely that such a capital would ever be required. George Brown rescinded his noble gesture, quit the Cabinet and resumed his feud with Macdonald. The euchre games and peashooters were forgotten. They did not speak to each other again.

Hope for Confederation faded. But help was on the way. Enter the Fenians, a crank conspiracy of moonstruck Irishmen. Their aim was to liberate Ireland from the English, and the leader of the American branch, John O'Mahoney, was directed that this could best be done by annexing Canada and turning it into an anti-British base. He was directed by the long-dead Celtic kings and heroes who gave him orders in visions. Arms were acquired from the disbanding Union armies and cached along the border. The Fenians didn't anticipate much of a fight. A blast of trumpets and the sound of marching feet would bring the oppressed Canadians rushing to their standard, shouting death to the British tyrant. This was still the popular view in much of the northern United States. You didn't have to be a romantic Irish crackpot to believe it; it just happened that the Fenians *were* romantic Irish crackpots.

They planned their invasion with lunatic care. Fenian warships were to guard Lakes Huron, Erie and Ontario while land forces moved from the Niagara peninsula down to Toronto and on to Montreal. Meanwhile, a west coast fleet would take Vancouver Island so that "New Ireland" — the name under which the new republic would be recognized by the United States — would stretch from sea to sea.

There was danger behind all this blarney. The U.S. authorities were doing nothing to stop the Fenians and some officials were helping them to get guns. Irish sentimentalists lavished money on them.

And so, on June 1, 1866, sure and begorra, the villagers of Fort Erie awoke to find armed men in their streets, waving a green and gold flag. They had crossed the Niagara River in two rented tugs and two barges. Now, their leader "General" John O'Neill informed the populace, they were open to Canadian recruits. None stepped forward. O'Neill was bewildered. He seems to have stayed in that condition for the two days his invasion lasted. Thanks to the incredible incompetence of the Canadian commanders sent to deal with him, he scored two victories, killing nine Canadian militiamen and capturing about sixty, to the cheers of the American spectators lining the U.S. bank of the river.

When he finally realized the Canadians were not ripe for revolt — thousands were pouring down the peninsula screaming for his blood — he fled with his Fenians across the river.

There were to be other Fenian raids, but none outraged Canadians like the Niagara happening. The provinces were humiliated. Their troops couldn't handle a handful of Irish comics in hired boats. Anti-Americanism flared to new heights. Nova Scotia and New Brunswick swung back to Confederation.

Next spring, a bored British Parliament passed the British North America Act and July 1, 1867 was set as the birthday of the new nation. There was no doubt who would lead it. The times had produced the man, and if some called John A. a rascal, well, they were rascally times.

Ottawa, the rough little lumber town, awoke promptly at midnight July 1 to begin its day of glory. A 101-gun salute shattered sleep. When the sun rose, the skies were a brilliant blue from Ontario to the Maritimes and in every town the burghers turned out in their best boots to cheer the parades and hear the reading of the Queen's Proclamation that told them they were now a nation.

Macdonald was sworn in as Prime Minister and proclaimed Knight Commander of the Bath — Sir John A. Five of his Cabinet were given the inferior title of Companion of the Bath and two of them, Cartier and Galt, were so annoyed they refused the honor. (Later they were soothed with baronetcies, putting them a rung higher than Macdonald, a mere knight.)

It is said of the modern American Presidency that the office expands and ennobles the man. Often it does. Sir John A.'s duty was to expand and ennoble the office of Prime Minister. It was a fragile thing, dependent upon shifting alliances, and the flattering and bribing of local chieftains. It needed armor more than a knighthood. It had to expand to survive. So did the new Dominion of Canada.

## II. *Old Tomorrow*

The Prime Minister and his new second wife made an imposing couple at the ceremonial opening of the first federal Parliament in November, 1867. Macdonald was 52, slim and debonair, with his comb of black curls piled atop his long humorous face, and his chest splashed with the scarlet band and star of the Garter. Agnes was in her early thirties, tall and stately, dark with large calm eyes. She worshipped him with a devotion that worried her because it was so complete it might be sinful. She mothered him and prayed over him. She gave up wine to set him an example. After the sorrows of his first marriage and nine years as a widower, Macdonald was to have two years of pleasant home life before the next tragedy struck. Agnes wrote in her diary, "Oftentimes he comes in with a very moody brow, tired and oppressed, his voice weak, his step slow; and ten minutes after he is making very clever jokes and laughing like any schoolboy, with his hands in his pockets and his head thrown back. . . . I tell him his good heart and amiable temper are the great secrets of his success."

This was a period of success. He had easily won the first national election in the late summer of 1867. His enemy George Brown was defeated at the polls and was never to run for office again. He was to torment the Tories from the security of his editorial chair at the *Globe*. Even that was not secure forever; thirteen years later he was murdered by a striking printer in the *Globe* office.

The Liberal opposition in the House was left leaderless by Brown's departure and for a time Macdonald's prestige was unchallengeable. He viewed the future with sardonic optimism. "By the exercise of common sense and a limited amount of that patriotism which goes by the name of self-interest," he wrote, "I have no doubt that the union will be for the common weal."

He spent much of his first year trying to arouse that patriotic self-interest in Joseph Howe who, with a band of fellow Nova Scotian members, had come to Ottawa bent on smashing the union. Finally, Nova Scotia was pacified and Howe hoisted into the Macdonald Cabinet. But while the Prime Minister was engaged in the east, he failed to see the growing threat from the vacuum of the northwest. He had never thought much of that wilderness. Although he was determined to keep it out of the hands of the Americans, he would have been content to let it remain a no-man's land. As late as 1865 he had written: "The country is of no present value to Canada."

It was not the Prime Minister, but William McDougall, one of Brown's Clear Grits, who set in motion an Address to the Queen requesting for Canada the enormous territory known as Rupert's Land that had been chartered to the Hudson's Bay Company since 1670. The U.S. was ready to pay $10,000,000 for it. But after two years' haggling Canada got the region for £300,000. With it came most of the present-day Northwest Territories. Macdonald suddenly woke up to the fact that he was absentee landlord of a third of the continent. "We have quietly and almost without observation annexed all the country between here and the Rocky Mountains," he wrote. This wasn't quite true. The goods had been bought, but they could not be delivered. Canadians would have to go and pick them up.

There was no government in the area, outside the 120 Hudson's Bay Company posts. The only force nearby was the U.S. Army, then busily fighting the Sioux Indians. Canada would have to colonize it — the new Dominion's first venture into imperialism. William McDougall, soon to be known as "Wandering Willie," was appointed Lieutenant-Governor of the huge territories. In the fall of 1869 he set forth, bearing a very small Union Jack, and expecting to be received with the deference due to his rank and pompous manner.

He travelled through the United States to St. Cloud, Minnesota, then northwest to Pembina, the border post leading to the Red River colony that was the heart of his new domain. At the American customs house, a *métis* (a half-breed Indian) handed him a note addressed to *Monsieur* McDougall. It ordered him, in the name of the Comité National des Métis, to stay out of the Northwest. Signed: John Bruce, President; Louis Riel, Secretary.

McDougall snorted and pressed forward with his aide, Captain D. R. Cameron, his councillors, his children, his servants and sixty wagon-loads of baggage. Two miles further north, he met a road block guarded by a group of armed *métis*. Captain Cameron reared up, adjusted his monocle and commanded: "Remove that blasted fence!"

The *métis* quietly turned the lead horses around and escorted the party back to the border. "Wandering Willie" took lodgings in a log cabin in Pembina. Winter set in.

The 11,500 *métis* of Red River were part Indian, part French-Canadian, part Scots and all Roman Catholic. They had their Church, their small farms and little else. In mid-1869 they learned they were to be sold like chickens to alien Protestant easterners. When the easterners sent surveyors in to measure their land, they feared they would lose everything.

So they seized control of the colony, formed a provisional
government, and began drawing up their own terms for union
with Canada.

Louis Riel, their leader, was 24 when he first stamped his
foot on a Canadian surveyor's measuring chain and ordered
him off the land. He was darkly handsome, and clever, if
unstable. As a half-breed, he could only find work as a carter.
Later he was to become a half-mad messiah, but when he set
up his first provisional government he behaved quite moder-
ately. He considered himself to be a loyal subject of the Queen,
just as entitled as Macdonald to rule an area where there had
been no rule. He had no red riband on his chest but he wore a
boiled white shirt, tail coat and striped trousers above his
moccasins when he turned back the new governor at the border. It was still October. Canada was not due to take over the
territory until December, so "Wandering Willie," despite his
little flag and his retinue, had no more rights than a private
citizen.

Had Macdonald ever met Riel and weighed and measured
him as a man instead of as a wretch trussed for the gallows, he
might have recognized a worthy opponent and soothed and
won him over as he did Howe. But no. The Prime Minister
saw only a "miserable half-breed" who had to be put down.
Here he reflected the feelings of the Victorian Scots and English in Ottawa. But that does not excuse his handling of the
northwestern situation. He often showed lack of vision but
rarely political stupidity.

McDougall, brooding in his cabin in twenty below weather,
made a last ludicrous attempt to exert his supposed authority.
His calendar told him it was December. He was now officially
the Queen's representative in the Northwest. As he didn't have
this spelled out in writing, he forged a royal proclamation and
a royal commission, and sneaked back two miles across the
border to read it. Darkness had fallen and a blizzard was raging. There were no *métis* out to stop his sleigh. His party of six
gathered in a shivering circle. McDougall pulled out his little

flag and read his parchment proclamation by lantern light. Then he got into his sleigh and slid silently back into the United States. He could now inform Ottawa that he was the established governor and Riel's men were in a state of rebellion. Not until December 6 did he learn that Macdonald had postponed the transfer of the territory to Canada until it could be handed over in a peaceful condition. McDougall was nobody. He slunk home, defeated.

Sir John A. had laughed at the initial misfortunes of "Wandering Willie." Now he was alarmed. The disorders in the Red River colony offered the Americans an excuse to move in and "restore order." Once there, they would never leave. Already Congress had passed a resolution demanding information from the State Department about McDougall's attempt to take over the colony "against the will of its inhabitants."

Macdonald calculated the U.S. would do everything short of declaring war to get the Northwest. Too late, he sent a large and powerful figure out to Red River to negotiate with Riel. The negotiator was Donald Smith, a monosyllabic Scot with a mighty beard and terrifying eyebrows who was to cut a swath across Canada. He is better known today as Lord Strathcona, the man who hammered home the last spike of the CPR at Craigellachie. At the time he was an ex-factor of the Hudson's Bay Company who had spent twenty years in the Labrador wilderness after a youthful dalliance with the young wife of the terrible governor of the Company, George Simpson. His mission to Riel was, in fact, recognition by Canada of the rebel government. He carried promises of an amnesty and preservation of *métis* property rights. He also carried bribes for their leaders.

He failed because of an outburst by a few gallant and idiotic Anglo-Saxon loyalists. A rambunctious Ontario Orangeman, Thomas Scott, said to have tried to strangle Riel, was shot by a partly-drunk *métis* firing squad. When the news reached Ontario, Macdonald's supporters screamed for blood and twelve thousand men were sent struggling across the prairies to get Riel. They took his headquarters, Fort Garry, but Riel had fled south. Four or five of the firing squad that shot Scott were later found and killed.

The military expedition, part British Regulars, part Canadian militia, was intended to prove that the British Empire could control the west. That year (1870) the region became the province of Manitoba. There was no further attempt to capture Riel. In fact, Macdonald offered him about one thousand pounds to stay away. But he returned. Although he was still a fugitive from justice, he was elected to Parliament and appeared briefly in Ottawa in 1874. Macdonald conceded that he was "a clever fellow," even if he was a half-breed.

Riel's achievement was to turn Ottawa's attention towards the west. In the grateful aftermath of the first prairie rebellion, the Dominion government was so overwhelmed by lust for this hitherto-unnoticed region that it made its famous promise to British Columbia: join us and we'll build a transcontinental railway within ten years. British Columbia had become a colony in 1866. Cut off behind its mountains, it saw no way of linking up with the provinces on the other side of the continent. The logical course was to join the coastal American States. Logic didn't work. In 1869 the ten thousand British Columbians were offered a petition demanding the annexation of the region by the United States. Only 104 signed. The rest wanted to defy geography and join Canada. They could have been persuaded to sign up with the promise of a good wagon trail. When Macdonald guaranteed a railway, they were ecstatic. In 1871, British Columbia became a Canadian province.

By that time, Macdonald was once again deep in personal tragedy. He and Agnes could no longer conceal from themselves the fact that their child Mary would never live a normal life. They had tried to ignore the baby's large, malformed head, the listless eyes. Now they knew there was no cure. John A. didn't even know whether he could provide for her. He was hopelessly in debt. He returned to the bottle.

He was drunk in the Commons, drunk in his office. At the

height of the Riel affair, the Governor-General passed the word to London: "Sir John A. has broken out again."

He shut himself in his bedroom with bottle after bottle of port. State papers were sent in to him but he stared at them vacantly. Much of the nation's business came to a halt. Overwork and frustration had turned the jolly toper into a despairing drunk. But the bouts ended. With tremendous effort he pulled himself together and walked shakily into the House. He was to face his first test as a Canadian statesman on the international stage.

Canada had no foreign policy. It was the first federation within the British Empire to be granted control of its internal affairs, but its dealings with other nations were handled by Britain. What the Dominion could do was protect its own borders and waters. So when the United States cancelled the reciprocal across-the-border trade agreement, Canada responded by cancelling U.S. fishing rights in Canadian waters.

In 1870 four little Canadian coastguard vessels seized 400 American fishing boats for trespassing. President Grant condemned "this colonial authority" which "as a semi-independent but irresponsible agent has exercised its delegated powers in an unfriendly way."

The fisheries row brought Canada to an international conference for the first time. Macdonald was permitted to join in the Anglo-American meeting in Washington called to clean up disputes left over from the Civil War. The United States wanted enormous damages for the destruction caused by the British-built Confederate raider *Alabama* plus fishing rights in Canada. Canada demanded compensation for the U.S.-based Fenian raids.

The British team, viewing the global situation, simply wanted to patch up all quarrels with the Americans and were prepared to throw them all the Canadian fish they could swallow. But John A., loyal and true-blue as he was, had no intention of giving the fisheries away just to please Britain. He became a lonely and unpopular figure in Washington. The

British and American delegates regarded him first with mild amusement, then irritation, then anger. The British howled "treachery" and "slippery moral behavior." Macdonald met a U.S. Senator's wife at a garden party. She didn't catch his name but, in conversation, informed him that a "perfect rascal" ruled Canada. John A. listened gravely and politely agreed.

In the end the fishing rights had to go, but Macdonald got the best possible price for them — not from the United States as it turned out. The weary British agreed to pay Canada's Fenian raid claims and Macdonald signed the treaty allowing American fishermen into Canadian waters for ten years. He did it with a sad and cynical smile. He had become the first Canadian statesman to attempt a flourish of independence in foreign policy and he had confirmed his distaste for "overwashed Englishmen."

"Macdonald has puzzled us all," wrote the chief British negotiator, Earl de Grey and Ripon. "I do not know whether he is really an able man or not; that he is one of the duskiest horses that ever ran on any course I am sure; and that he has been playing his own game all along with unswerving steadiness is plain enough."

For all this noble disdain it was de Grey's government, not the shady colonials, that tried to welsh on the deal. It took six months to get the promised Fenian payments out of London. Until he had the cash, Macdonald did not dare to put the dubious fisheries treaty before Parliament for ratification. By that time he had worse problems. It was six weeks to election day 1872 and the bloom was off the Macdonald government. He was broke, his party was broke. His tariff policy was not one that could be put plainly to the voters. Doubletalk was needed. The farmers had to be lulled with hopes of international trade; the manufacturers had to have hints of high tariffs. And all Canadians had to see at least the beginnings of a transcontinental railway or lose faith in a nation from sea to sea. Little had been done about the railway. It was uneconomical and might prove impossible to carve a route north of the Great Lakes and through the Rockies — the survey teams had yet to find a way across the mountains. Yet that was what "Old Tomorrow" had promised. He tried to get the railway moving in a hurry, and he blundered.

The Canadian Pacific Railway Company, set up by the Montreal shipowner, Sir Hugh Allan, was prepared to do the job. But it was financed by American capital. The classic Canadian dilemma had begun: how much U.S. money can you take before you get U.S. control? Macdonald was much clearer on this point than most of his successors. The Canadian railway involved the biggest engineering enterprise in North America and the biggest private land deal since the Hudson's Bay charter. If Americans grabbed control of that, they could grab all of Canada. He demanded that Allan drop his American backers and Allan agreed.

With this understanding, Macdonald lurched into the election campaign against a re-organized Liberal party led by Alexander Mackenzie and masterminded by the brilliant Edward Blake. Cartier, the great French ally, was dying but still campaigned for re-election. He needed Allan's support in Quebec. Allan still wanted the railway contract on his own terms, so he offered to bankroll the impoverished Conservatives.

Macdonald was dazed, sick and drinking heavily. He and his candidates spent $300,000 of Allan's money, but wanted more. He sent Allan a fatal telegram: "I must have another ten thousand. Will be the last time of calling. Do not fail me. Answer today."

Narrowly, he won the election. Then came the reckoning. Allan had not dumped his American backers, but only hidden them. A Chicago financier arrived in Macdonald's office to prove this; unless the original U.S.-backed plan went through, he would reveal the source of the Tory campaign funds. The wily Prime Minister, now victorious and sober, knew how to handle blackmailers. There was a discreet dinner party in Montreal; the Americans were paid off and Allan sailed for London to look for fresh British capital for his railway.

Macdonald relaxed. He didn't know that a quiet young

clerk in the office of Allan's solicitor, John Abbott, had rifled the safe. The papers he found were being peddled around the Liberal camp for $5,000 cash.

When an insignificant Liberal Member rose to tell the House that the CPR was a U.S. company in disguise, the Prime Minister smiled easily. Then came the charge: the CPR charter had been bought by campaign funds.

Macdonald fought it off. He set up a committee to investigate these allegations. Then out came the telegram "I must have another ten thousand. . . ." The charge would stick. He made one great speech in his defence, but in the debate even his friend Donald Smith turned against him and that was the end.

John A. presented his resignation to the Governor-General and returned to his bottles of port. He was seen "tottering down the hill to the East Gate alone, others passing him with a wide sweep."

He wrote: "My fighting days are over, I think."

Alexander Mackenzie, a sober grey stonemason, became the second Prime Minister of Canada. And the majestic plan for a transcontinental railway disintegrated into a series of puddle-jumping transportation systems. After five years of Mackenzie government, it took seventeen changes of vehicle to get from Fort William to Winnipeg. You climbed from steamer to covered wagon to rowboat to tugboat to stagecoach. Not until 1877 did the first locomotive, the wood-burning Countess of Dufferin, reach Winnipeg. She got there on the deck of a steamboat.

For two years "Old Tomorrow" laid low. He made plans to get out of public life entirely and to re-open a law practice in Toronto. But the tempting sight of a split in Mackenzie's party stirred the old political juices. He had offered to give up the Tory leadership; the party had refused. He told himself he would never again suffer the agonies of the prime ministership. Still, there was no harm in baiting the Liberals for failing to build the railway he had failed to build. As Mackenzie flustered and faded, Macdonald's strength came back. The "old cat," as Brown called him, began stalking his prey, searching for an issue. Loyalty to the Crown was one. He smelled a tinge of "little Canadianism" in a Liberal amendment to a bill setting up the Supreme Court of Canada. "Those who disliked the colonial connection," he declaimed, "spoke of it as a chain. But it was a golden chain (and he, Macdonald, was) proud to wear its fetters."

He sallied forth to the towns and villages, waving the flag and the golden chain, damning the Liberals and creating a new Canadian institution — the political picnic. The first meeting of the Fathers of Confederation had been upstaged by a travelling circus. John A. had learned something there. Politics was entertainment. It should not be reserved for the jaded pros and apathetic loggers of Ottawa or doled out to the constituents at election time. Put on a good show — a brass band parade, a hefty cold chicken and ham meal in a park, provide handshakes for the faithful and jokes for the rustics — and the town would remember for years.

Macdonald's picnics were solid satisfying affairs, unlike the whistle-stop train tours and jet-hopping campaigns of our time. They had the same purpose — to present the leader to the people, not as a distant tile-hatted symbol but as a warm, touchable man. The picnics did not blot out the image of John A., villain of the CPR scandal but, in Ontario at least, they made him a pleasant, folksy villain. Mackenzie, square, honest and humorless as his tombstones, could not compete.

Macdonald's new "National Policy" was a work of art — sufficiently inspiring and magnificently vague enough to offer something for everyone. Read backwards, forwards or sideways, it seemed to offer lower tariffs for the farmers and higher tariffs for the manufacturers. All it specified was "a judicious re-adjustment of the tariff." Canada was slipping into a depression; Mackenzie lacked the guile to hold his party together, let alone outfox John A.

In their rented Toronto house, Macdonald told Agnes: Get

ready to move back to Ottawa. In September, 1878, the Tories
swept back into power. The leader was defeated in Kingston
for the first time in 34 years but this meant little; a by-election
could be arranged. For a few weeks he relaxed with some
bottles of brandy. He was flat out in bed in Halifax when a
secretary tried to rouse him to greet the new Governor-General,
whose ship was pulling in to the dock. Macdonald reared
slowly on one elbow, scattering brandy-soaked state documents
among the bedclothes. "Vamoose from this ranch," he growled.

The British Colonial Secretary remarked that "he should
have lived in the good old times of two-bottle men." He was,
in some ways, a figure from the previous century. Mid-Vic-
torian statesmen were expected to be stuffy and sober in
public. Macdonald had work to do and jokes to tell and grief
to forget. He had no time to be earnest. He was 64 and he had
been granted a second chance to build his nation.

The depression lifted and the sun shone on the economy.
The National Policy, it transpired, meant tariff protection for
almost any manufacturer who wanted it — particularly manufacturers who had supported the Conservatives. On the land,
John A. declared solemnly, a farmer told him his Conservative
cow gave three quarts of milk more a day after the election
than before.

The challenge of the Pacific railway remained: a strip of
steel must skewer the country together. This time Macdonald
made a deal with a group headed by George Stephen, a melan-
choly Scot of humble origin who was president of the Bank of
Montreal. The group would build the railway for $25 million
cash and 25 million acres of land. The name of Stephen's
cousin, Donald Smith, was carefully left off the contract and
he remained a silent partner. Macdonald had not forgiven
Smith for his betrayal during the railway scandal debate. He
had described him in the Commons as "the biggest liar I ever
met."

Stephen and Smith found the man to build the impossible
railway — William Cornelius Van Horne, a giant American
of many talents. He was musician, painter and slave-driver —

a gourmet who said he ate, drank and smoked all he could and didn't give a damn for any man. "If you want anything done," he said, "name the day when it must be finished." The deadline was set — 1891 — and Van Horne roared ahead, driving his rails forward at two and a half miles per day. Later, it became three and a half miles and on one tearing, sweating day, twenty miles of track were hammered into the hostile ground. Villages and towns sprang up along the railway as it clanked and battered westward, aiming its steel lance at a seemingly impenetrable barrier of rock — the Selkirk range. At the last moment the bewhiskered American surveyor Major "Bishop" Rogers found a way through the mountains.

Then the money ran out. CPR stock fell. The banks refused further loans. Van Horne telegraphed in code: "Cannot pay crews." Parliament, fearing another scandal, told Macdonald it would not vote another penny for Stephen and Smith to squander. An advisor woke John A. to tell him: "The day the CPR busts, the Conservative party busts the day after." He already knew that. For good and sufficient reasons railway building had taken on the aroma the used car trade was to acquire in the next century. Everyone associated with it, including Stephen, Smith and Macdonald, was tarnished to some extent. Yet the railroaders had courage. Stephen and Smith pledged their own funds to the hilt. They vowed that if the project collapsed they would be found broke by the tracks, without a dollar. At the blackest moment Stephen was in London searching for funds. He cabled Smith in Montreal: "Stand fast, Craigellachie!" It was the battle-cry of the Clan Grant to which they both belonged. Macdonald, too, stood fast. And the three Scots were saved — not by one of "Jock Tamson's bairns" but by the mad *métis* Louis Riel. At this desperate moment, he launched his second rebellion.

Riel was 40 now, a mystic haunted by visions, not long released from a lunatic asylum. He called himself Louis "David" Riel for that was how his spirits addressed him. He was obsessed by the holiness of the ultra rightwing Bishop of Montreal, Msgr. Ignace Bourget, who had written him a letter urging him to fulfill his God-given mission. He now believed God directed him to free the *métis*, destroy the existing Catholic hierarchy, and promote Bishop Bourget to Pope. The Red River valley half-breeds had called him back from his American exile — this was fact, not fantasy — in a letter which stated: "The whole race is calling for you." They had moved westward to south Saskatchewan.

On July 1, 1884, the village of Batoche, now the main *métis* settlement in the prairies, turned out to cheer his return. Batoche, two hundred miles north of Regina, was to be the capital of his new kingdom. Ten miles from Batoche in the dreary trading post of Duck Lake, his riders clashed with 57 Mounties and 41 volunteers, and killed a dozen of them. The *métis* had surrounded the police detachment, intending to take hostages and compel the Dominion government to negotiate. The fighting began with a hand-to-hand struggle between an Indian on Riel's side and a police interpreter. The Mounties fired first. Riel was unarmed, except for a large cross which he had torn from the spire of the Duck Lake church. The *métis* routed the Mounties, and every white in the Northwest shuddered at the thought of a half-breed and Indian war.

That day Riel saved the CPR. Van Horne offered to rush Canadian troops along his new rails — and transport them across the gaps — to put down the rebellion. He would move the troops west to Saskatchewan in eleven days. As ever, he met his deadline. Within eleven days they were there, sped by sleigh, by regular railway and across tracks hurriedly laid over frozen rivers. They spilled off their flatcars, put down the rebellion and captured Riel.

It took 8,000 militiamen to crush Riel's 500 ill-armed *métis*. Yet without the railway it could not have been done. There would have been a full scale Indian uprising. The Blackfoot Confederacy Indians were restless, stirred up by Riel's envoys; but when they saw the speed with which the Canadian militia arrived, they calmed down.

Back east, public and Parliament moved towards approval

of another mighty CPR loan. The last spike at Craigellachie was assured and with it Macdonald's band of steel from sea to sea. Yet in his triumph the old chieftain forgot that in his Dominion, sentiment was stronger than steel and religious ties more solid than the hewn wood. Despite his years of crafty construction, the career of evasion and compromise, he behaved like a querulous Sultan. He chose to kill Riel, the messenger of destiny. "He shall hang," he declared, "though every dog in Quebec should bark in his favor."

Three doctors said Riel was sane; but by any common standard he was mad. He would not have been put to death under today's sanity rules. But there was more to the Riel decision than legal quirks, insanity or humanity. He was the French-speaking leader of an oppressed Canadian minority, a Roman Catholic who left the Church but returned to it in his death cell. He was the first French martyr since Confederation. Six days after he dropped to his death at Regina, on November 18, 1885, he was being compared with Joan of Arc. Macdonald was burned in effigy in Montreal. And a young Liberal, Wilfrid Laurier, told an audience of thousands in the Champs de Mars: "Had I been born on the banks of the Saskatchewan I would myself have shouldered a musket to fight against the neglect of the government and the shameless greed of the speculators." Macdonald's true successor had arrived on the scene. He was beginning his career on the foundation of Macdonald's great mistake.

When John A. with Agnes rode the CPR across the mountains the following year he could see the physical evidence of a continent linked together. But he knew that in their minds and their various loyalties the peoples of the continent were still far apart.

The old man grew bitter. The broad mind which had weighed every side of every argument, narrowed until it focused, perhaps unfairly, on one fundamental point: Would his Canada survive or be annexed by the United States? When the election of 1891 came upon him, "Old Tomorrow" had no tomorrows left. His political machine was failing, his party fading. Young Laurier, who now led the Liberals, looked like a handsomer reincarnation of the early John A. He demanded unbridled free trade, and a commercial union with the United States.

Macdonald kindled up the last embers of the old imperial fire. "A British subject I was born, a British subject I hope to die." With his last breath he vowed to oppose the "veiled treason" which attempted to steal his people's allegiance. The old man was magnificent. Laurier stood accused as a traitor, a "sellout" to the Americans, in the same way that Mackenzie King and Lester Pearson would be accused. All Macdonald needed was evidence to prove the charge.

His henchmen stole it just as the Liberals stole the telegram that laid him low in 1873. An editor of the Toronto *Globe,* James Farrer, had visited the U.S. Secretary of State, apparently as an unofficial agent of the Liberal party, to get his views on over-the-border trade. Being a journalist, Farrer committed his views to paper and printed them in a pamphlet which the Tories discovered. It was intended to be an objective study, conveying the American point of view. In it, Farrer even suggested ways in which the United States could retaliate economically against Canada's trade and fisheries policies.

Macdonald used it ruthlessly, the way the Grits had used his telegram. There was, he charged, a conspiracy "by force or by fraud" to force Canada into the American Union.

On March 5, 1891, he routed the Liberals once again. But he was in bed, grey and quavering as the results came in. Two months later he was dead. Tomorrow had come. There was no Canadian of his stature ready to face it.

MACKENZIE
1873-78

# III. *Plain Sandy*

For only three pounds, Sandy Mackenzie was told, he could leave the poverty of Scotland behind and cross the seas to a land of boundless opportunity. Millions of acres were waiting to be settled; towns and cities would spring up. A visiting Upper Canada Cabinet minister promised: "I will furnish you with mail coach roads, macadamized roads, plank roads, nay even railroads. Our frontier towns like Toronto, London, Hamilton, Bytown will prosper . . . our lakes will be covered with vessels . . . our streets filled with shops."

Mackenzie had three pounds and he was interested. He was twenty, a qualified stonemason with his own tools. Born in a Highland croft at the Pass of Killiecrankie, he had moved to Ayrshire, Robert Burns' country, and was doing quite well. But there was misery all around him. He had read a Chartist pamphlet which declared: "Yes! the destiny of Great Britain is to be the instrument, under Divine Providence, of spreading civilization and Christianity, by means of Colonization and the Emigration of her Anglo-Saxon children over the whole globe."

The stonemason was willing to follow this destiny. He was a stern, sober Christian who had just left the grim shelter of the Church of Scotland for the greater zeal of the Baptists. He expected to find a still deeper faith amid the God-fearing people of the distant frontier.

One other factor drove him to Canada. He was in love with seventeen-year-old Helen Neil and she was emigrating there with her family. Sandy Mackenzie packed his tools and sailed with the Neils in April, 1842.

He was to find the boundless opportunity he had been promised. Just 31 years later he became master of the new land — its second Prime Minister. He brought to that office a square solidity and uncompromising morality it had lacked before. He had chiselled granite slabs and something of the hard sureness of that grey rock had entered his character.

Bruce Hutchison assesses him as a lesser but more honest and in some ways better man than Macdonald. He first settled in Kingston where John A., the rakish young lawyer, was cutting a swathe in local society, but they did not meet. Dull, plodding Mackenzie married his Helen, prayed to his teetotalling God, and contentedly hewed his stone. Yet the stonemason was to share the same sorrows as the lawyer. Two of Helen's three children died and she, too, faded away like Macdonald's Isa. Both men were plagued by illness and worn down by the frustrations of office; but Mackenzie sought solace in prayer instead of port.

Unlike Macdonald, who worshipped no man, Mackenzie made a hero of George Brown. He never thought of himself as a leader, only as a follower and organizer. He entered politics to support his brother, Hope, and stayed in out of loyalty to Brown.

After three years in Kingston he had moved to Port Sarnia, a mainly-Scots settlement on the St. Clair River, and had begun to prosper as a builder. Starting with the Port Sarnia Episcopal Church, which he constructed for $766, he went on to build the first Bank of Upper Canada in the town, the courthouse and jail in Chatham. He read until his eyes ached and his grammar and spelling improved. He was active in the local Temperance Society, the St. Andrew's Society and the debating club. He managed George Brown's successful campaign for election as Reform candidate in Kent and Lambton and handled patronage appointments for him. For a time he ran a crusading Brownite newspaper, the *Lambton Shield*. His hero sent him the occasional encouraging letter from Quebec, where the Assembly was meeting: "Do you Heelanders keep your blood warm on the banks of the St. Clair. I am half a Mackenzie man myself."

The "Heelanders" lived by principle and prejudice. To Mackenzie, Britain was still "home," Frenchmen, *métis* and all papists were naturally inferior. Free Trade was ordained by gospel and Tory tariffs were "the acme of human selfishness — relics of barbarism."

Now and then, sombre Sandy could summon a quiet streak of wit. When a Tory accused him of disloyalty to the Queen, he turned his massive head and declared with blank earnestness: "Loyalty to the Queen does not require a man to bow down to her manservant, or her maidservant — or her ass."

He was elected to the first Canadian Parliament in 1867. George Brown was defeated, but he remained nominal party leader and the Grits expected him to return. The brilliant but erratic Edward Blake dominated the party in his absence and Mackenzie deferred to him. He served as his treasurer in the Ontario provincial government, while remaining in the federal House, and governed the province while Blake was away in England.

When Brown at last made it clear that he was not coming back to elective politics, Mackenzie had no desire to succeed him. He proposed Blake for party leader, or, failing him, the Grits' leading French-Canadian, Antoine Aimée Dorion. But both men turned to him. It had never occurred to him that in his monumental integrity he possessed a quality that any party might covet.

Reluctantly, he took the leadership. "We'll see how matters go," he said, "and if everything does not go well I will endeavor to shake it off yet." Nine months later the Pacific scandal laid Macdonald low and the Governor-General, the Earl of Dufferin, summoned Mackenzie. "A poor creature," Dufferin called him.

From the start Mackenzie lacked an adequate Cabinet. Blake rode off in all directions. Having pushed Mackenzie into the leadership (which had suddenly become the prime ministership), he began to demand it for himself and refused a Cabinet seat. When finally corralled and brought in as Minister of Justice, he proved an uncertain colleague. According to Macdonald's first rule of Canadian government, every English-speaking prime minister needed a strong Quebec chieftain in his Cabinet and Mackenzie couldn't find one. Dorion, the logical man, had gone to be Chief Justice of Quebec. Worst of all, the times were against the stonemason. The country was entering a depression and Macdonald had got out just in time. Mackenzie took the tariff, the acme of human selfishness, and raised it from 15 to 17½ percent.

At least the depression provided an excuse to put off the building of Macdonald's railway, which Mackenzie disliked with the visceral repulsion felt for creepy crawly things. There was something essentially dishonest about railways. The promise to start construction by 1873 was "an insane" act according to the sober pay-as-you-go Scot. He knew it couldn't be paid for, and by all the rules of pre-Keynesian economics he was right.

Blake the brain went farther. He said the railway would never pay for its own axle-grease. So began the Liberals' half-hearted railway policy. Instead of tracks, they would utilize the great stretches of water that happened to be there anyway. It was boat-train-boat for the traveller, and the greedy British

Columbians could wait. When they sent their blackmailers to Ottawa, threatening to leave the union, Mackenzie told them that the Liberals were businessmen and threw them out. Plain Sandy never appreciated the fact that Canada was not, and never could be run as a sensible business. It was an illogical enterprise whose balance sheet would never add up.

Courageously, he stood up to the impressive Lord Dufferin when he took it upon himself to meddle in railway politics. The Governor-General promised the British Columbians that he would fight their battle. He proposed that the Colonial Secretary in London should intervene to settle the differences between British Columbia and Ottawa.

This brought a series of stormy confrontations between Dufferin and his dour Prime Minister, supported by the excitable, sometimes tearful, Blake. Mackenzie told him he was to remember that Canada was no longer a colony and would not be dealt with as small communities had been — "that we were capable of managing our own affairs . . . and that no government would survive who would attempt even at the insistence of a Colonial Secretary to trifle with Parliamentary decisions."

Dufferin shot back, "you are not a Crown Colony . . . neither are you a Republic. If you were, you would find a President, imposed upon you by the popular vote, a much more troublesome master than I am ever likely to be." He said he had as much right to argue his opinion as his ministers had and they must not expect him to accept their advice just because they gave it.

This was heresy. Mackenzie and Blake offered to resign and Dufferin made a partial apology. From then on, he was a model of respect for the constitution. He had long since changed his opinion of Mackenzie as "a poor creature." Instead, he was "pure as crystal and strong as steel."

Pure he was, and hard. His decisions thumped forth with the authority of stone tablets. But he was never happy in office. The men around him were not pure, or even loyal. He disliked the Tories, but he detested the Liberal hacks who plagued him with their mean little demands. At home with his second wife, Jane, he was a different man, childishly and playfully content. When they were apart he wrote her touching love letters. "I was crying . . . I use up a handkerchief daily. I think of using a towel after this for economical reasons. If you stay long away it may become a sheet."

The Tory papers, he told her, said he was eaten up with ambition. He gave his own self-appraisal: "I am ambitious to succeed in governing the country well and without any reproach but beyond that my ambition is of a very humble kind. . . . I think I have ambition enough, however, to strengthen me to fight in, I hope, a manly way, the base herd of hireling scribes who would for political gain write away a man's character, and courage enough to back up that ambition."

Macdonald could assess his own frailties; Mackenzie saw his own limitations. He was too proud and too religious to blame his failures on pure bad luck. The United States Senate rejected the Liberal government's ardent proposals for freer trade. The depression threatened to bankrupt Canadian industries and Mackenzie was forced, against his principles, to increase their tariff protection. But he gained little political credit for this move; Macdonald's National Policy took care of that. At his political picnics, "Old Tomorrow" joked that his idea of protection was like a drunken squaw's view of liquor — "a little too much is just enough."

The one piece of luck that helped bolster Mackenzie's place in history was the formation of the Northwest Mounted Police. Macdonald had brought in a bill to set up the force on July 8, 1874. That was a decisive date in the history of Canada.

The west was gaping open. American traders were crossing the unmarked borders of Manitoba, bringing whiskey and rapid-fire rifles for the Indians and toting back fortunes in buffalo hides. The Blackfeet went crazy on "whoop-up bugjuice." They would trade away anything they had for it and then riot. It was very bad whiskey. One variety was made by mixing a quart of rye with a pound of chewing tobacco, a bottle of Jamaica ginger and a quart of molasses. Another was watered wine with tea leaves and tobacco.

Whiskey Gap, Robber's Roost and Slideout were centers of the bug-juice trade. The biggest was Fort Whoop-up, eleven miles south of present-day Lethbridge, Alberta. It was the first target of the Mounted Police. The white man's booze — and his smallpox — had rotted the Blackfeet, without arousing much response from Ottawa. A series of outrages, culminating in the Cypress Hills massacre, in which a group of American wolf-hunters drunkenly butchered 30 Indians, finally brought action. Two hundred and seventy-five Mounties in scarlet tunics and pillbox hats left Fort Dufferin, near Emerson, Manitoba, and headed for Fort Whoop-up to save the west for Canada. After two months they were lost and the first snow was falling. Their first contact with civilization was a lone Yankee trader who sold them flour and sugar — at outrageous prices.

In October they found Fort Whoop-up, took up battle stations and aimed their one cannon at that citadel of corruption. It was deserted but for one old man and a few squaws.

Although the enemy had gone, the long march was a success. By constant movement, this very thin red line covered as much as possible of the huge savage land. By their stiffnecked courage, implacable pursuits and astonishing fairness, these few hundred men tamed the territory and scattered the whiskey traders. They convinced the Indians that for the first time they could get equal justice with the whites. Said Blackfoot Chief Crowfoot: "If the police had not come to the country where would we all be now? The police have protected us as the feathers of the bird protect it from the frosts of winter."

From the start the Northwest Mounted Police showed relentless determination to "get their man." It took them two years to gather sufficient evidence to accuse the murderers of Cypress Hills. There were fourteen of them, "wolfers" from the U.S. outpost of Fort Benton. In May, 1873, they were in Cypress Hills in the wilderness of south Saskatchewan looking for horses that had been stolen from them. Since they couldn't find the horse-stealers, they camped and got drunk. Nearby a band of Indians was doing likewise. One wolfer shouted that his horse was missing (it was grazing nearby) and the whites rushed the Indian camp. They fired a volley; the Indians charged and one white was killed. That night the wolfers stormed into the Indian camp, raped the squaws, cut off the chief's head to stick on a post, and killed about thirty men, women and children.

Back in Fort Benton they were received as heroes. The Montana newspapers supported the killings as a bit of firmness needed to keep the Indians in their place. In June, 1875, the Mounties applied for the extradition of the fourteen to stand trial in Canada. On orders from Washington a hearing was held in Fort Benton. The men were discharged, a parade was held in their honor, and a Mountie colonel was picked up by local police for making a false arrest. John Evans, leader of the murder gang, opened a tavern and called it the Extradition Saloon.

The following year three of the gang boldly returned to Canada and were promptly arrested and charged with "wanton and atrocious slaughter of peaceable and inoffensive people." They complained to the United States consul in Winnipeg, the State Department intervened, the trial was postponed for a year, and, in June, 1876, the men were acquitted.

The courts, not the Mounties, had failed. Their law was more effective than the gun-slinging of the Wild West sheriffs; and it was practically bloodless. They were a source of pride to a new nation that badly needed pride of its own.

In the summer of 1875, Mackenzie and Jane sailed to Britain, to meet the Queen and the Imperial Government, the belted knights and ermined dukes who represented the British tradition he had sworn to uphold. He found them all annoyingly stuck-up and uninterested in the Empire. The dukes, he found, were social tyrants and the knights mere flunkies.

A duchess complained to him during lunch at Windsor

Castle: "It's a very trying thing now to deal with Society. There are so many people forced upon you whom you don't want to see, people who have no position." The ex-stonemason concluded that before long there would be a blow-up between the two extremes of society in Britain.

Meeting the aristocracy confirmed his suspicion that Canadians should not be given titles. (He was the only one among the first eight Canadian prime ministers who never took one.)

He told Disraeli, "we were all but ruined from first to last by English diplomacy and treaty-making and we would have no more of it at any price." After two weeks of talks in London he decided that Canada was more British than Britain and told Dufferin so. He even found himself defending the American system. Despite its faults, their society was free of the class system that cramped ambition.

These doubts and irritations vanished with his triumphal return to Scotland. Every town and village where he had lived as a boy turned out to cheer the emigrant lad who had made good.

In his speeches he echoed the visiting Canadian tub-thumper of 33 years before: "It is the mission of the Anglo-Saxon race to carry the power of Anglo-Saxon civilization over every country in the world." Canada, he promised, would one day surpass England, not only in territory and population but in political grandeur too. Back in his birthplace, in the Pass of Killiecrankie, he told his clansmen that the years had changed his allegiance. He was still a loyal Scot, but Canada came first. He sailed back across the Atlantic, this time travelling first class.

Back in Ottawa he faced the dilemma every national leader encounters sooner or later. The depression was hitting hard. Unemployment was up; the farmers were hungry; the treasury was low. Should he tell the people exactly how bad things were? Or would that only make things worse?

He hesitated only for an instant. "The truth must be told," he said. "I have no faith in pretensions of any sort." This honesty was plain Alexander's contribution to Canadian politics. With it he brought the Clear Grit principles of free trade, good housekeeping, and his Scots narrowness of outlook. These were not enough to cure the depression, expand the country or ward off the Tories. And the shaky Dominion was not ready for a leader of uncompromising morality. Tory banners proclaimed "Sandy's no sic a man as our Sir John."

As the 1878 election approached, his red beard was greying fast and his eyes glittered feverishly. He looked, wrote Dufferin, "a washed-out rag and limp enough to hang upon a clothes line." Parliament was fighting day and night over the railway. Macdonald could survive these sessions with a short nap, a glass of wine and a dozen oysters; Mackenzie was dazed and ill.

One incredible sitting lasted 27 hours and turned into slapstick comedy with members roaring songs, blowing toy trumpets, and throwing blue books across the floor at one another. Despite the uproar some stayed asleep on their desks. Sir John A. was flat out on a couch in a committee room — "simply drunk, in the plain ordinary sense of that word," according to the Toronto *Globe*. Twice Lady Dufferin appeared in the gallery, and the House sang "God Save the Queen" and waved handkerchiefs until she left in embarrassment. A Quebec member, M. Cheval, had a squeaking instrument, described by a reporter as a toy bagpipe. With it, he led a percussion band.

When someone tried to stop M. Cheval's squeaking he appealed to the Speaker: "Mr. Speaker, I wish to know which is more worse, de man dat trows blue books 'cross de House or de man dat goes in for a small leedle music." The Speaker said both were unparliamentary. Prime Minister Mackenzie demanded that the Sergeant-at-arms be called to restore order but he was hiding in some private nook, enjoying the fun.

The 1878 session ended in the midst of a howling row between Macdonald, Sir Charles Tupper and Donald Smith. As Black Rod entered the chamber Tupper was yelling "mean treacherous coward." Macdonald shouted "that fellow Smith is the biggest liar I ever met" and pushed across the aisle after the towering railway-builder. As other members held him back he muttered in fury, "I could lick him quicker than hell could scorch a feather."

Mackenzie recovered somewhat after Parliament adjourned. When the election came that fall he was confident. The depression was ending at last and the Liberals had solved their Quebec leadership problem. Laurier had moved in as second man in the government. Blake had resigned and left Ottawa without bidding farewell — a great loss, but a welcome one. Five years of honest government were about to pay off.

The returns left Mackenzie gasping. Honesty was discredited and the Liberals swept out. The party, he wrote bitterly, must find a new leader, a man who had "graduated as a horse-thief or at least distinguished himself as having chiselled a municipality or robbed a railway company."

Brown persuaded him to remain as leader and he lasted two years, a raddled monument to failure. Then Laurier told him, "it is only human nature that a defeated army should seek another general." The Liberal caucus chose Blake to succeed him, and he lived to see Blake fail too.

He died in 1892, a few months after Macdonald, whispering, "Oh, take me home."

His lasting memorial is the Mackenzie Tower in the West Block of the Parliament Buildings. It contains a secret staircase which the stonemason had built so that he could escape from his second-floor office down into the courtyard without passing the favor-seeking businessmen and party hacks who camped in his outer office. Later Macdonald used it to dodge his creditors. And in 1968 Pierre Trudeau slipped out that way to avoid the press while he went to call an election.

ABBOTT
1891-92

THOMPSON
1892-94

BOWELL
1894-96

TUPPER
1896 (May-July)

# IV.  *The Pall Bearers*

Macdonald's government should have died with him in 1891, but it lingered on through five years and four unsuccessful prime ministers while Laurier, the next nation-builder, waited in the wings. There were two possible successors to Sir John A.

There was 70-year-old Sir Charles Tupper, a Father of Confederation, now living sumptuously in London as Canadian High Commissioner. Or there was young Sir John Thompson, whom Macdonald had described as his brightest political discovery. Neither wanted the job — or so they said at the time; both were to accept it later. Tupper was enjoying his reward in London. Thompson, at 47, felt he was too young. Besides, he was a Nova Scotian and a convert to Catholicism — characteristics made to lose votes in Ontario where converts were called perverts.

So the demoralized Tories came up with the candidate who

v.anted the job least of all. Said Senator John Abbott, "I hate politics and what are considered their appropriate measures. I hate notoriety, public meetings, public speeches, caucuses and everything that I know of which is apparently the necessary incident of politics — except doing public work to the best of my ability. Why should I go where the doing of public work will only make me hated . . . and where I can gain reputation and credit by practising arts which I detest to acquire popularity?"

Why indeed? Yet it is an eternal fact, never properly explained, that the people's call to office is always answered, often before it is sounded. Senator Abbott's declaration ranks with General Sherman's classic formula for declining the U.S. Presidency: "If nominated I will not run and if elected I will not serve." Or conservative wit William Buckley's statement made while running for mayor of New York: "If elected I shall demand a recount."

Yet Abbott, a grim, tired old corporation lawyer, took up the burden, carried it for eighteen months and found it every bit as bad as he had predicted. At the start he told the Senate that the prime ministership was beyond his hopes, aspirations or merits. He had been chosen as a compromise, "because I am not particularly obnoxious to anybody, something like the principle on which it is reported some men are selected as candidates for the Presidency of the United States . . . that they are harmless and have not made any enemies."

As Macdonald brought skill to the job and Mackenzie added honesty, Abbott, in his brief term, contributed an appalling frankness.

He was 70 and could have been spared the rigors that ruined the health of his two predecessors. He had achieved the safe haven of the Senate after years in the rough politics of the English minority in Quebec. He had opposed Confederation. As a young man he had signed the infamous Annexation Manifesto of 1849 which urged British North America to join the United States. It was a hotheaded outburst by a group of young Conservatives who felt deserted by Britain when she abandoned preferential tariffs. Abbott explained it away as the act of a child who strikes his nurse but doesn't really mean to murder her. His worst political drawback was the musty smell of the CPR boardroom which still clung to him. He had been an associate of Sir Hugh Allan in the first railway scheme of 1873. It was from his safe that the scandalous Macdonald telegram — "I must have another ten thousand" — was stolen.

He took office as a caretaker, ruling from the Senate. Even by then it was obvious that the Upper House would never become the center of action in any government. A leader had to sit in the Commons to control events as they arose. Abbott and Mackenzie Bowell proved that. And as Arthur Meighen was to discover during the constitutional crisis of 1926, when he was temporarily without a seat, it was no use lurking behind a curtain outside the chamber, composing speeches that he couldn't deliver inside.

Long before Abbott resigned, Thompson, as Justice Minister, was in effective control of the government. The nominal leader of the House, Sir Hector Langevin, was under a cloud which soon smothered him and brought his resignation. He was caught up in a mess of crooked public works contracts, graft and kick-backs to the Conservative machine in Quebec which scandalized the nation — until it learned of even greater corruption in the Liberal provincial government of Quebec and of the subsequent dismissal of its Liberal Premier.

Abbott had every reason to be Canada's most pessimistic Prime Minister. Depression loomed once more. Blake, the Liberal leader, came out for commercial union with the United States and wondered aloud if political union would follow. Laurier wrote that the premature dissolution of Canada seemed to be at hand. A writer in the New York *World* estimated that the country could be annexed for a "judicious" expenditure of five or six million dollars. That would be about a dollar per Canadian. At that gloomy period, many Canadians would have gone for less.

And in the west, a fundamental, insoluble Canadian problem was coming to a head once more. The Manitoba schools question was an elaborate conundrum that set everyone arguing — Church versus State, provincial rights versus federal rights, Catholic versus Protestant, French versus English.

The 1870 Act which established Manitoba as a province provided that no law should be passed to prejudice the rights of the existing denominational schools. This meant in effect that French-speaking, Catholic, separate schools would continue to be supported by public funds. In the next twenty years English-speaking Protestants from Ontario poured into the new province. By 1890 only one Manitoban in seven was Catholic. In that year the Liberal provincial government abolished French as an official language and set up a single system of non-sectarian public schools.

The man behind this was one of the new arrivals from Ontario, Clifford Sifton, Attorney General of Manitoba, a militant Irish Protestant and without doubt the toughest legal gun in the Canadian west. The Catholic bishops of Manitoba and Quebec screamed "foul" and demanded that the Manitoba law be disallowed in Ottawa. Macdonald, who had handled the racial and religious issue since before the nation began, performed one of his adroit side-steps and suggested the Manitoba act be tested in the courts.

This was "Old Tomorrow's" last bequest to his successors. They could relax for a year and do nothing, hoping the courts would overrule the Manitoba government. Obligingly the Supreme Court of Canada did so. But the Manitoba Catholics appealed to the Privy Council. And in the summer of 1892, Thompson, Minister of Justice, stared in blank dismay at a telegram from London. The Privy Council had upheld Manitoba's law. This spelled eventual doom for the Conservatives.

Abbott, having gained a knighthood and lost his health, decided to get out. He had taken the job because he was not obnoxious to anybody. Now, with the Manitoba decision tossed at him, he would have to become obnoxious to one side or the other. He resigned in November, 1892, went to Europe in an attempt to restore his health, but failed and died the following year.

Sir John Thompson put the best possible face on things. "I have never shrunk in my calling as a member of the Bar," he had said, "from taking any man's case, no matter how desperate it might be." With his woolly sideburns and massive jaw he had all the airs of a judge and knight and prime minister. He had the makings, too, of a statesman, if only he could improve as a politician. His tongue was too sharp and so was his sense of the ridiculous. "He is a little too fond of satire," Macdonald said, "and a little too much of a Nova Scotian."

Born in Halifax, the son of an Irish immigrant, he worked his way up through the local school board to the Nova Scotia Assembly. At 38, happily married with five children, he left politics to become a judge of the provincial Supreme Court. Macdonald, who was looking for a young face to brighten his hoary Cabinet, brought him to Ottawa and made him Minister of Justice at 42. In 1887 he was sent to Washington to prepare the British case at a conference on Atlantic fishing rights. There he delivered himself of a notable verdict. "These Yankee politicians," he wrote his wife, "are the lowest race of thieves in existence." He was knighted by Queen Victoria for his attempts to deal with them.

He made his name in Parliament with a brilliant defence of Macdonald's decision to hang Louis Riel. It was a fine example of the defence counsel's craft, but as far as Quebec was concerned, it put him on the side of the hangman.

He could handle the fiercest Grit in the House, but he sounded more like a judge than a leader. He once admitted that there were many facts in Canadian history of which he was not aware and on which he could not deliver an opinion. A leader was supposed to know everything, or at least have an opinion on everything. He was too young and too clever to manipulate the machine built by creaky and crafty old men. One of his Tory colleagues remarked disapprovingly: "He won't even consider whether a thing is good for the party until he is quite sure it is good for the country."

He did manage to avoid making any clear decision on the Manitoba schools question. Here his air of judicial impartiality came in useful. Once the Privy Council had established that Manitoba had the right to pass its school act, the next question was: did Ottawa have the right to overturn it? The Manitoba Catholics put their case to Thompson's Cabinet. The Cabinet asked the Supreme Court for an opinion on whether it could intervene. The Court said no, but once again the matter went to the Privy Council's Judicial Committee. All this took another two years. The Liberals attacked the government for its indecision, but Thompson sat back waiting, with no impatience at all, to let the law take its course.

We will never know what this Catholic leader of a mainly Protestant party might have done when the moment of truth came. In December, 1894, aged 50, he went to London to be sworn in as a member of the Privy Council. At a luncheon in Windsor Castle he suddenly dropped dead.

As a sign of respect for the Dominion and of admiration for this promising and charming Prime Minister, the Queen ordered a full-dress ceremonial funeral. The battleship *Blenheim* brought his body back to Halifax to be buried in a small Roman Catholic cemetery.

The Conservatives had lost their best man. To replace him they produced one of their worst. Sir Mackenzie Bowell is remembered, if at all, as a stupid, bigoted, conceited and slightly paranoic little man. Yet he made the great decision in the Protestant-Catholic schools question. It went against his upbringing and his instincts, and it didn't do his career or his party any good at the time. Still, he did it, and if anyone emerged with any credit from the final crumbling of the Tory government it was he.

Bowell was an Orangeman. He was initiated into the mysteries of the Order at nineteen, ten years after he landed in Canada from Suffolk, England. From his local lodge in Belleville he progressed to the post of Grand Master of Upper Canada and finally to the exalted title of Grand Master for British North America. The great thumping Orange drums led many an Upper Canada lad to fame in the professions and the Tory party. While some slipped out of the parade in their middle years, Bowell marched on proudly to the end. The lodge was more imperialist than the Queen-Empress, loudly anti-Catholic and anti-French. It helped young Bowell to climb from printer's devil on the Belleville *Intelligencer* to editor and publisher of the paper. The crust of its ancient prejudices formed and hardened on him with the years.

Occasionally he missed a beat of the drum. When he first ran for election as a Tory he was up against George Brown's vitriolic anti-Catholic crusade so he forced himself to take a moderate, almost pro-Catholic stand. He lost that election. As Macdonald's Belleville ward boss he recognized that Catholics had votes. He once advised his chief to attend a Catholic picnic and deliver "an anti-Huxley speech with a slight sprinkling of politics."

If he disliked Catholics, he positively hated Grits, including the violently anti-Catholic ones. When he reached Parliament in 1867, he fell naturally into the leadership of the extreme rightwing of Macdonald's party. John A. brought him into his 1878 Cabinet to hold the lunatic fringe in order. As Minister of Customs he supervised the collection of the new tariff duties which were the foundation of the National Policy. Abbott used him as Minister of Militia, for he was a proud founder of the Belleville Rifle Company and had seen service during the Fenian raids. Thompson made him a Senator, and moved him to the new Ministry of Trade and Commerce, which he ran from the Senate. There, he showed a certain administrative ability. He led a trade mission to Australia, promoted a submarine cable link between the two continents, and organized a colonial conference in Ottawa.

So far, so good. Mackenzie Bowell had gone as far as his talents would take him. The call from Governor-General Lord Aberdeen took him one step over the edge and down into the abyss of his own conceit. Macdonald's old secretary, Sir Joseph Pope, then a clerk to the Cabinet, noted that Bowell was as little qualified to be Prime Minister as Aberdeen (an ardent Liberal) was to be Governor-General. What followed, he wrote, were "days which I never recall without a blush, days of weak and incompetent administration by a Cabinet presided over by a man whose sudden and unlooked-for elevation had visibly turned his head . . . a ministry without unity or cohesion of any kind, a prey to internal dissensions until they became a spectacle to the world, to angels and to men."

Lady Aberdeen noted that he could not even make up his mind on an inscription for Thompson's wreath from the Cabinet. "Only," he instructed, "do not put 'With Kind Regards'."

Bowell hurried around, a tiny figure with a jagged grey beard and hooded eyes set in a parchment face. The Montreal *Herald* described him as "an irascible old gentleman (he was 61) who despite his long political experience works himself into a white heat on very slight provocation."

He had plenty of provocation. He was attacked by the moderates in his own party who had either chosen him as leader or accepted him as the choice of the Liberal Lord Aberdeen. (It is still not clear just what did happen.)

He had been in office just over a month when on January 29, 1895, the Manitoba schools question reached the end of the legal road. The Privy Council ruled that the government of Canada could, if it wished, intervene in Manitoba and pass "remedial" legislation to give the Catholics back their schools. It was a landmark in federal-provincial relations, establishing the supremacy of the central government, but at the time it merely intensified the religious row. As Laurier's biographer, Prof. O. D. Skelton, points out, the dispute had little to do with education: "Rarely is the public roused to a lively interest in the problems of education. The school was merely the arena where the religious gladiators displayed their powers, an occasion for stirring the religious convictions and religious prejudices of thousands, and of demonstrating how little either their education or their religion had done to make them tolerant citizens."

Weak though he was, Bowell resolved to settle the matter. He signed an order-in-council instructing Manitoba (pop. 150,000) to re-establish separate schools for its 20,000 Catholics. Manitoba refused. Sifton was not about to give in to the raging little incompetent in Ottawa. If Catholics should have public school money, he argued, why not Presbyterians, Anglicans, Mennonites and everyone else?

Bowell was cornered. Although every Orange inch of him rebelled at the thought, the Grand Master was now on the side of the Pope. Worse, he was aligned with the Quebec bishops who were decidedly more Catholic than His Holiness. His only consoling thought was that Laurier would have to stick by his church and his province and support Bowell's action in the election due the following year. Bowell pushed ahead, trying to get the distasteful business over before the vote. He tried to ram through a remedial bill restoring the schools. In an attempt to placate his Protestants, he argued that the Privy Council decision was an order for the Canadian government to intervene. But it all smacked of popery — much more than his Cabinet could stand, even from an Orangeman.

Seven of them resigned. When he attempted to replace them they staged a Cabinet strike. The seven bewhiskered figures in top hats picketed trains arriving at Ottawa station, button-holing every Tory that Bowell might try to recruit, and urging him not to join the Cabinet. Working conditions for ministers were impossible, they declared. They combed the Ottawa hotels for potential Cabinet ministers and warned them off. "A nest of traitors," howled Bowell as he gave in. He was to keep the tattered trappings of office for the remaining weeks of the Parliamentary session, then resign to make way for Sir Charles Tupper.

In May, 1896, he returned to the Senate where he sat, nursing his grievances, for another 23 years. He became ever more brittle and bitter with the years, but he lived to be 94, while the "nest of traitors" died off one by one.

Tupper was back from London well before the Cabinet strike. Obviously he knew it was breaking up because his son, Sir Charles H., was a leader of the rebels. Ostensibly, he was back to promote an Atlantic shipping project, but there is more than a suspicion that he came, at last, to claim his heritage. More than any Tory, he held the deeds to the Tory prime ministership. He had talked of a continent-wide nation, linked by a railway, seven years before Confederation. He had won Nova Scotia for the union and John A. He had refused to press his claim for high office in the first Macdonald Cabinet because there wasn't room. Now there was room enough at the Tory top. The old bull-mastiff of Empire had come to claim the honor due to him, even if it was to be a temporary one. More than that, he felt the tug of duty and his homeland.

He was one month short of his 75th birthday — a fine, rounded man, a doctor from Nova Scotia. He was born in Amherst, son of a Baptist minister with Puritan ancestors. Three years in Edinburgh in the old body-snatching days of medical school taught him all that was needed to make a backwoods medico in Cumberland, Nova Scotia.

At 34 he ran as a Conservative against the mighty Maritime tribune Joseph Howe, heard his speeches dismissed by the great man as "the feeble mewing of a kitten," but beat him. In 1864 he became Premier of Nova Scotia. When Howe reversed himself and tried to block Confederation, Tupper became Macdonald's lieutenant down East; and he clung to his chieftain through good times and bad. He took on the thankless task of wooing Howe. He followed Donald Smith by sleigh to Fort Garry to negotiate with Louis Riel. He devised the label "National Policy." At one time he was considered to be Macdonald's heir and successor, but when the old Chieftain died he hung back in his comfortable London post, happy in semi-retirement. He encouraged Thompson, the young hope of the party, not knowing that Lady Thompson (who presumably got her views from her husband) called him "that old tramp." When, after 40 years in politics, he came to the prime ministership, he remembered a speech he made in the early days: "The human mind naturally adapts itself to the position it occupies. The most gigantic intellect may be dwarfed by being cabin'd, cribbed, and confined. It requires a great country and great circumstances to develop great men."

When he roared into his last campaign to save the party he was already one of its great men. His tenure in office was the shortest of all prime ministers — three months — but his claim to it was incontestable.

Square-jowled and fearless, he advanced against the Liberal hordes, saddled with the impossible Bowell policy of coercing a Protestant province to accept Catholic schools in the name of the Protestant Queen. That election of 1896 was the weirdest upside-down episode in the Dominion's history. Laurier, the Quebec Catholic, supported the Manitoba Protestants against his own bishops. Yet he won Quebec and lost Manitoba. Tupper lost Ontario, the Tory homeland and the rest of the west.

It marked the delayed finish of the years of Sir John A. Macdonald and the old British immigrant leaders. When Tupper was defeated, not just by the Catholic schools issue but by the shining personality of Wilfrid Laurier, the first stage of the Canadian prime ministership came to an end.

**LAURIER**
1896-1911

# V.  *Knight of the White Plume*

The village of St. Lin was a gentle place where little happened and precious little changed with the generations. In 1841, when Laurier was born there, it remained as deeply rooted in the ways of New France as its elms and maples were sunk in the soil of the Laurentian plain. The Achigan River slurped over the water-wheel above the mill pond. The big stone church loomed over the creaky wooden shacks on St. Lin's two streets. Its priests ruled the spiritual and temporal lives of the villagers and made little distinction between the two. The Church had survived the British conquest of Quebec and was in a position even stronger than when Laurier's first Canadian ancestor sailed from Caen in Normandy 200 years before to hear, with Maisonneuve, the first mass sung on the Island of Montreal. Its authority was not affected by the 1841 Act of Union which joined the two Canadas in the year Laurier was born. Union itself, while it caused a stir in

Montreal, a few miles to the south, passed by St. Lin as
casually as a log floating down the Achigan.

The villagers were untroubled by the passions and conflict-
ing loyalties that racked the strange folk outside. The Scots
and Irish settlers blared forth their loyalty to the Crown or
their hatred of it and their fear or fondness of the United
States. To the Canadiens, they were new arrivals. When they
thought of home, it was somewhere across the ocean. The
Canadiens *were* at home. They had no ties with France. Not
only had France abandoned all 60,000 of their forefathers in
the snows after the Plains of Abraham, it had since gone
through a revolution. Anti-clerical feeling was rife over there,
so the Canadian-born clergy shielded their flocks from the
pernicious ideas emanating from Paris. There had been no
immigration from France since the British conquest, and only
a sprinkling in the last years of the French régime. The Canadiens had found their place and their identity by themselves.

Laurier's father was a land surveyor, a person of note in the
village, although he lived in what would now be called poverty.
The boy slept on a narrow shelf in a closet of the cramped
little house, but considered himself well-off. There was fishing
in the summer, woods and streams to explore. In the winter,
there were books. Laurier had a happy home life followed by
a happy marriage, with none of the domestic agonies suffered
by Macdonald and Mackenzie. There was about him a sun-
niness of soul that brightened his time.

If he had stayed longer in St. Lin, he might have become
the greatest of French-Canadian leaders but he would not
have become Prime Minister. Instead, at the age of eleven, he
made the tremendous jump from one culture to another.

Seven miles west along the Achigan lay the all-Scottish
village of New Glasgow, recently settled by Presbyterian old
soldiers who had served in the New World with various
British regiments.

Laurier's father sent him there to learn English and through
it the mysteries of the world outside St. Lin. He boarded in a

Presbyterian home and studied under the remarkable Sandy Maclean, who kept a hefty strap on his desk and a hefty glass of Scotch beside it. One drew attention from the pupils, the other drew from Maclean's full mind long flowing quotations from the English poets. From him, Laurier acquired the perfect English he was later to use to fascinate, soothe or torment Parliament. With it came an understanding of "the English" unsurpassed by any French-Canadian leader.

After New Glasgow, he returned to his native tongue and religious atmosphere. He spent seven years studying classics and French literature at L'Assomption college. He was the best student there, but something of a heretic. He argued before the college debating society the proposition that the French king should have permitted the Huguenots to settle in early Quebec. The priests settled that debate by closing down the debating society. That was the last time Laurier permitted priests to silence him.

He moved to Montreal, working in a law office by day and studying law at night, preparing for the career in politics that was then the obvious outlet for a brilliant young French-Canadian who didn't aspire to the Church.

The Quebec wing of the Liberal party, which he was to lead, grew out of nationalism, anti-clericalism and the abortive rebellion against the British led by Louis Joseph Papineau in 1837. The rebellion was quashed by 2,000 British Regulars at St. Eustache, twenty miles from St. Lin. Papineau fled to France, but ten years later he was back, still lusting for the lost glories of New France, and now influenced by European notions of democracy and half-convinced of the need to jolt Quebec out of its seventeenth century lassitude. His group of Democrats, better known as *Rouges* (Reds) attracted ardent young men who saw a new republic of Quebec on American lines, probably, but not necessarily, a part of the United States.

Their ardor cooled gradually. Once convinced they could not break the new union with Ontario, they chose the secondary goal of better representation for Quebec in the combined

Assembly. They attempted to reform the province by attacking church privileges such as tithes and by questioning church control of education. From revolutionaries, they softened into reformers and left old Papineau to his ancient dreams of seigneury. But the Quebec bishops fought reform as fiercely as they fought revolution. The most extreme was Msgr. Ignace Bourget, Bishop of Montreal, who was to be Louis Riel's candidate for Pope. He banned a *Rouge* literary society to which young Laurier belonged and in 1869 refused the last rites of the church to another member, Joseph Guibord. On his death bed, Guibord, a life-long devout Catholic, refused to disown his *Rouge* friends. He died unshriven and the priests refused to bury him in a Montreal cemetery.

His friends took the case to the courts, up to the Privy Council in London, while Guibord's body rotted in a vault. Five years later the Council ruled that Guibord had done nothing, even under the ecclesiastical laws of New France, that would deny him Christian burial. Yet mobs barred the gates of the cemetery when his body was brought there. He was finally buried with an escort of 1,200 troops but without benefit of clergy.

After the soldiers had gone and builders had placed concrete and iron covers to protect the grave, Bishop Bourget swooped like an avenging angel to declare the ground formally interdicted and unconsecrated.

This was the climate in which Laurier joined the *Rouge* party. He steered it away from republicanism and the drift towards annexation by the United States. The bishops pursued him from Montreal to the Eastern Townships, where he edited a Liberal weekly. Although his editorials were mild and scarcely anti-clerical, local priests advised their parishioners not to buy the paper, and it died. The experience remained with Laurier, the mature politician. At the mention of Bourget's name his noble forehead would wrinkle and his gentle eyes harden. Still loyal to his religion, his race and his province, he could weigh the case for and against the Canadian Catholic hierarchy in the Manitoba schools question and coolly decide what was politically right.

That was how he became Prime Minister in the amazing election of 1896.

When Mackenzie Bowell made his incredible decision to back the Quebec bishops and coerce the Manitoba Protestants, he was double-crossing his own side and was to founder because of it. He never suspected that Laurier was capable of matching him by betraying *his* side.

Yet from the time he entered the first Liberal Cabinet of Alexander Mackenzie, Laurier knew where he stood with the bishops. He wrote to a friend in 1875: "The moment I accept office I will go into it actively and earnestly and from that moment my quietness and happiness will be gone. It will be a war with the clergy, a war of every day, of every moment. I will be denounced as Anti-Christ."

He defined his principles of Liberalism in an address to the *Club Canadien* of Quebec in 1877. The bishops, he said, were trying to organize the faithful into one Catholic Conservative party. They had condemned Catholic Liberals as heretics. Did they not realize that this would weld the Protestant majority, too, into one party and open the way to a terrible religious war?

"More revolutions," he said, "have been caused by conservative obstinacy than by liberal exaggeration. . . . Wherever there is compression there will be explosion, violence and ruin. . . .

"I am a Liberal. I am one of those who think that everywhere in human things there are abuses to be reformed, new horizons to be opened up and new forces to be developed . . . there is always room for the perfecting of our nature and for the attainment by a larger number of an easier way of life. This in my eyes is what constitutes the superiority of Liberalism."

Laurier was searching for a middle course between anti-clericalism and subservience to the reactionary priests. He would move the *Rouges* from battles at cemetery gates to the high ground of parliamentary debate. He was ready to lead French Canada out of the seventeenth century, putting his own Canadianism ahead of his racial and religious ties. But would Quebec follow him?

In 1896, he put the matter to the test; he defied the bishops and supported Manitoba's right to close its Catholic schools. His campaign was a rare blend of principle and cynicism, the high road and the low. His Quebec organizer, Israel Tarte, told Liberal candidates outside Quebec to go ahead and be as anti-Catholic as their voters wanted them to be. "Make the party policy suit the campaign in other provinces," he said, "and leave Quebec to Laurier and me." So in the west, Clifford Sifton and his Grits lambasted the bishops and Laurier himself stood for provincial rights against federal coercion.

Inside Quebec, Laurier told his people the Conservatives had so mismanaged the situation that the Manitoba Catholics were already beyond help. Better elect a Liberal government with a Catholic leader who would try to smooth things over by and by.

The bishops blasted back. A *mandement* read in all Quebec Catholic churches warned all Catholics to vote only for candidates who pledged to vote for a return of the Manitoba schools. Individual priests declared that it was a sin to vote for Laurier. One threatened his flock with the fate of a neighboring village that had been buried by a landslide if they voted Liberal. These threats did the Liberals no end of good in Protestant Canada. But Laurier had to convince both Canadas. Again, would Quebec stick by the bishops or vote for the handsome heretic?

The returns showed that the Quebeckers had voted, neither against their bishops nor for Laurier, but against the Tories who had hanged Louis Riel. They remembered Laurier's passionate speech: "Had I been born on the banks of the Saskatchewan. . . ." Perhaps, too, they were tired of being pushed around by the priests.

Tarte's cynical strategy worked. Laurier came to the prime ministership as a conciliator who had brought the two Canadas together, the only rôle any successful leader can play. The methods he used were dubious, but the only way to get the two opposites to unite was to confuse or betray them. In 1896 the end justified the means — for a while.

Having defeated the power of the bishops at the polls, Laurier proceeded to undermine the power at its source. He sent two envoys to Rome to argue that the Manitoba schools settlement was the best available. The provincial government agreed to permit religious instruction in public schools "by any Christian clergyman" for the last half-hour of the school day. The Quebec hierarchy sent its men to Rome, too, and Laurier's representatives found "half ecclesiastical Canada there before us."

Intricate pin-dancing arguments droned through the dark chambers of the Vatican. Laurier's men dragged out 200 cases of political intimidation by Quebec bishops and priests. Antique papal bureaucrats nodded and mumbled. "The signal of retreat will never come from Rome," Bishop Bourget prophesied. But it did. After an apostolic delegate, Msgr. Merry del Val, had been dispatched to Canada, investigated and made his report, the Pope issued an encyclical to be read in all Canadian pulpits. It urged moderation, meekness, and brotherly charity. The bishops had shot their bolt. The attacks stopped.

In the lovely summer of 1897, Laurier and his wife Zöe sailed to London for Queen Victoria's Diamond Jubilee, knowing that he had calmed Quebec. Now he had the British to worry about.

The Jubilee was a spectacle to overwhelm kings and emperors, much less the man from St. Lin. There had never been anything like it, nor would there be again. It was the glaring high noon of the Empire. From the farthest ragged fringe of the red splotches on the world map, the Queen's subjects had come to do homage. Three million people cheered the miles of might and magnificence that tramped and trumpeted

through the streets of London. There were headhunters from
Borneo, befezzed Zaptiehs from Cyprus, big bearded Sikhs,
Jamaican Zouaves gleaming in red and blue, Hong Kong
Chinese in pointed hats, and Haussas from the Gold Coast
who had never worn shoes before. All were soldiers of the
Queen.

At the head of the colonial procession rode the tall,
slender Prime Minister of Canada and his lady, escorted by
the Governor-General's Guards, the Toronto Grenadiers in
their black busbies and the kilted Royal Canadian High-
landers. He was Sir Wilfrid now, the title sprung upon him too
late to refuse without offending the Queen. As first among
colonials, Canada's leader rode directly behind the state coach
of the little old Queen-Empress, rating a special roll of cheers.
Laurier wore the gold-trimmed cocked hat, gold lace, knee-
breeches and white stockings of an Imperial Privy Councillor.
Zöe was regal in grey silk with diamonds in her hair. It was a
heady day. If the pageantry could rouse beggars and cut-
purses to tears of fervor, what must it do to a shining new
knight?

Laurier's subsequent banquet speeches in Britain showed
what it did: "If a day were ever to come when England was in
danger, let the bugle sound, let the fires be lighted on the
hills and in all parts of the colonies . . . whatever we can do
shall be done . . . to help her."

"It would be the proudest moment of my life if I could see
a Canadian of French descent affirming the principles of
freedom in the Parliament of Great Britain."

These were just the sentiments the wily Colonial Secretary,
Joseph Chamberlain, wanted to hear. At the Colonial Conference that was to follow the Jubilee he intended to ask
Canada to contribute towards the Royal Navy. And he envis-
aged an imperial super-parliament in London that would take
over some of the responsibilities of the colonial assemblies.

Laurier conquered London society overnight. A figure so
stately, so gentle and charming yet dignified and remote, a

natural aristocrat from the backwoods, an orator of such depth and erudition (and loquacity — he could out talk anybody), a voice of such liquid purity deliciously tinged with French intonation — he was made to be lionized. The halfpenny *Daily Mail* noted, with unconscious condescension: "For the first time on record a politician of the New World has been recognized as the equal of the great men of the Old Country." No subsequent Canadian leader made such an impact — until Pierre Trudeau hit London in 1969.

By the time the bargaining began, Sir Wilfrid had his feet back on the ground. The champagne had worn off. He posed for the last of the colonial group photographs — old Joe Chamberlain seated in the center, monocled with top hat beside him, while his lieutenants of Empire stood around him. But Joe got nowhere with Laurier. He was a florid imperialist by night, when carried away by the mood of his audience and the moment. But next morning, at the conference, he would be a cold fish. As undisputed leader of the colonials he killed, ever so politely, the idea of an Imperial Parliament. There would be no Canadian money for the Royal Navy — Laurier planned to build his own navy one day. Although Laurier, being the best orator, outdid all the other colonial leaders in his expressions of loyalty, the question of support for England's imperialist wars was left hanging.

He looked back coolly on the British attempts to woo him and assessed them in a letter: "We were looked upon not so much as individual men but as colonial statesmen to be impressed and hobbled. . . . It is hard to stand up against the flattery of a gracious duchess. Weak men's heads are turned in an evening and there are few who can resist long. We were dined and wined by royalty and aristocracy and plutocracy and always the talk was of empire, empire, empire."

Chamberlain of the hard-nosed Birmingham merchant family (that later produced Neville of Munich) was outhaggled by the courtly gentleman from St. Lin. Laurier offered Imperial Preference, a trading arrangement between

Britain (and its colonies) and the Dominion, which would
supersede existing deals with Germany and Belgium. Sir
Charles Tupper, still the Tory leader, came to London to
denounce the scheme as absurd. But Britain renounced its
agreements with Germany and Belgium.

Laurier sailed home, via Paris and Rome. He had challenged the lords of the Empire at the height of their power,
drunk their heady wine, tickled the fancy of their duchesses,
and returned home with money in the bank. Few Canadian
leaders accomplished so much at so little cost. Laurier's secret
lay somewhere in the two dirt streets of St. Lin.

Charmed and charming as he was on these great British
occasions, he remembered he was not British. When Joe
Chamberlain rampaged on about the glories of a world order
based on British pluck and the superiority of the Anglo-
Saxons, he forgot that Laurier was a Gaul. There was no mind
so cool as that of the Canadien who had defied his bishops.
Laurier weighed and thought and determined. He envisioned
a Canadian nation under the British Crown but equal in status
with the tiny British Isles. He knew he was thinking far ahead.
These thoughts could not be expressed in the Kiplingesque
year of 1897 when the sun of Empire reached its height. But
an instant after noon the setting begins. Eleven years later
Laurier could tell the Toronto Tories at their Ontario Club:
"We are under the suzerainty of the King of England. We are
his loyal subjects. We bow the knee to him. But the King of
England has no more rights over us than are allowed by our
own Canadian Parliament. If this is not a nation, what then,
is a nation?"

From the glories of Europe, Laurier returned to the squalid
politics of Ottawa. The imperial hangover was upon him. "I
am not sure whether the British Empire needs a new constitution," he wrote wearily, "but I am certain that every
Jubilee guest will need one."

He had little time to recover from the imperial champagne
before the first imperial decision faced him: should Canada

send its few young men to fight Britain's wars of conquest? The Boer War had begun and Tupper was pushing to get Canadians over there. As ever, the British-Canadians were more loyal than the Queen. The French-Canadians saw no need to get into a distant little war which held no threat for Canada.

Chamberlain angled for a firm commitment that Canada would send troops as a matter of course, not just to South Africa but anywhere else they might be needed in future "small" wars. Laurier had promised to defend the Empire if it was threatened, but he saw little threat in forty thousand Dutch farmers opposing forty million Britons. He compromised. Canada would equip and transport a contingent of volunteers. A battalion of 1,100 men was raised and shipped off, followed by three squadrons of cavalry and three artillery batteries. In addition, Donald Smith, now Lord Strathcona the spike-driver, paid for 600 mounted rifles, to be named Strathcona's Horse. Altogether 7,300 Canadians fought in South Africa, as Canadian units, but under British orders.

Not enough, cried the Tories. They jeered Laurier as the first to ride in the Jubilee parade but the last to ride into action. On the French side, Henri Bourassa, grandson of the rebel Papineau, resigned from the House in protest against any Canadian involvement in Britain's war.

Laurier answered both tartly: "I have no sympathy for that mad, noisy, dull-witted and short-sighted throng who clamor for war . . . whilst I cannot admit that Canada should take part in all the wars of Britain, neither am I prepared to say that she should not take part in any war at all." Canada alone had the right to decide when to act and when to remain aloof.

Old Tupper banged the British drum across Ontario in the 1900 election. Laurier, he informed the Toronto Tories, was "not half British enough." Then he trundled into Quebec to cosy up to the extreme conservative *Bleus* and made the remarkable discovery that Laurier was "too English for me." Communications had improved in Tupper's 80 years and the two statements eventually filtered across the provincial boundary to meet with a jarring clang. The old Canadian game of bi-cultural doubletalk had to be played more cautiously from then on.

The nation was prospering for a change. Most of its people were proud of the performance of their troops in South Africa and of the war that had just been won. The Liberals returned comfortably to office and Tupper retired from politics, to be succeeded by a dogged Halifax lawyer, Robert Laird Borden.

The war issue had produced a more deadly threat than the protestations of Tory patriots. The day the decision was taken to send Canadian troops, a young Quebec M.P. walked into the Prime Minister's office and asked, "Mr. Laurier, do you take account of opinion in the Province of Quebec?"

He was Henri Bourassa, a small dandyish young man with an aggressive black beard and burning dark eyes. A harmless enthusiast, Laurier thought. He and Israel Tarte had brought him along in the party, partly out of nostalgia, because he was Papineau's grandson.

Laurier smiled. "My dear Henri, the province of Quebec does not have opinions; it only has sentiments." Bourassa burst into a violent tirade. The courtly Prime Minister put his hand on the smaller man's shoulder, "Ah, my dear young friend, you do not have a practical mind."

He shrugged as Bourassa stamped out and resigned his Commons seat. He did not know he had just met his nemesis. Bourassa was a rarity in the cool Canadian climate — a fanatic. He believed that he, not Laurier, embodied the spirit of French Canada — conservative, racist, separatist. His nationalist party was to burn away at Laurier's base in Quebec and tear at his political roots.

This lay ahead. At the time Laurier was embroiled with the Americans. Gold had been found in the Yukon; men were maddened by it and the madness spread to Ottawa and Washington.

The nuggets that George Carmack, the squaw man, found in August 1896 turned men's brains into baked beans. He found them, with Tagish Charlie and Skookum Jim, in Rabbit Creek, a trickling tributary of the Klondike river, soon to be renamed Bonanza Creek. Within two years the adventurers of the world were clawing their way to Dawson City in the Canadian Yukon territory, the heart of the new gold field. They brought to this fearful sub-zero desolation their women, their grand pianos, and their craziness.

But not their lawlessness. A handful of Mounties kept order. No gunslinging was allowed and the gambling hells closed each Sunday; no one bothered to lock his cabin door. The contrast with Skagway and Dyea, the American towns on the coastal approach routes to the Yukon, was extreme. There flourished absolute individuality, absolute crookedness and absolute depravity. Soapy Smith, the gangster, fleeced every traveller who turned his back. But once over the awesome passes into Canada the adventurer was safe from everyone but himself. The only enemies were greed, stupidity, loneliness, and the soul-shattering cold.

The Klondike put the Northwest on the map and revived an old boundary dispute between the United States and Canada. It inspired Laurier to make the premature claim: "The twentieth century belongs to Canada." And it raised the hackles of that classic American Tory President, Theodore Roosevelt. He had read Kipling, too, but his vision of Empire was all American. He wanted undisputed rights to the Alaska Panhandle which ran down the west coast, separating the Yukon treasure-house from the sea. Canada claimed ports of entry on the Panhandle to reach the interior of British Columbia and the Yukon.

So, in 1903, Britain negotiated for Canada once again, and handed the prize over to the United States. Big powers had to be placated; colonies could struggle along. Laurier, like Macdonald before him, had to watch a sell-out. But, unlike Macdonald, he wore no golden fetter. The temper of Canada was changing and the British Empire was no longer the only sun in the firmament.

In 1909 he started the first flutterings of an independent

foreign policy. He set up the Department of External Affairs, a faint, shadowy Foreign Office of his own. He told Parliament: "So long as Canada remains a dependency of the British Crown, the present powers that we have are not sufficient for the maintenance of our rights."

The nation was filling up, at last. In 1896, 16,800 immigrants arrived, in 1897, 32,000. During Laurier's fifteen years, more than two million came in, about 38 percent from Britain, 34 percent from the United States and the rest from Europe. The population jumped from under four million at Confederation to five million in 1901 and more than seven in 1911. Most of the newcomers went west, lured by free land — 160 acres per head — and the enthusiastic advertising of Clifford Sifton. As Minister of the Interior he reached out to grab immigrants where he could find them. Nine Canadian offices were opened in the U.S., each displaying the recently-developed hard wheat which could be grown profitably on the prairies. He brought American editors up to see for themselves, and offered Canadian junkets to selected British M.P.s. He reached into Europe, found no Frenchmen, few Scandinavians but enough Germans that the German government complained about attempts to lure their people to "this desolate sub-arctic region." The English cities yielded an unlikely assortment of furriers, hat-makers, grocers and butchers, few of whom had seen a farm.

Sifton struck it rich in the Ukraine. His agents there were given a bonus of five dollars per head of household and two dollars per family member delivered F.O.B. at a Canadian port. They were "peasants in sheepskin coats," he said, but of "good quality." Between 1887 and 1914 more than 200,000 of them were delivered, with their sheepskins, to Manitoba and Alberta. They could farm and they tore a living from the land. The years leading up to 1914 put some flesh on the nation's bare bones. Then came the Great War and immigration stopped.

While the Laurier government was packing in people, it was

dabbling in power. Power in the early 1900s meant a navy. Teddy Roosevelt had just demonstrated what might was all about by sending his Great White Fleet bucketing smokily around the world. Britain had more dreadnoughts (the best battleship going) than anyone else, but the German Kaiser was catching up in the naval race.

Britain needed more warships and Laurier rose to the occasion. "The supremacy of the British Empire is absolutely essential," he said. Canada would supply ships, but they would be Canadian ships.

Borden, the new Tory leader, had to agree. Hearts of Canadian oak, jolly Canadian tars — this was the stuff to daunt the Hun.

Well, almost. What Britain really wanted was cash to build her own ships on Clydebank, on the Tyne and the Mersey, and to man them with the pride of Portsmouth. As this message reached Canada, the Tories lambasted Borden for supporting Laurier's "tin pot navy." Such were the sorry beginnings of the Royal Canadian Navy which was to be forcibly submerged into the Pearson government's homogeneous armed forces a half-century later.

It was to start with five cruisers and six destroyers — cost, eleven million dollars or a three percent increase in the national budget. Laurier explained, in his best ambidextrous style, that when Britain went to war, Canada would go to war but the new navy would not go unless Canada sent it. Borden, looking for something to disagree with, examined statements like this in dismay. Finally he decided that the Canadian naval scheme had come too late. It must be shelved, he said, while Canada gave Britain the 35 million dollars urgently needed to buy three new dreadnoughts.

The tin pot navy survived such tin pot attacks. But then Bourassa brought his racist broadsides to bear. The navy would be used in every British war across the globe, he warned. The *habitant* would be shanghaied from his peaceful fields to shed his blood wherever the British whim should carry him. There was no German peril, said Bourassa, and if there were it was England's own fault.

At this point Laurier stumbled. He appointed to the Senate the member for Drummond-Arthabaska, causing a by-election in this safest of all Liberal seats in Quebec. Bourassa's new Quebec Nationalist party had to put up a candidate or shut up. Reluctantly Bourassa entered a challenger, an unknown local farmer. The riding was Laurier's old fiefdom and Bourassa was so certain of defeat that he prepared in advance an editorial for his new paper *Le Devoir,* explaining that "drunkenness, debauchery and tumult" had cost his party the election.

The Nationalists sent men in soldier's uniform from door to door, listing men of military age. They told the householders it was just to have the information ready when the Laurier Naval Act went into force. The *habitants* were warned that 50,000 heads of family would be shipped to Asia to fight for Britain. Bourassa's leaflets advised: "Those who disembowelled your fathers on the Plains of Abraham are asking you today to go and get killed for them." With such terror tactics the Nationalists won by 207 votes. Laurier was losing his hold on his native heath. His biographer, O. D. Skelton, called it the most important by-election in Canadian history.

The naval bill passed, but Laurier was scarred on both sides — as a would-be dispatcher of Canadian cannon-fodder and as a bath-tub Nelson. His independent fleet compares with the St. Laurent government's attempt to build Canada's own supersonic warplane, the Avro Arrow. Neither weapon contributed much to the science of war or the balance of world power. But each was, in its time, a tremendous morale booster for a small country. Arms are made to be brandished, not used. This is even truer today than it was at the turn of the century. But Laurier knew it; Diefenbaker, who killed the Arrow, did not.

After Drummond-Arthabaska, Laurier could feel power slipping away. The Liberals had been in power for fifteen years, having survived three elections since 1896. Sifton had left the Cabinet, claiming he had been double-crossed over the Manitoba schools affair. Apart from a promising young Labor minister called William Lyon Mackenzie King, the Cabinet lacked new blood. Something new must be added to the Laurier formula.

It was the U.S. President, William Howard Taft, who supplied it — reciprocity again, low tariffs, a chance to go back to the simon-pure Liberalism of the last century and secure the farm vote. The Republican Taft had been a high-tariff man. Now, in 1911, he had a sudden change of heart. Secretly, he offered to reduce the barriers to across-the-border trade without adding the usual American demand that Canada stop giving preference to British imports.

The word "tariff" has a political magic in Canada almost unknown anywhere else. Other lands have their sacred cows, their graven images, their flags, their martyrs. Canada survived on a delicate balance between the need for trade and the need for protection from the encroaching Yank. Now that the encroachment is nearly complete and he owns more than half of the manufacturers, the situation has changed. But there is eternal verity in the words of President Taft in a private letter to Teddy Roosevelt in 1910. Reciprocity, he wrote, would cause "a current of business between Western Canada and the United States that would make Canada only an adjunct of the United States."

Taft could see this as a Canadian argument against the deal he was offering and, he admitted "I think it is a good one." Laurier did not learn of the letter until after the election. Nor did he appreciate the demon he had conjured up with the tariff isue.

When word of the Taft offer leaked out all the old Canadian suspicions reawoke. What was Taft up to? Why had he changed his mind?

Laurier's own Liberals began the agitation. Sifton, the prairie strongman, denounced reciprocity in a manifesto signed by seventeen other party stalwarts. Bourassa's dark mind was still obsessed by the imperialist navy, but if attacking reciprocity was a way of getting at Laurier, fine, he would join in. The Liberal defectors turned to the bewildered Borden, imploring him to behave like a real Tory and wave Sir John A.'s Union Jack. He had always used the flag as a wrapper for a high-tariff policy.

As Ralph Allen pointed out in *Ordeal by Fire*, "When Sir John A. cried the immortal words 'A British subject I was born, a British subject I will die,' he was thinking in the immediate and specific sense not of Raleigh, Wolfe or Nelson, but of the tax on ladies' dresses from New York."

The campaign against Laurier now fell into place. "I am branded in Quebec as a traitor to the French," he said sadly, "and in Ontario as a traitor to the English. In Quebec I am branded as a jingo and in Ontario as a separatist. In Quebec I am attacked as an imperialist and in Ontario as an anti-imperialist. I am neither. I am Canadian. Canada has been the inspiration of my life."

Disdainfully, he combed his silver locks and strode forth to the fray, echoing the battle-cry of Henry of Navarre at Ivry: "Follow my white plume and you will find it always in the forefront of honor."

If the campaign had been fought on a field of honor, Canada's most perfect knight would have triumphed once again. But it was set on a continental stage. For the first time, the Americans were watching intently. Worse, they were barracking from the sidelines, offering Laurier the kind of support he could best do without.

The Speaker of the U.S. House of Representatives, J. Beauchamp ("Champ") Clark, achieved his place in any Canadian chamber of horrors by declaring, "I hope to see the day when the American flag will float over every square foot of the British North American possessions clear to the North Pole.... I have no doubt whatever that the day is not far distant when

Great Britain will joyfully see all her North American possessions become part of this Republic."

He added later: "We are preparing to annex Canada."

The Canadian Tories sang "Yankee Doodle Laurier." A
Conservative campaign poem read:

> Rise, rise up ere it falls, Lord and save us
> And blast with the fire of Thy mouth.
> The treason that barters our birthright
> For the gold of the Kings of the South.

Rudyard Kipling, the poet of Empire, cabled from London,
"It is her own soul that Canada risks today." On election night
someone threw a brick through the window of the Toronto
*Globe* office where the great Grit Brown had been murdered.

It was all over for Laurier. The unassuming Borden ascended to power on a fire not of his lighting. The first and greatest
French Canadian leader, now 70, stepped out gracefully. He
had moved Canada forward and beyond the narrow confines
of a cold colony. He had, for a time, breached the racial barrier between French and English, and he had carried on the
work of Macdonald, filling the empty spaces he left. It was
when he looked south and back to traditional Liberal continentalism — a trade deal with the Americans — that he fell.
But he did not see this. Statesman and sophisticate though he
was, he remained in his heart the man from St. Lin. "It is
becoming more and more manifest to me," he wrote, "that it
was not reciprocity that was turned down, but a Catholic
Premier."

**BORDEN**
1911-20

# VI.  *This Infernal Life*

Modest Robert Borden, who liked to ride to work on his bicycle, was welcomed back to Ottawa like a Caesar. One hundred happy Tories pulled his carriage through the streets, while thousands cheered and waved their Union Jacks. After fifteen years the suave, too-brilliant Frenchman had been laid low; the Conservatives had regained the leadership which they considered their natural heritage. A solid homespun Nova Scotian was now in charge.

Borden carried the blood-lines of the Canadian majority. The original Bordens came from the Weald of Kent and moved to New England in the seventeenth century. The Lairds, his mother's people, came from Scotland, via Ireland. Both sides migrated to Nova Scotia and Robert was born in 1854 on a small farm at Grand Pré near the Bay of Fundy. In his memoirs he remembered "the orchards, the upland fields, the distant meadows and the quiet village streets with their fine

Lombardy poplars and old willows. . . . The surf on the shores of Long Island, which lay north of the Grand Pré meadow, and the soughing of the south wind in the evening often lulling me to sleep."

Hè had little schooling. He worked all day on the farm and studied Latin, French and German on his own in the evenings. Yet at 14 he had a job as an assistant schoolmaster and a few years later, while teaching in New Jersey, heard himself addressed with the giddy title of "Professor." (The school, he said, had a weakness for high-sounding titles.) He never went to university but studied law as an articled clerk, and by the age of 40 he was a leading Halifax lawyer. His family were all Liberals; Robert turned Tory in his indignation at Liberal threats to take Nova Scotia out of Confederation.

He was to drive himself beyond the breaking-point and wreck his health, but in appearance he was always as tough as teak, the picture of Anglo-Saxon honesty and reliability. He never fought for the party leadership. It fell into his hands as the only reasonable candidate around. He was astonished, as he confessed to his diary, "at the multitudinous difficulties and embarrassments with which I was called upon to deal day after day."

He became Prime Minister at 58, when most men's minds and characters are settled for life. His was not a brilliant mind and there seemed no likelihood of its expanding. The one-time farm boy who still chewed tobacco, the meticulous lawyer and quiet politician was set in his ways. Three years later, when Europe exploded into war, rocking and nearly shattering Canada, his sturdy figure absorbed the impact.

In building his Cabinet he tried to include all elements of the unlikely alliance that had turned Laurier out — the Ontario Tories, the Bourassa Quebec nationalists, and Sifton's rebel Liberals. The Cabinet was a shaky structure with one truly notable member, the Minister of Militia and National Defence, Colonel Sam Hughes. He was notable because he was more than slightly mad.

Sam was an Irish Orangeman from Lindsay, Ontario, with a cold-eyed certainty of purpose, a fertile, if cloudy, imagination and no sense of humor at all. He had rushed into the Boer War determined to lead his own battalion of Canadians, but his arrogant antics so antagonized the British brass that he was for a time denied his command and even forbidden to wear uniform. What he actually did when he reached the front as a supply officer is not clear. According to his own dispatches, published in his own weekly paper, the Lindsay *Warder,* Colonel Sam and his faithful batman, Turley, practically won the war between them and undoubtedly earned two Victoria Crosses. These decorations never arrived, however, and for years Sam pestered Prime Minister Laurier to get them from the Imperial War Office. He became Canada's best-known unrewarded hero. He was a hard man to handle, as Borden knew when he took him into his Cabinet.

In 1911 he was still after his missing VCs. The new Governor-General, the royal Duke of Connaught, was horrified to get a letter from this jumped-up militia colonel recounting his ancient wrongs. Hughes now wrote of himself in the third person. In every one of a long list of engagements, "it fell to the lot of Hughes to direct the British forces and in each and every instance victory fell to their lot, although the numbers and positions were invariably in favor of the Boers." When Hughes left the battlefront, he wrote, the British General Warren was "sobbing like a child."

Connaught, a Field Marshal and third son of Queen Victoria, suggested pointedly to Borden that he get rid of Colonel Sam. But despite his incipient paranoia, Sam was doing a remarkable job of organizing the militia. All Canadian males, he declared, were to become marksmen by the age of twelve. "Give me one million men who can hit a target at 500 yards and we would not have a foe who could invade our country."

Invasion was no longer the threat. The Kaiser was marshalling troops and building dreadnoughts. The Empire was moving towards war. The naval argument began again in

Ottawa. Laurier was recovering from his defeat. "I don't feel ripe for Heaven," he said, "and at all events I want another tussle with the Tories." Borden stood before him, politically insecure and open to attack. The two men respected each other and would continue to do so. There was none of the loathing that was to pervade the King-Meighen or Pearson-Diefenbaker feuds. But it was Laurier's duty and pleasure to oppose.

Why, he began mildly, was there no mention of the navy in the first Throne Speech of the Borden government? A year before Borden had talked of dire emergency. There had been no time to build a Canadian navy. Laurier's naval bill was now law. Did the Tories propose to replace it?

Neatly, he chiselled a gap between the Tory imperialists and the Bourassa nationalists. If Borden truly wanted to help Britain he would have to ditch his fiery Quebec supporters.

Later leaders would refer such awkward questions as naval needs to a royal commission. Borden investigated it himself. He went to London to study sea-power and Canada's role in it. Like Macdonald and Laurier before him he began to perceive the need for an independent Canadian policy — no taxation without representation, no guns without a finger on the trigger. It would take four years of war and thousands of Canadian dead before he could demand these things. British Canada was still blindly loyal, and Borden was the essence of British Canada. The First Lord of the Admiralty, Winston Churchill, convinced him that war was indeed near and Borden agreed to ask Parliament for $35 million to present three dreadnoughts to the Royal Navy. As a slight sop to the Liberals, he insisted that Canadian officers must command the ships.

"O, ye Tory Jingoes," Laurier declaimed. "Is that the amount of sacrifice you are prepared to make? You are ready to do anything except the fighting."

The Tories ground their teeth.

Churchill sent them a message to bolster their case —

Canada, in the First Lord's estimation, could neither build its own fleet, sail it, or even keep it seaworthy. It was a classic insult, though probably true. The Liberals seized their chance to defend the national honor against this sneering Englishman (who, at the time, was a Liberal too). One M.P. said the message marked the start of Canada's separation from the Empire. Laurier staged a filibuster to hold up the $35 million. For two weeks he kept the House in session 24 hours a day until Borden, with an odd flash of subtlety, pulled a complex trick, forced a division and closed off the debate. The $35 million bill passed the House but was killed by the Liberal Senate. When war came fourteen months later Canada had two ancient training cruisers, one of which was seaworthy.

In the last days of July, 1914, Borden was holidaying on a Muskoka lake, tired, disillusioned and plagued by aching carbuncles. Laurier was sulking under his quiet maples at Arthabaska. An archduke had been assassinated at Sarajevo but that event was miles and seemingly centuries removed from the uncertain, quarrelsome land that claimed title to the twentieth century. Within a week Canada's political troubles were stilled; there was a sudden sense of uplift and unity. Borden never doubted that his British nation would follow the motherland into war without hesitation. Laurier agreed. When the life of the Empire was at stake, the French-Canadian patriarch would lead his men down the path of duty. Even Bourassa supported the war. He had been on holiday in Germany and had escaped on foot across the border just before it began. He opposed the spilling of Quebec blood in Britain's small wars, but not in a big one.

Parliament rallied solidly behind Borden and Britain — for the time being — and the government was given all the money it wanted for munitions. Sam Hughes, the possible hero of the Boer War, became the brass-bound copper-bottomed general-purpose hero of the moment. He had endured his day of doubt. On August 3, when it appeared Britain would not declare war, he roared, "They are going to skunk it. Oh, what a shameful state of things! By God, I don't want to be a Britisher under such conditions!" He ordered the flag lowered from its staff at the Ministry of Militia.

Next day the dogs of war were unleashed, and with them Sam. He charged out, sometimes in feathered hat, sometimes on horseback with a sword, grandly promoting officers on the spot — he promoted himself to Lieutenant-General within two years — bawling out commanders and arranging one of the fastest and most disorderly mobilizations in history. Within six weeks he had bundled 31,000 men with 8,500 horses aboard thirty ships in the St. Lawrence. They had boots that didn't fit, equipment that didn't work and many horses that didn't either. It took the Canadian commander, General E. A. H. Alderson, weeks to sort out the floating mess when it arrived in England. All that could be said about the first Canadian contingent upon arrival was that the men were keen, sober, furious at the enemy, and furious at Sam Hughes. Teetotalling Sam had forbidden beer in their canteens.

The battlefields of France and Belgium would turn these volunteers into soldiers unsurpassed anywhere. Hughes' contribution was that he got them there. By Regular Army standards he was only partly an officer and by no means a gentleman. He cursed colonels in front of their captains and subalterns before their men. One commander broke military rules to write to Borden, "Please get rid of this objectionable cad." Borden worried about Hughes, his generals, his men, and his prime ministership, which had grown into a job he had never imagined. Like a reluctant elected sheriff called upon to preside at his first execution, he now had to send thousands of men to their deaths. He needed a personality as strong as Hughes to attend to the gruesome mechanics.

For the first two years of war Hughes was in his element. He dismissed his critics as "yelping puppydogs chasing an express train." He, alone among officers on the Allied side, had the nerve to face the awesome Field Marshal Lord Kitchener in the Imperial War Office.

The official history of the Canadian Army in the First World War records the scene:

Kitchener: "Hughes, I see you have brought over a number of men from Canada. They are, of course, without training and this would apply to their officers. I have decided to divide them up among the British regiments; they will be very little use to us as they are."

Hughes: "Sir, do I understand you to say that you are going to break up these Canadian regiments that came over? Why, it will kill recruiting in Canada."

Kitchener: "You have your orders, carry them out."

Hughes: "I'll be damned if I will!"

Exit Colonel Sam, bigot, megalomaniac — and Canadian. He marched to the offices of Prime Minister Asquith and Chancellor of the Exchequer Lloyd George, and got his way. The Canadians stayed together. Borden needed such a man — for the time being.

Hughes was toppled by two enormous scandals that shattered the patriotic political unity in Ottawa — overpriced shells, and a bad rifle. Of all the honorary colonels Hughes created out of paunchy businessmen, his favorite was Col. J. Wesley Allison, who, he maintained to the end, was "the biggest and best man in Canada, and the cleanest, too." Allison was given what almost amounted to a licence to steal as a commission agent for the Shell Committee which bought munitions. Liberal investigators discovered that he had used it. The entire Shell Committee was a dubious operation — it bought, for example, twenty million dollars worth of fuses at four dollars apiece when the going rate was three dollars. Allison had gone further. For arranging a $1,500,000 loan and $10,000,000 in orders for a New York firm with a capital of $3,000, he took a kick-back of $220,000.

For a time Borden fobbed off the scandal by explaining that it wasn't Canadian money that was lost; the Shell Committee was buying for Britain. The Royal Commission that investigated was less disturbed by the dishonesty involved than by

the fact that American and not Canadian firms were getting
the benefit of it. Hughes was cleared of any complicity, but his
friend Allison was found guilty of "inexcusable conduct." He
kept his $220,000 but lost his honorary colonelcy.

At least nobody was killed as a result of that chicanery.
The tale of the Ross rifle was more serious. To an infantryman
his rifle is his livelihood and his life. The Ross was not the
soldier's best friend. Out of the 5,000 Canadians at Ypres,
1,452 threw away their Rosses and grabbed British Lee-
Enfields from the dead. General Alderson reported this
cautiously. It would be indelicate to suggest that this Cana-
dian-made weapon was not as serviceable as the British rifle.
But there was the verdict of the infantryman.

Hughes did not originate the Ross rifle; it was a holdover
from the Laurier administration. But, as a marksman, he fired
it and loved it. It was a fine target rifle; but when it was made
to fire 125 rounds in quick succession it overheated, jammed,
and even melted its foresight. Modifications designed to cure
this made it a pound heavier and seven inches longer than the
Lee-Enfield. When the troops complained, Hughes argued
that the ammunition was at fault. The Ross, he said, had never
been known to jam with good ammunition. The Canadians
who died kicking the stuck bolts of the hefty weapon could
not reply. Finally Sir Douglas Haig, the Imperial Commander-
in-Chief in the field, decided :"The Ross is less trustworthy
than the Lee-Enfield."

At the time Allison was exposed as a profiteering rogue,
the Canadians in the trenches thankfully handed in their Ross
rifles. The two scandals, exploding together, made Borden
decide that he would have to get rid of Colonel Sam — now
General Sir Sam Hughes. Four months later he demanded his
resignation. In his memoirs, written in 1928, Borden reflected,
"I discussed with Hughes when I appointed him his extraordinary eccentricities. . . . In my experience his mood might
be divided into three categories: during about half of the time
he was an able, reasoned and useful colleague working with

excellent judgment and indefatigable energy; for a certain other portion he was extremely excitable, impatient of control and almost impossible to work with; and during the remainder his conduct and speech were so eccentric as to justify the conclusion that his mind was unbalanced."

Sir Sam was safely dead when Borden made that judgment. He would not have risked it when Hughes was a public idol. As the old warhorse lay dying in Ottawa in 1921, some official remembered his love of special trains and ordered one to carry him home to Lindsay. The conductor asked Sir Sam if the train should go slowly on his last ride. "No," he replied, "tell 'em to go like blazes."

If the Minister of Militia had been slightly mad, his was nothing compared to the madness going on in France. By 1916 millions of men were sunk in putrid mud and water, moving perhaps a few yards back or forwards at a cost of piles of freshly dead, gassed, torn, burned, and bayoneted men. It was the biggest and worst of land wars and neither side was getting anywhere. The generals had no answer but more and more bodies, first alive and then dead. The politicians at home had to support the generals, for the generals represented the boys in the trenches, and there was no other channel of communication. The Canadians were dying, miserably or heroically, sometimes thankfully after the chlorine gas got to them. They were winning the respect of the Allied establishment. Lloyd George called the Canadian Corps "storm troopers" and acknowledged that after their performance at the Somme in 1916 "they were brought along to head the assault in one great battle after another."

This was gratifying to Borden but not much use in his growing troubles. Canada was still wholeheartedly behind the war but the unthinking fervor of 1914 had gone. The only reliable news that filtered home from the front was the butcher's bill. Only one officer and twelve men were left of the first battalion of the Princess Patricia's. (The officer was Captain Talbot Papineau, Henri Bourassa's cousin.) By May

1915, 20,000 Canadians were dead, wounded, or lost in the gas clouds.

In Britain, censorship, rage, and loyalty to dead comrades stifled most criticism of the war effort. Canada, being next door to the United States, was never sealed off from anti-war opinion. The mothers of America were singing, "I didn't raise my boy to be a soldier." And Bourassa — dubbed von Bourassa by the Montreal *Star* — was back at his old stand. He said the war effort was being run by "boodlers, vampires, the furnishers of bribes and electoral funds." Laurier pledged again his support of the war but added: "To all wrongs, to all frauds, we shall offer determined opposition." The normal political process had begun again.

There had been war frauds aplenty — profiteering in bad boots, bad horses, drugs, field dressings, trucks, bicycles, even jam. More costly still was the domestic scandal of the second transcontinental railway, the Canadian Northern, which would eventually become part of the Canadian National. In 1888 the CPR's monopoly was revoked by the Tories, and by 1902 the Canadian Northern system in the west and the Grand Trunk in the east were clamoring to set up cross-Canada lines. An attempt to amalgamate them failed and two new transcontinental systems were chartered in 1903. Both finally went broke during the Great War and were taken over by the nation to form the CNR. But before that, the promoters of the Canadian Northern, the Ontario Scots, William Mackenzie and Donald Mann, had gouged more from the taxpayer than any two men before. Their railway was always out of cash but they got richer and richer. The financial complications were baffling and the clearest picture that emerged was of Mackenzie and Mann, the magnificent debtors. Never was so much owed by so few to so many. Their company kept running out of funds and failing to pay its laborers, but M. and M. did very well.

This railroad row split the Tory party. Two future leaders emerged, each with a hand on the other's throat. Richard

Bedford Bennett accused M. and M. of "shameless mendacity." Borden's solicitor-general, Arthur Meighen, defended them. M. and M. passed the hat around once again and collected another $45 million from the taxpayers. On the face of it Meighen won, but in winning he acquired the reputation of Borden's hatchet man, the grim, acidulous defender of the rich and unscrupulous. Bennett, who was to become extremely rich as a corporation lawyer and confederate of the bold, bad Baron Beaverbrook, came out looking like the people's friend.

Laurier watched this Tory squabble with quiet pleasure and did not interfere. He was busy mounting a new attack on the Anglo-Saxons on the old gut issue of race and language in schools. In the Manitoba schools affair he had supported provincial rights against his own people. Now Ontario had ruled that English must be the language of all its schools, including those where all the pupils were French. The second language would be taught only in the first two grades. The ruling had been passed in 1912 and Bourassa had been making hay with it for years, denouncing Ontarians as "Canadian Prussians" and demanding relief for "the wounded of Ontario."

Why now, in the darkest period of the war, did Laurier, the uniter of the races, choose to drag this rotten piece of laundry-work before the Commons? Bruce Hutchison maintains that he did it to unhorse Bourassa and regain his own place as hero and father of French Canada: "To assure that place in history he would sacrifice office, power, policy, national reputation and life too."

In one of his soaring speeches he combined the battlefield and the Ontario classrooms: "It is true alas, that there are in my province men of French origin who, . . . when France is fighting the fight of heroism which stirs the blood of mankind, remain with their blood cold, who tell us 'No, we will not lift a finger to assist Britain in defending the integrity of France, but we want our wrongs to be righted in Ontario'. Wrongs or no wrongs, there is a field of honor, there is a call of duty."

Laurier was trying to spur recruiting in Quebec while keeping the Ontario schools question alight. He failed to get recruits and the Borden government refused to coerce Ontario into mending its ways. The Ontario Liberals agreed with Borden. Laurier brooded over his past career and offered his resignation as party leader. "I have lived too long," he said, "I have outlived Liberalism. The forces of prejudice in Ontario have been too much for my friends. It was a mistake for a French Roman Catholic to take the leadership. . . . I told Blake that thirty years ago." His resignation was refused, but he continued to feel sorry for himself.

Borden felt the same way. He couldn't sleep. He had sciatica, lumbago and neuritis. He wrote: "How tired and sick I am of this infernal life."

He had accomplished remarkable things. He had created a relatively enormous munitions industry and sent 280,000 volunteers to France out of a nation of eight million. He went to France to visit these men. He toured the trenches and he talked with the torn remnants of Canadian soldiers in a dozen hospitals. He maintained the square Nova Scotian gruffness of his war leader image as he bent over the beds of the dying but, he wrote in his diary, he could hardly restrain his tears.

When he returned to Canada he was convinced, rightly or wrongly, that only conscription could supply sufficient replacements to keep the Canadian units going. The Empire needed more men, and the Empire must have them. He would never understand Laurier. Staunch as any Anglo-Saxon on his "field of honor," rousing his kinsmen to fight, the great Liberal could still find time to argue about French lessons in schools. Perhaps the two leaders were sending men to die for different causes. Laurier sent knights to joust for the glory of their homeland; Borden sent infantrymen to die for this portion of the British Empire. Their final confrontation was near.

Borden tried to avoid it by forming a coalition with Laurier's Liberals. They had agreed to extend the life of Parliament for one year, but there had to be an election before the end of 1917 and a wartime campaign on the conscription issue would strain the country's vitals. Young Mackenzie King warned Laurier it might wreck the Liberal party, but Laurier refused a coalition.

Borden set Arthur Meighen to work drawing up a conscription bill while he redeployed his support into a so-called Union government. The Quebec nationalists had left him; Clifford Sifton and his English-speaking Liberals replaced them. The bill was introduced to Parliament with a trumpet call from Borden — Don't betray our boys in the field. If it were rejected, he warned, they might come home "with fierce resentment and even rage in their hearts."

This brought into the open the bitter certainty of the Anglo-Saxons that the French-Canadians were shirking their duty, or considered fighting not to be their duty at all. This was not entirely true.

In the first rush to the colors, two of every three recruits were not native Canadians but immigrants from the British Isles. True, only 1,200 French-Canadians joined the first Canadian contingent of 30,000, but Quebeckers were mainly rural people and rural recruiting was low everywhere. And Sam Hughes' recruiting methods in Quebec were deplorable. The Orangeman sent too-British Protestant tub-thumpers out to rouse the *habitants.* His chief recruiting officer in the Province was an English-speaking Baptist pastor. He was against French-Canadian regiments and French-Canadians as such. The Quebecker who joined his original forces could expect to forfeit his religion and French identity as well as his life. Sam Hughes had been dumped from the Cabinet but he was still in Parliament, bellicose as ever.

By 1917 the choleric English curses he heard on all sides had convinced the *habitant* that he was regarded as a traitor in Ontario whether he joined up or not. Bourassa screamed that he was protecting the disembowellers of his forebears. Laurier told him conscription was an Ontario Tory weapon aimed at Quebec: "Everyone who favors conscription favors the movement not because he believes it necessary but because Quebec is represented to be against it."

It was a savage election campaign. Tory posters proclaimed "A Vote for Laurier is a Vote for the Kaiser." A Toronto Tory committee called Laurier "the tool of Bourassa," while Bourassa himself called him "the most nefarious man in Canada."

The Liberals argued that voluntary enlistment was working — between six and seven thousand were joining up each month — and tried to divert the campaign to Tory graft and mismanagement of the war. But the real issue was whether Borden could be trusted. Just to make sure, Borden pushed through a wartime election bill that took the vote away from conscientious objectors and immigrants who had been in Canada less than fifteen years (people who might vote Liberal) and gave it to wives and mothers of soldiers (who would certainly vote Conservative). And the soldiers' vote, mainly Tory, was split up and used in the constituencies where it would do the government supporters most good. This crude and blatant bit of gerrymandering was Meighen's work and it would come back to haunt him.

When the returns were in and properly salted with the soldiers' ballots, Borden had 153 seats out of 235. He held all the provinces except Quebec. As Mackenzie King had warned, the Liberal party was wrecked as a national vehicle; it was now a French-Canadian splinter.

Conscription was the law of the land, supported by the majority, but it still had to be enforced. The Catholic Church in Quebec had backed the war up to a point; now it saw its rights endangered and its young men about to be taken away. "We are nearing racial and religious war," said Montreal's Archbishop Bruchési. In Quebec City, mobs smashed and burned a recruiting office, a police station and two newspaper offices. Troops from Toronto were sent in and charged the rioters with cavalry swords and bayonets. When snipers shot at them from housetops they replied with machine-gun fire.

Four civilians were killed, five soldiers wounded, and hundreds of young Quebeckers fled to the hills.

The trouble was not confined to Quebec. Five thousand farmers, mostly from Ontario, marched on Ottawa demanding the exemption for farm boys be restored. And a Tory Cabinet Minister told the Commons: "There are thousands, yes hundreds of thousands of people in the rest of Canada (outside Quebec) who have tried assiduously to evade military service."

Even when the riots had been put down and squads of police sent to hunt draft-dodgers, conscription did not work. Out of 404,000 unmarried men between 20 and 34 who registered by the end of 1917, 380,000 claimed exemption. Out of 125,000 registered in Ontario, 118,000 tried to avoid serving. In Quebec 117,000 registered and 115,000 tried to get out. By the end of the year, conscription had added a mere 83,000 men to the army, of whom 47,000 got overseas. The monthly rate of enlistment was lower than under the voluntary system.

The Great War cost Canada 60,000 dead and a split in the national fabric that never completely healed. All Laurier's work of bringing French and English together was destroyed. His party was confined to Quebec, powerless beyond the Ottawa River. The Tories lost French Canada and with it the hope of governing the nation as a whole. When Laurier died of a sudden stroke in February, 1919, he left only the memory of great words and a shining personality. His deeds had been overtaken. His last words, as he pressed his wife's hand, were "*C'est fini.*"

\*     \*     \*     \*

Deep in the middle of the war a British liner steamed across the Atlantic, blacked out, its crew alert for U-boats. On the bridge was a large canvas bag, heavily weighted with lead. The captain had orders to throw it overboard if there were any danger of the ship being captured. It contained the first British secrets of any military value to be entrusted to a

Canadian Prime Minister. They were sent because the stolid workaday Borden staged what was, for him, a tantrum.

For years he had torn his nerves, his health, and his political position to pieces to help the British war effort. Yet all he had learned of the progress of the war came from the censored British newspapers. He asked the Colonial Secretary, Andrew Bonar Law, to remedy this but Law, a Canadian himself, knew how to handle colonials. It was not practicable to keep Borden informed, he wrote. What's more, the question should not have been raised.

At this insult from an insufferable expatriate, Borden blew up. He wrote to his High Commissioner in London: "It can hardly be expected that we shall put four hundred thousand or five hundred thousand men in the field and willingly accept the position of having no more voice and receiving no more consideration than if we were toy automata. . . . Is this war being waged by the United Kingdom alone, or is it being waged by the whole Empire? Procrastination, indecision, inertia, doubt and hesitation and many other undesirable qualities have made themselves entirely too conspicuous in this war." He quoted a British Cabinet minister's opinion — the chief shortage in the war effort was of brains. Some of those running the show in London could not have handled things worse if they were traitors.

This got results. First came the bag of secret papers, then an announcement by Bonar Law's successor that His Majesty's government felt fuller information should be given — a weekly confidential letter would be sent to Canada. About the same time an Imperial War Cabinet was formed to give Borden and other Empire leaders at least an appearance of participation in important decisions. His membership in this new body gave Borden his chance to gain for Canada a bigger say in world affairs.

In London he teamed up with Jan Christiaan Smuts the South African leader to write a momentous resolution. It demanded "full recognition of the Dominions as autonomous nations," with complete control of their domestic affairs and the right to "an adequate vote in foreign policy and foreign relations." Borden proposed it, Smuts seconded it and it had the support of Australia, New Zealand and Newfoundland. They hardly dared to hope that Prime Minister Lloyd George and his Cabinet would agree. But they did. Britain and the Empire were fighting for their lives and the Dominions were needed. Smuts told Borden: "You and I have transformed the British Empire." That effort led to the Declaration of 1926 and the Statute of Westminster, 1931, the charters of Canadian independence and the beginnings of the Commonwealth.

These were the results of Borden's first great outburst of temper. He had one more left in him that would be equally effective. When Armistice came on the eleventh hour of the eleventh day of the eleventh month of 1918, the Prime Minister, now a tired but toughened leader, told his Cabinet he would not settle for second best at the forthcoming peace conference. The nation that had lost 60,000 men would demand its own independent delegation — not merely a few seats on the British side of the table. He got it, despite the deep suspicion of the American President Woodrow Wilson and French Prime Minister Georges Clemenceau. Why, they inquired, was the British Empire demanding seats for its various pieces? Was Lloyd George trying to pack the conference and grab control of the postwar world? Wilson didn't wait for an answer. When the next step was ready, a meeting of all the Great Powers to create his dream of a League of Nations, he prepared to pack it with little U.S. satellites who had never fought in the war to preserve democracy and wouldn't recognize democracy if it hit them in the face.

Again Borden raged. "The Dominions," he said, "have maintained their place before the world during the past five years through sacrifices which no nation outside of Europe has known. I am confident that the people of Canada will not tamely submit to a dictation which declares that Liberia or Cuba, Panama or Hedjaz, Haiti or Ecuador must have a

**MEIGHEN**
1920-21
1926

# VII. *Arthur the Ready*

In the early spring of 1919 the boys came marching home. They paraded one last time for their cheering hometown folks, dismissed and looked around for jobs. Jobs were scarce and heroes found themselves at the back of the queue. The land was wide and welcoming as ever, but the innocent years were gone. The nature of Canadian society was being challenged — not violently, as in Europe, but insistently. The One Big Union had arrived in Canada.

Two months after the remnants of Princess Patricia's Canadian Light Infantry marched through Ottawa to receive their due welcome from the Governor-General, a general strike broke out in Winnipeg. It began with 2,000 metal workers and spread to 35,000 people, including streetcar operators, cooks, waiters, bakers, truck drivers, plumbers, carpenters, postmen, firemen — enough to paralyse Canada's third largest city which then had a population of 200,000. The police voted to strike, but the strike committee which ran the city like a military junta, asked them to keep order. Sympathy strikes were called in Toronto, Vancouver, Edmonton and Calgary, but these cities did not come to a halt.

So began the sad, short regime of Arthur Meighen. He was not yet Prime Minister — Borden was on holiday trying to regain the strength sapped by the war — but as Minister of Justice and of the Interior he was minding the store.

The Industrial Workers of the World, the Wobblies or One Big Union, was probably the most successful band of revolutionaries North America had seen since the band of arch-Tory aristocrats and horny-handed farmers George Washington led. The IWW still exists in a seedy little office in Chicago. Its surviving functionaries were holding a sentimental meeting while that city was torn apart by bearded young revolutionaries and savage cops during the 1968 Democratic Party Convention. It is now a faded memory, but in 1919 it was a force in Canada. Its basic plan — to supplant craft unions with the one big union that would strike when any segment of labor was threatened — worked in Winnipeg. Its ultimate goals were the end of the profit system and a soviet form of government. To start with, it wanted a six-hour day and a five-day week.

Meighen sniffed at these winds of change and smelled bolshevik conspiracy. The United States was gripped by its first great Red scare and its Attorney-General, Mitchell Palmer, was finding Reds under every bed. Five immigrants with Russian-sounding names were active in Winnipeg and that was enough to persuade Meighen to follow Palmer's method. In a dramatic dawn raid 50 Mounties and 100 special police crashed into the homes of the strike leaders and carted a dozen of them off to the federal penitentiary at Stony Mountain. News of the arrests caused a six-hour riot in which two died, but the Mounties crushed it and the strike was put down.

The five alleged Russians had to be released for lack of

evidence, and the government was left with ten supposed seditious conspirators, including two city aldermen, a member of the Manitoba Legislature and the Rev. James Shaver Woodsworth, who was to become the father of the anti-Communist social democratic movement in Canada.

Meighen unwisely revealed his motives in a telegram to a local Justice Department agent: "Notwithstanding any doubt I have as to the technical legality of the arrests and detention at Stony Mountain, I feel that rapid deportation is the best course now that the arrests are made, and later we can consider ratification." After Winnipeg, Meighen could add labor to his growing list of enemies. Quebec already hated him for pushing conscription; non-Anglo-Saxon immigrants cursed him for taking their vote away to give to soldiers' wives; and the farmers knew him for an unreconstructed high-tariff Tory. When he succeeded Borden as Prime Minister in July, 1920, his failure was assured. He accomplished practically nothing and his mistakes, blazing like misdirected rockets, served only to illuminate the drab beginnings of that most successful of all Canadian politicians, Mackenzie King.

Meighen loathed King with a physical revulsion he barely bothered to conceal. He first met him in debate as a fellow-student at the University of Toronto — a small, fat lad with an oily manner, nicknamed Rex. Both came from small-town Ontario families but Meighen's father was a poor farmer; King's a sharp lawyer-politician.

The Meighens, who stemmed from Ulster, were unbending hell-fearing Presbyterians and their Arthur was a remote, shy scholar with a quarrelsome manner. His gift of words was a weapon which he honed and polished until he could attack the world with it. He rehearsed his speeches for school debates in the woods with only birds and squirrels for an audience. He revelled in Shakespeare and could quote whole scenes from his plays without a slip. "While language is the vehicle of thought," he said, "it is a great deal more. It is part of the texture. It is inseparable from the thought itself."

Meighen taught school for a time, then quarreled with the trustees and quit. He moved west, failed as a smalltime business entrepreneur, then took up law and became an instant success at the Manitoba bar. He married and settled in Portage la Prairie. The first of his three children was christened Theodore Roosevelt Meighen — an early indication of his theory of leadership. Borden met him during a trip out west, liked his gaunt integrity and hard mind, and brought him along rapidly as his protégé. When something swift and ruthless had to be done, Meighen's mathematically-balanced brain would devise it and his fine sarcastic tongue defend it. He attacked the arms profiteers and braved the soldierly wrath of Sam Hughes. He also dug up yet another government loan for the bankrupt railway millionaires Mackenzie and Mann, and in so doing skewered and lambasted their attacker, R. B. Bennett. Like all those who were scarred by Meighen's wonderful weapon of words, Bennett remembered and waited. Old wounds are the slowest to heal. Politicians remember best the hurts inflicted upon them in their early insecure years before the case-hardening process begins.

Mackenzie King's maiden speech as Liberal leader in 1919 was no masterpiece. Meighen listened to the dreadful little Rex, his antagonist of the U. of T. debates who had somehow stumbled into ridiculous prominence, then fell upon him.

"If I have one suggestion to offer to the fair rose of expectancy of His Majesty's loyal Opposition," he sneered, "it is that when we have a concrete subject for debate before the House he would be good enough to offer some remarks which really bear upon the merits of the issue and leave out of consideration, if he possibly can, these old hackneyed phrases 'democracy', 'autocracy of executives' and all the rest of it, which have no more relevancy to this discussion than were he to discuss the merits of the government of Japan." Little King, the very junior, practically unknown leader, looked suitably abashed at this brilliance. Nobody could tell what he was thinking. Nobody ever could.

A few months later when Meighen formally succeeded Borden as Prime Minister, King rose to offer his compliments with a cherubic smile. "On personal grounds," he oozed, "it was to me both a source of pride and pleasure to learn that His Excellency had chosen as his first adviser one who in university days was a fellow undergraduate and whose friendship, through a quarter of a century, has survived the vicissitudes of time, not excepting the differences of party warfare and the acrimonies of political debate."

There was not a hint of sarcasm, not a weak spot on this bubble of hypocrisy that Meighen could stab. He listened and was sickened. Perhaps Rex meant it. If so, he was more contemptible than ever.

(Rex didn't mean it. He confided to his diary that it was a bad thing for the country that Meighen had become Tory leader but a fine thing for the Liberals. "It is too good to be true," he chortled. "I can fight him naturally. The issues will become clear and distinct. It is the beginning of a speedy end to the Unionist administration.")

Meighen and King cleared the decks for the 1921 election. It was to be the first three-way struggle since Confederation. The farmers had taken a long look at the two major parties and found them wanting. The Tories, as ever, would protect the eastern moguls; the Liberals had been stung so badly over reciprocity in 1911 that their new fellow King no longer talked of free trade but had invented something called "freer trade." So out of the cornfields came a new force — the Progressive party, led by a long lean westerner called Thomas Alexander Crerar. The farmers had done well during the war, when acreage nearly doubled and prices tripled. Now the price of wheat was down from $2.50 to $1 a bushel, but the farmers had no intention of returning to the bad old days.

The sun and the rain determined the crops, but the government determined the prices, so the farmers determined to get into the government. In October, 1919, the Conservative government of Ontario was suddenly overwhelmed by the

United Farmers' party, which jumped from three to forty-five provincial seats. On the same day, farm candidates won five Federal by-elections. Three months later, 100 farm delegates met in Winnipeg to launch the national Progressive Party, dedicated to free trade.

Meighen, a farmer's son born in good old-fashioned Christian poverty, lectured the farmers on the error of their ways. "The public mind is confused with a veritable babble of uninformed tongues," he began in his best superior manner. "Thousands of people are mentally chasing rainbows, striving for the unattainable, anxious to better their lot but seemingly unwilling to do it in the old-fashioned way by hard, honest intelligent effort."

Free trade, he warned, had depopulated rural England, filled the emigrant ships, starved Ireland and ended Britain's supremacy in industry. It would ruin Canada too.

Huge colored posters proclaimed "Canada Needs Meighen" and showed his domed schoolmasterish figure dragging a shipwrecked Canada ashore.

Canada felt neither shipwrecked nor in need of Meighen. It wanted change and hope, not penny lectures. Hard, honest toil was all right, but war profiteers had made fortunes under a Tory government without recourse to it.

While Meighen was flailing at harvesters out west, King quietly repaired the Liberal party in the east. He had written off the prairies to the Progressives. He would not fight them or argue with them about tariffs. They were friends and allies against the outrageous Tories and should be treated as Liberals who had gone slightly astray but would soon come home, wagging their tails behind them. Although Crerar rejected King's offer of deals — he offered to withdraw his Liberal candidates from some contests if Crerar would do likewise — King was sure he could swallow the Progressives eventually. And eventually he did. In 1921 they beat the Conservatives for him — they and the changing mood of the times which Meighen never understood.

When the votes were counted in December, 1921, 117

Liberals were elected, 65 Progressives and only 50 Conservatives. Meighen and nine of his ministers lost their seats. The Tories were not even entitled to form the official Opposition, although they did so after Crerar refused.

The defeat was not so much Meighen's fault as his destiny. He steamed forward on his ordained course while the country went the other way. He never tried to shed his image as the dour dominie. Only his family and close friends knew that the private man was cheerful, humorous and never put on airs.

The image of another ruthless prosecutor, Robert Kennedy, was to be softened by his habit of turning up on State occasions wearing sneakers. Meighen once showed up in the House absentmindedly wearing bedroom slippers, but the event went almost unnoticed. So did the story of his overcoat — a garment so old and disreputable that his colleagues once stole it from him on a train and threw it out the window. A railwayman found it on the track and returned it; Meighen wore it for several more years.

If he had stayed longer in the prime minister's office, there would have been time for his more endearing qualities to shine through. As it was, he endured the frustrations of the job without the rewards. After a few months in it he remarked that he felt like the bookstore clerk who, when asked if he had *The Life of St. Paul*, replied that he hadn't the life of a dog and intended to quit the damn' job on Saturday night. His intellect won him admirers but few friends. Those who stayed around him, braving the blazing candlepower of his convictions, discovered an amiable companion and a loyal friend. Crerar, who fought him in 1921, ended by worshipping him and detesting King. Yet this private warmth never radiated from Meighen the Prime Minister. His state uniform was secondhand, bought from a retired statesman, and his principles came straight from the copperplate maxims in his schoolboy copy-books. From one of them sprang the slogan by which the wordsmith is best remembered "Ready, aye, ready!"

In September, 1922, Canada was vaguely aware of a small

crisis in the Dardanelles, the strait commanding the sea link between the Mediterranean and the Black Sea, scene of a great Allied disaster in the Great War. The Greeks and Turks had been massacring each other in the area. Now, an Allied garrison left over from the war was trapped at Chanak, liable to be wiped out by the Turks. No Canadians were involved and the government, once again, knew nothing of the crisis but what it read in the newspapers. On September 15 it read with horror an Associated Press dispatch from London: "Great Britain has invited Canada and the other British Dominions to be represented by contingents in the British force taking part in an effective defence of the neutral zone in the Near East, it was authoritatively reported today."

Winston Churchill, now Colonial Secretary, had struck again. The invitation to shed blood in a small war appeared in the press before a secret cable to that effect reached Ottawa. What had happened to all the arrangements for consultation contrived by Borden during the War? Did the British think all they had to do was whistle and Canada would jump?

Some jumped. The Montreal *Star* and the Toronto *Globe* promptly clicked their heels and said Britain knew best. Volunteers rushed to militia depots in British Canada. French Canada watched with amazement and some alarm. Overnight the country was back in the mood of the conscription crisis of 1917-18.

Mackenzie King was furious both at the Churchill request and the way it had been made — by press leak, appealing to the Dominions over the heads of their leaders. He wrote, "It is drafted designedly to play the imperial game, to test out centralization versus autonomy as regards European wars. . . . I am sure the people of Canada are against participation in this European war." As always, King could see the move after next. The Progressives would be against sending troops. Now might be the time to bring them into the government. Quebec, of course, was against. This was a chance to comfort Quebec. For the time being, King would do nothing.

Not so Meighen. He spoke from his British heart and schoolboy loyalty: "When Britain's message came, then Canada should have said 'Ready, aye, ready: we stand by you'."

The crisis died down in a few days. There was no fighting and Chanak was soon forgotten everywhere but in Canada. Meighen was branded forever as a knee-jerk imperialist.

He never regretted his patriotic broadside; he was not given to second thoughts. King, in his revolting waffling way might have won that round, but just retribution was waiting around the corner. Honesty was the Best Policy and Crime Did Not Pay, Meighen knew, and Rex would soon find that out. The great Customs scandal was bubbling up like a batch of bad booze.

When the United States, as one man, swore off drink in January, 1920, Canadians happily cashed in. Canada became the biggest smugglers' cove in history. As succeeding governments, federal and provincial, pointed out, it was all perfectly legal. The Americans, through the Eighteenth Amendment to their Constitution, had outlawed all alcoholic beverages and created a hundred-million-headed monster of thirst. Organized crime began with Prohibition; so did the Canadian whiskey industry which still dominates the U.S. market the way practically every other U.S. manufacturing industry dominates Canada.

Although the Canadian provinces followed the American example in banning strong drink, it was done in a piecemeal way. The country was never completely wet or completely dry and never was profit sacrificed to principle. While Ontario and Quebec denied hard liquor to their residents, they encouraged the building of the world's biggest distilleries to pump bootleg booze across the border. The "noble experiment" corrupted the United States and brought the gangster era. It also corrupted Canadians more than any subsequent American aberration from flagpole-sitting to the seizing of universities. Along 4,000 miles of border and by sea from Nova Scotia to the quiet coves of Maine or from Victoria to Puget

Sound, Canadian smugglers plied their neighbors with forbidden bottles. The sturdy Atlantic fishermen left their nets
to carry rum; the prairie farmers took time off to lug jugs
southward by wagon or bicycle.

The Meighen and King governments grinned, remembering
how the U.S. authorities turned a blind eye to the Fenian
raids. There had always been something romantic about
smuggling and now it was all in a good cause. The Americans
had made themselves particularly unpopular in Canada since
the war by claiming that they had won it singlehanded. Now
they had obviously gone collectively mad and they had it
coming to them. Britain and Canada shouted "freedom of the
seas" when U.S. customs boats pursued their rum-runners outside territorial waters. Canada disdainfully rejected American
appeals to stop the shipment of liquor at its source.

It was three years before the King government woke up to
the fact that you can't run a billion dollar smuggling business
without breeding some disrespect for the law — not just the
American law — anybody's law. The boats were returning
from Rum Row laden with American goods to be smuggled
into Canada. Enormous quantities of Canadian liquor were
being consumed duty-free in Canada because the government
assumed it was manufactured to be bootlegged to the States.
(There were forged papers to prove it left the country, but by
this time the Customs men assumed as a matter of course that
all papers relating to whiskey were forged. They hardly blinked
at documents proving a ship had been to the Caribbean and
back three times in one week, or had made the round trip to
Peru in two days.)

Black anarchy enveloped the Customs houses. Obviously,
somebody was going to make a dollar, and somebody did.
Joseph Bisaillon, Chief Preventive Officer at Montreal, knew
his trade backwards. In his off-duty hours he ran a private
customs brokerage and he owned two old houses in Rock
Island, a smuggling village where the properties conveniently

straddle the Canadian-U.S. border. His name figures in two strange cases — the disappearance of $35,000 worth of narcotics that had been seized by the Customs, and the saga of the barge *Tremblay*, whose crew and cargo of 16,000 gallons of spirits had been grabbed by the Quebec Liquor Commission, only to be liberated by Bisaillon in the name of the Crown. The 16,000 gallons were subsequently sold by the Customs Department as rubbing alcohol, priced 36 cents a gallon, to a well-known legal bootlegger who then exported it to the States as drinking alcohol. The Meighen Conservatives charged in Parliament that the government lost $200,000 in revenue on that one shipment.

King had removed his veteran Minister of Customs to the Senate — nine filing cases full of allegedly damaging evidence went with him. Now the new Minister, George Boivin, was up to his neck in the *Tremblay* affair. Worse, he had been caught with his thumb on the scales of justice: springing from jail a convicted smalltime bootlegger who happened to be a Liberal party organizer.

King called an election before the Customs scandal reached full bloom but lost it just the same. Meighen's Conservatives won an incredible 116 seats to the Liberals' 99 and the 24 Progressives were in control of the House. King was defeated in his own constituency, but he proposed to find another seat in a by-election, stay on as Prime Minister and govern with the support of the Progressives. There are two versions of his conversation with the Governor-General, Lord Byng, but whatever actually was said, Byng agreed to let him carry on. King arranged a seat for himself in Prince Albert.

Meighen was sure the day of judgment was at hand. The Tories had marshalled evidence of wholesale graft—a government department not only linked with but practically operating a giant smuggling ring. The facts were simmering in the Customs Committee. It only remained to pour them out and the wretched King was done for.

When the Committee duly convicted the Customs Department of graft and corruption but spared the Liberal government as a whole, Meighen moved in for the kill. The Tories put a motion of censure against the Prime Minister for failing to take action in the scandal and against Boivin for interfering with the course of justice. If passed, this would destroy King more completely than Macdonald in the Pacific Railway scandal. No prime minister had yet been overthrown by a vote in the House. When it became clear that the motion would pass, King ducked for the only exit. He went to the Governor-General and demanded the dissolution of Parliament and a new election.

Lord Byng refused. An hour later King entered the House, eyed the vultures in the galleries who had come to watch his demise, bowed to the Speaker and announced that his government had resigned because the Governor-General refused his advice to dissolve Parliament. He moved the adjournment of the House and added grimly, "I might say that this motion is not debatable."

Meighen was summoned by Lord Byng and asked to form a government. He had glimmerings of the trap he was entering but the call of duty was clear. Ready, aye, ready, Meighen picked up the tarnished but tempting torch.

Now it was his turn to govern from behind a curtain. Under the rules of the day, a newly-appointed Prime Minister and his Cabinet had to resign their seats and seek re-election. Yet if he and the seven men he had picked as ministers were to leave the House it would destroy his hope of a majority. He tried to get around this by appointing them acting unpaid ministers. They remained in their seats while he resigned his. Until a by-election could be called, he had to lurk in the corridors outside the House, composing the great speeches he should be making inside, but unable to deliver them.

For two days the Meighen government went about its business. The House passed the Customs censure motion against the now-dead King government but the savor had gone out of that victory since King had ducked out before the blow fell. On the second night, as the House settled down to boring supply motions — salaries, purchase of copies of the Parliamentary Guide — Mackenzie King rose, to inquire blandly and pleasantly, if the acting ministers on the Treasury Benches had taken their oaths of office. No, they had not, they said, but they were entitled to sit there, as they were not drawing Cabinet pay.

In a moment, King was transformed. He roared and raged. The House, he shouted, was voting large sums of money to these men who had no right to govern. They were mocking the Constitution. The Meighen government was illegal. Meighen was destroying a thousand years of tradition. Liberty and freedom were threatened.

The Tories laughed but the Progressives listened. If King was right, this was a bigger scandal than 16,000 gallons of liquor.

King went on to challenge the Governor-General's right to refuse dissolution. For a century no British monarch had refused his Prime Minister's advice. If Byng got away with it Canada would be back in the status of a Crown colony. Meighen, by accepting responsibility for Byng's refusal, had mocked everything Canada held dear.

Meighen stormed helplessly behind his curtain. He could shatter the little charlatan with words, bury him with arguments, slice him with scorn. But he couldn't get at him. He had no seat in the House. The constitutional debate which King had suddenly created thundered on. The Progressives drifted back to the Liberal fold. When the crunch came — a Liberal motion declaring the Tory acting Cabinet illegal — the vote was 96 to 95 against Meighen. Defeated, he went to Lord Byng and asked for dissolution. This time it was granted.

Meighen was free to go out on the hustings and say what he thought of King's constitutional trickery. "It was a work of guile," he said. "It was a plant; it was a piece of verbal chicanery; it was a wily sinister artifice to take advantage of men untrained in legal reasoning; it was, in plain language, a fraud." King had tried to cling to office "like a lobster with lockjaw."

He tried to revive the Customs scandal but there was little interest in graft when the Liberals were ranting about independence and sovereignty in Quebec and the British Parliamentary tradition in Ontario. They were damning the monarch's representative and praising the monarchy. They had it all ways. They charged Meighen with the worst Customs offence of all — smuggling an illegal government into the House.

The Liberals swept Quebec and piled up 116 seats to Meighen's 91, plus the support of 30-odd Farm and Progressive candidates. King's constitutional issue, however contrived and overblown, had been real to the voters. King knew the dark levers that made Canadian democracy work.

Meighen called him "the most contemptible charlatan ever to darken the annals of Canadian politics," but Meighen was through. His party chose a new leader — his old antagonist R. B. Bennett — and he began a new career as an investment banker in Toronto. In 1932 Bennett appointed him to the Senate where he stayed for nearly a decade, launching occasional shafts at King which were lost or ignored in the barren reaches of the Upper Chamber.

In 1941 he made his last bid for revenge. He resigned from the Senate, was elected Conservative leader once again by the party caucus in the Commons, and awaited election in the safe Tory seat of South York.

The old hatred had not mellowed in either man. After fifteen years in office, King was cranky and cantankerous, caught in the conscription trap he had watched Borden squirm in during the previous war. Watching Meighen ride back, mounted on that dreadful pale horse, and calling for an immediate call-up for overseas service, King came close to hysteria. He wrote,

"I am getting past the time when I can fight in public with a man of Meighen's type who is sarcastic, vitriolic and the meanest type of politician."

As no Liberal could possibly win South York, King threw his party's full resources behind the Cooperative Commonwealth Federation candidate and got him elected. King chortled, "When I think of Meighen trying to usurp his way into Parliament . . . and of his being now completely defeated and out of public life . . . I have indeed reason to be thankful."

After that brief, sad epilogue, Arthur Meighen went back to business in Toronto, where he died in 1960.

**KING**
1921-26
1926-30
1935-48

# VIII. *God and King*

William Lyon Mackenzie's house, now a museum, stands near the corner of Bond and Dundas Streets in Toronto. There on display are the Mackenzie family piano and the old flatbed press on which the Little Rebel turned out his violent broadsheets. When the house was being restored in the late 1950s two caretakers quit because they said they could hear the press clanking and churning and the piano tinkling at night. But by the time the restorers had gutted what was left of the original house, the ghost, be it Mackenzie or his daughter Isabel, had quit too.

Ghost stories get little credence in Toronto, and less in the newer parts of Canada. Yet for nearly thirty years those ghosts ruled the nation through the weird haunted figure of William Lyon Mackenzie King. His life, as he saw it, was an extension of the Rebel's, through Isabel, who was King's mother. He was born old; he lived with the dead, talked with them and often longed to join them. So his story begins with his grandfather, the Rebel, who died 13 years before he was born.

Mackenzie, a pedlar's lad from the Scottish Highlands, might have been the great liberator of Upper Canada if that colony had been ready for liberation. Instead, he was exiled as a traitor, a tiny, fierce, fanatical nuisance. A fearless publisher and unpurchasable politician, he had terrorized the churchmen, the Colonial Office and the respectable prigs who 'made up the ruling establishment known as the Family Compact.

He hated banks and joint-stock companies because he truly believed that money was evil, and, unlike so many fellow-believers, he didn't want any for himself. In 1837, a time of depression when the poor were being exploited more than usual, he declared himself leader of the "mechanics and free-holders" of Upper Canada and demanded responsible government for the people. He assembled a band of farmers with pikes and muskets at Montgomery's Tavern, just above Eglinton on Yonge Street and began a straggling march downhill towards the center of power, which nowadays is 14 minutes away by subway.

The rebellion failed, not just because the Family Compact had sharp bayonets at its disposal but because the average Upper Canadian wanted no part of the scruffy libertarian nonsense preached below the border; he wanted to be a respectable prig with a share of the evil cash.

Mackenzie escaped to the States, his political and philosophic home, disguised as an old woman. In his nine years of exile, he concluded that American democracy had produced an establishment more vicious and more wretched than that he left behind. Then he was pardoned and returned to Toronto to quarrel again and again with the new responsible government set up in his absence.

Isabel, his thirteenth child, was born in poverty and distress in the United States. While she stayed loyal to her father, she shed his atheism and dislike of money. She married a respectable Canadian lawyer, John King, son of an officer who had helped put down the Mackenzie rebellion, and she became a pillar of the Presbyterian Church. Her first son was born in Berlin (later Kitchener), Ontario. Plump Willie King worshipped his mother. At 25 he would write, "Mother is such a little girl. She is so bright, cheerful, good, happy and lovely. She has so much grit and courage in her. I have met no woman so true and lovely a woman as my mother."

While other boys read adventure tales, he read the royal proclamation that had offered one thousand pounds for the capture of his grandfather. Isabel, the cosy middle-class matron, filled the boy's head with the words of the romantic rebel whose name he bore. He was small and unimpressive in appearance but swaggered noisily at school and won more than his share of playground fights. When he moved from quiet Berlin to the University of Toronto he showed promise as a scholar. Although no orator, he pushed himself into the debating society where he met and offended Arthur Meighen.

There and in post-graduate studies in economics at Chicago and Harvard, he developed that concern for the oppressed workers that was his grandfather's heritage and became the stepping-stone to his political career.

In Chicago he fell in love with a nurse. After a year of wrangling with his conscience and his family he almost decided to propose to her. He convinced his diary that old Mackenzie would approve: "His mantle has fallen upon me and it shall be taken up and worn. I never felt it could be done before; I see it now. With Miss — at my side I can stand out against all the world and stand out I will." Marry a nurse? A creature lower than a governess? The Rebel's middle-class daughter was shocked. "I have built castles without number for you," she wrote Willie. "Are all these dreams but to end in dreams? I am getting old now, Willie, and disappointment wearies and the heart grows sick . . . charity begins at home . . . I am not grasping for myself but I do feel for your sisters and I know you who have such a big heart will not forsake me."

Torn between desire for Miss — and the colossal mother

complex that was to dominate his life, King sacrificed the nurse. After breaking with her, he wrote, "If I can only win such a wife as I have a mother, how infinitely happy!" No such paragon was to be found. King never married.

There were minor flirtations and cuddlings by moonlight, but even when on the way towards becoming a millionaire he convinced himself that he couldn't afford a bride. Not even political advantage could lure him. His mentor, Laurier, produced a young widow for his inspection, explaining that "the right person" would be a great help in public life. King fled.

When he was in his early thirties he lost his closest friend, Henry Albert Harper. Harper drowned trying to rescue a child in the freezing Ottawa River. King wrote a tribute to him in a sad, soul-searching little book *The Secret of Heroism*. From then on he seemed to lose the capacity for close friendship. Destiny, the dead, and a series of terriers called Pat were his companions.

His brief career as a muckraking journalist was remarkably successful. In 1897 he wrote a series of articles for the Toronto *Mail and Empire* exposing the fearful condition of sweated immigrant labor in the city's garment industry. He seems to have grasped one essential secret of the exposé-writer's trade: always hold back one appalling disclosure to threaten the exposed with when they try to sue you. King held back the fact that the Canadian Post Office was buying its uniforms from sweat-shops. His father introduced him to the Liberal Postmaster-General, William Mulock; he told his tale and was given the job of preparing a report on government clothing contracts. Journalism had served its purpose; young King was on his way into the civil service. Not for him the ephemeral glory of a day's headline. He wanted to be where the power was and the wrongs could be righted.

The Post Office stopped buying uniforms from the swinish employers. At King's suggestion, the government inserted a fair-wage clause into future contracts. In 1900 he was called to Ottawa to become Deputy Minister in the new Department of Labor. For eight years, the industrious, sober and religious young man hurried around the country as a conciliator of labor disputes, telling employers and workers what to do. Strikes were something new in Canada and government intervention newer still.

In 1908 Laurier advised him to run for election in his hometown constituency, North Waterloo. He won easily and made the leap from the civil service to the Cabinet, from Deputy Minister to Minister of Labor. It was an important Cabinet post but he became general government handyman — one of the youngest and brightest of Laurier's talented collection. In 1911, Laurier was swept out and King lost his job, his seat and, it seemed, his career. Like the rebel Mackenzie before him, he was cast into exile. Still, he was convinced God intended to make him Prime Minister some day.

He floundered for three years, doing odd jobs for the Liberal party. Then the Rockefeller Foundation brought him to the United States as a conciliator. The champion of the oppressed was now working for the biggest of the bosses. He advised John D. Rockefeller, Jr., son of the most hated man in America, on how to improve his image, and he helped settle fierce mining strikes out west.

He was to be accused of running out on Canada during the war, but he was fat and forty and would have been little use at the front. The Rockefellers allowed him to continue his work with the Liberal organization and he spent much of his time in Ottawa.

In 1917 he ran again for Parliament, out of loyalty to Laurier, because he was sure he would lose. When he was off campaigning, his mother died. Even in this time of black despair King's wonderful political intuition told him that with Laurier defeated and finished he would become Prime Minister. There was no longer any doubt.

He went back to the States as industrial consultant to the giants of Big Business — Standard Oil of New Jersey, General Electric, Bethlehem Steel. At the same time he was writing a

book on what was wrong with Big Business, urging a measure
of state control over private enterprise. If *Industry and Humanity* had been more readable or more carefully read by the
leading Canadian Liberals, King might never have been chosen
to lead the party. The book strayed far beyond the orthodox
Liberalism of the times. It blamed free competition for an
economic system that enriched the few, debased society and
made wars inevitable.

King wrote: "In the conflict between the temporary interests
of selfish individuals and the permanent welfare of nations,
the latter alone is entitled to consideration. Wherever in social
or industrial relations the claims of Industry and Humanity
are opposed, those of Industry must make way."

Industry, which King was then serving for fees of $1,000
a week, was a Frankenstein monster — "something other than
was intended by those who contributed to its creation, when
it can be transformed into a monster so demoniacal as to breed
a terror unparalleled in human thought and bring desolation to
the very heart of the human race."

King would control the monster, not by nationalizing it, as
the Communists or Socialists wanted, or by handing it over
to the workers on the syndicalist plan. Industries would be run
by directorates containing representatives of capital, labor,
management and the community. These four would put the
welfare of the community ahead of all else, abolish all-out
competition and set up a minimum standard of life for everybody. This system would spread out beyond national boundaries until countries co-operated in commerce for the general
good.

The plan, King saw, could not be realized by material means
alone. "It is from the reverence for life which men get from
their mothers and from the faith which a religion pure and
undefiled imparts, that there comes the spirit of mutual aid
through which the material interests of the world make way
for the nobler aspirations of the soul."

In this overlong, turgid and pious book, King laid down a

philosophy that was radical for its day. There was comfort in it for both bosses and workers and too much reliance placed on the Deity and organized religion, but it was a revolutionary document. King, the friend of the Rockefellers and the sweated workers, King, the waffler and instrument of supernatural forces, was still King, the Rebel's grandson. *Industry and Humanity* has been described as his *Mein Kampf* — a statement of aims so extraordinary that nobody took them seriously. Apart from the obvious differences between the authors — King was driven by benevolent ghosts rather than demons — Hitler's book was easier to understand. *Industry and Humanity* was heavy going.

When Laurier died in 1919, King entrusted his campaign for the Liberal leadership to God and sailed to England to study labor conditions for Rockefeller. He barely made it back to Ottawa in time for the party convention. He was confident. On the morning of the balloting he read in his favorite inspirational book: "Nothing shall be impossible to you." The victory came as a matter of divinely inspired course. "It is to His work that I am called," he wrote. "The dear loved ones know and are about, they are alive and with me in the great everlasting Now and Here."

He was 45 and seemed very much alone. His mother and father were gone, his brother was dying. He had little hope of finding a suitable wife. He had few outside interests in this world, and as he rose to power he began to withdraw into himself. The glad-handing of politics had served its purpose. He held the most public of offices but he was to become almost a recluse. He would still bounce into the Commons or on to a platform, but when the public appearance was over he would retreat to be alone with his secret. He had found communication with the dead and none of his colleagues must know that he was now a practising spiritualist. Only one of his secretaries discovered it. The mediums in Canada and England, through whom he talked with his parents and others, kept the secret for nearly thirty years.

He moved into Laurier's old house — a present from Laurier's widow — and stuffed it with horrifying Victorian bric-a-brac, paid for by his rich supporters. There he roosted amid spidery little tables, huge vases, scarlet plush chairs, gilt mirrors, his mother's piano and her portrait, which was always lit by a small lamp. He slept in Laurier's brass bed, a terrier curled in a basket beside it. (Not only Liberals slept in each other's beds; Tory John Diefenbaker proudly occupies one that belonged to Sir John A. Macdonald.)

At weekends King moved across the river to Kingsmere, his Gatineau estate. He had been attracted there by the gentle beauty of the hills and lake as much as by the name, which had no family connection. He bought one farm, then several more, and finally acquired seven houses in all. His unique monument is the collection of man-made ruins he built on a hill above the lake. Stones from wrecked buildings in Ottawa, the front of a bank, pieces of the original burned-down Parliament Buildings, the arch of a hotel window — these pieces were cemented together under King's meticulous direction but with no form or purpose that the masons could understand. At first sight they could be the ruins of an ancient Highland church, but at a closer look the chunks don't match or blend. But King loved them and fussed over them. Statesmen from around the world spent weekends at Kingsmere and King showed them his ruins. He never explained what they meant.

He once told Parliament that there was a real world and an imaginary one, and that statesmen must operate in the real one. In the deliberate vagueness of King's speeches this may have been intended to explain why the ideals of *Industry and Humanity* had to be put aside for a more propitious time when something might be done about them. Certainly there was no greater master of the "real" world than King, who could knife an opponent so gently he hardly felt the pain, or smother him slowly with the velvet pillow of his cultivated dullness. If this most durable and successful of prime ministers was coached by ghostly voices from the beyond, perhaps men like Meighen,

Bennett, Diefenbaker and Pearson should have listened too.

His first task on taking power was the one that faced and faces every incoming administration since Macdonald: to unite the country. (Other nations merely change governments as a lady changes dancing partners: Canada contrives to fall in a dead faint every time the music stops.) For practical purposes "achieving unity" usually means reaching an accommodation with Quebec. King neither spoke French nor pretended to understand French Canada, so he appointed an ambassador, who became more of a viceroy, to handle the province as he saw fit. Ernest Lapointe, a huge, self-taught farmer became his alter ego, the second man in his government and the only colleague who dared call him "Rex." The two stumped the country together — the small droning Prime Minister and the orotund Gallic giant — an unlikely combination and living proof that the two Canadas could get along.

The second task, which had faced most of his predecessors, was the first trip to the perfumed drawing rooms of London to joust with the imperialists and to brave the flattery of the now-aging duchesses. King weathered it well. When he arrived for an Imperial Conference in 1923, he had already shown what he thought of peremptory British demands for troops in the Dardanelles (Chanak) affair of the previous year. And Lapointe had been dispatched to Washington to sign a fisheries agreement, the first to be concluded without any participation by Britain.

At the wartime conference, Borden and South Africa's Smuts had won for the Dominions a right to a say in imperial foreign policy. Now King had his say. He wanted an independent Canadian policy, unaffected by any Imperial "cabinet." Britain still hoped the Empire would speak "with a single voice." King refused to join in the chorus. Smuts was delegated to talk him round but gave up, saying, "Mr. King, you are a very terrible person." King did not enjoy the conference. He told the members he might have to pass up future ones if their purpose was to commit the Dominions in advance to policies over which their Parliaments had no control. Apart from that he was a hearty eater and didn't like the irregularity of the meals. . . .

At the next conference, in 1926, he dominated the proceedings. He had pulled off his constitutional card-trick, squashed the Tories and was now the calm master of his nation. The conference produced the declaration that "every self-governing member of the Empire is now master of its destiny. In fact, if not always in form, it is subject to no compulsion whatever." This principle was the sum of the points scored in London by Macdonald and Laurier and, more heavily, by Borden and King. It became law with the Statute of Westminster, signed by Bennett in 1931.

Canada celebrated the Diamond Jubilee of Confederation in 1927. The Prince of Wales came to visit. Charles Lindbergh flew his transatlantic plane, the "Spirit of St. Louis," to Ottawa. Schoolchildren waved their flags, licked their ice creams, and chattered with the excitement of the old royal pageantry and the thrill of the marvellous modern age. The carillon in the new Peace Tower played "The Maple Leaf Forever" and "O Canada," and its chimes were carried across the land by radio network.

Dedicating the tower, Mackenzie King described the fall of the old one in the fire of 1916, then rose to rare heights of eloquence: "When the clock which is now installed begins to sound forth the hours of this day it will take the flaming torch thrown to it over a space of years by the old sentinel at midnight and, holding it aloft, will strike at high noon the hour of twelve in commemoration alike of the birth and resurrection." There was nothing to add but "tick-tock."

King was sunnily confident. He went to Geneva and signed for Canada the Kellogg-Briand Pact, which rejected war as an instrument of policy. Now, he said, there were "no wars to be averted, or rumors of war to be quieted." The Tories had doubts about this and King rounded on them: why would they distrust other nations? "Because," said Bennett, their leader, "we have had experience."

The Wall Street crash of 1929 confounded both men. King, who had diagnosed the faults of the capitalist system 12 years before, had no answer. He waited for the crisis to go away. Bennett, the capitalist, had an answer but it was the wrong one — enormous tariffs would stop foreign competition with Canadian goods, "blast" Canada into the world market, and Canada would "cure unemployment or perish in the attempt."

As unemployment rose and businesses failed, King prepared for an election in the summer of 1930. Long bland speeches were drawn up. The cutting edges were rounded off and any telling phrases muddied over. A King speech was intended to wash pleasantly over the hearer and flow away, leaving no sediment of specific commitments behind. He dodged from platform to platform, never mentioning unemployment. If such a problem existed it wasn't bad enough to warrant intervention from Ottawa. It wasn't King's baby.

In the final session of Parliament he was forced to discuss it and the blandness was shorn away. The provinces were demanding Ottawa's money for their jobless. King refused this because, he said, taking such federal cash would interfere with their provincial rights under the constitution. Besides, he remarked, why were the provincial premiers crying poverty? Every one of them had delivered a New Year's message to his people boasting of prosperity in his fiefdom.

J. S. Woodsworth, the "conspirator" of the Winnipeg strike who was now the saintly socialist conscience of Parliament, asked him: "Do governments ever declare that there is anything but prosperity during their regime?"

The question pierced through to King's private doubts. He burst forth in a welter of self-justification. The Liberals had given good government since 1921. Now provincial premiers — *Tory* premiers — wanted *him* to raise taxes so that *they* could get the money. The unemployment crisis became a Tory plot. King waded deeper, destroying his constitutional argument against providing federal money. Yes, he said, he might consider giving cash to one or two western provinces which had Progressive governments — "but I would not give one cent to any Tory government!"

"Shame," howled the delighted Tories. King plunged on to ruin. "May I repeat what I have said? With respect to giving monies out of the federal treasury to any Tory government for these alleged unemployment purposes, with these governments situated as they are today, with policies diametrically opposed to those of this government, I would not give them a five-cent piece!"

That one telling phrase — "five-cent piece" — cost King the election. In one burst of temper he had laid bare the current theory of federal-provincial relations: Thou shalt give to the provincial government of thy choice and political persuasion. "Nine years of wasted effort before the great betrayal," Bennett roared. "It didn't take Judas that long."

King had played politics with the poorbox. Every speech he made was destroyed by hecklers shouting "five-cent piece." The unemployed turned out to vote for Bennett, a multi-millionaire in striped pants. The Liberal government melted in the voters' wrath. Bennett took office with 137 seats to King's 91, with 17 Independents.

If the author of *Industry and Humanity* had tried to lose the election he could not have done it better. He had misjudged the nature of the crisis and the mood of the people, just as Meighen had done in 1921. He had even omitted to read his own textbook. As he brooded by his lovely ruins at Kingsmere he decided that God had planned his defeat. So it was all for the best. As the workings of God and King were so closely linked, he soon convinced others, and perhaps himself, that he had deliberately thrown the election for the future good of the Liberals and the country. Bennett was now saddled with the Great Depression, publicly pledged to cure it or perish. He would surely perish.

King's confidence flowed back. He was now leader of the Opposition at a time when opposition could be sheer joy. All the daggers which God thrust into his hand could be used in the House. And in his quiet moments, in his walks through the Gatineau meadows or the cluttered rooms of Laurier House, he could use this God-given interlude to remould the philosophy of his party. Laissez-faire Liberalism had failed as high-tariff Toryism was about to fail. It was time to re-read and revise *Industry and Humanity* and remember he was still the Rebel's grandson. It was also ordained, and rightly, that he should be scourged and endure the worst indignity of his life. He called it "the valley of humiliation."

The St. Lawrence Seaway, the mighty waterway which opened up the Great Lakes to ocean-going ships in April, 1959, had a long and quarrelsome history. Negotiations between Canada and the United States for a joint project jogged along through the 1920s, reached the treaty stage in 1932, then collapsed when the U.S. Senate rejected the treaty. Speculators lay in wait along the route, among them the Beauharnois Power Corporation Ltd., a private concern that held valuable power rights on part of the St. Lawrence River near Montreal. To exploit them, the company needed, and got, Canadian government approval to build a canal. This approval, according to statements in the House, became a licence to swindle the public of thirty million dollars. Farm M.P.s raised the scandal. Bennett took it up on learning that Beauharnois had been paying off the Liberal party, then quickly dropped it when he learned that the Conservatives were in on it too.

After a year of stalling by the two big parties, the farmers forced the matter into the open. A Parliamentary committee soon discovered that Beauharnois had paid at least $700,000 into Liberal campaign funds; a mere $30,000 to the Tories. In addition, prominent Liberals had helped themselves lavishly. Senator Wilfrid Laurier McDougald made millions out of Beauharnois while serving on four separate public bodies that helped decide upon the company's application for a priceless piece of river. Once the application was granted, he breezed out into the open and became the chairman of the board of Beauharnois. Painfully prodded out of his Senate immunity, McDougald testified before the Commons investigators, was "strongly condemned," and resigned from the Senate — to enjoy a comfortable old age.

But not before a receipt was produced — McDougald's business expenses charged to and paid for by the Beauharnois Company: "Expenses of trip to Bermuda, Hon. W. L. Mackenzie King and self: Hotel, Bermuda, $288.53. Fare, Montreal to Bermuda and return, $395.04. Hotel, New York, $168.75. Total $852.32."

It seemed hideously clear. The rogues who had bribed the government had paid a large bill for its Prime Minister.

A pathetic figure rose to explain to the House. King's bitterest enemies felt only sympathy for the grey, shaking, suddenly-old man touched personally by scandal for the first time. Even Bennett nodded his understanding. When he went to pay his bill in Bermuda, King said, he found that his companion, McDougald, had already taken care of it. He considered this to be a personal matter. McDougald had paid as a friend, not a company officer. He was horrified to hear the bill had gone back to Beauharnois. As McDougald had testified, this was a secretary's mistake.

There was mild applause from both sides of the House as King sat down. He had made his painful, personal amends.

Ten days later a quite different King arose to defend his party's sins in the Beauharnois affair. He was surprised and pained to hear his friends had taken money, but there was no proof that this had influenced government policy in any way. The payments for "gratefulness" had been made months before the government made its decision on the Beauharnois application. As he, King, never discussed Cabinet business outside Cabinet meetings he knew nothing of the source of campaign funds and had no idea Senator McDougald was connected with the supplicant company.

Nonetheless he was penitent — "The Liberal party has not been disgraced but it is in the valley of humiliation. I tell the people of this country today that as its leader I feel humiliated and I know my following is humiliated."

On the other hand — a small knife appeared from under the penitent's sackcloth — what about Bennett? If he *stopped* his Tories taking money from Beauharnois, he must have known they were taking money in the first place. The Liberals were a poor party who could barely afford to get their program printed. The Tories, of course, were the friends of Big Business — they got ten times as much in contributions. So it was all the more important that the Tory leader must never know who paid how much to his party.

King glowed with sweet reason. "If it be true that my Rt. Hon. friend had knowledge of all who were contributors to his party funds, what will the country be thinking today of the changes which have been made in the tariff in connection with cottons, . . woollens, . . rayons and silk?" King warmed up. "What about iron and steel, boots and shoes, gasoline, magazines, sugar refining; what about income taxes, agricultural manufacturers, motorcar manufacturers, electrical goods manufacturers?" Maybe one little power company paid off the Liberals. King implied that every manufacturer in the country was paying off the Tories.

Bennett had nodded sympathetically at poor King's debasement. Now he could stand no more. "This is disgraceful," he yelled.

It was King's turn to show sympathy. He had implicit faith in Bennett's integrity, he assured the House. "I honor him as a man." But did he honestly think a party leader should be expected to count campaign contributions?

"I have always held," said Bennett, the lawyer, "that the receiver of stolen goods was a criminal."

King talked calmly on into the night, the guilty lecturing the innocent. The proper thing, he suggested, was to appoint a Royal Commission to investigate the campaign expenses of the last three elections. He talked of "the sacred relationship of human friendship," world peace, Canadian unity and the glories of the Diamond Jubilee. The real world receded ever farther from the imaginary world. It was a masterful performance, not convincing, but wonderfully distracting. Bennett cut it to pieces next day but the Beauharnois canal was now clogged with red herrings and decoy ducks. The scandal was over and King could now get back to the business of the depression, which was now Bennett's depression, and was getting worse every day.

**BENNETT**
1930-35

# IX.  *Goodnight, My Lord*

Thanksgiving Day, 1934. Choking clouds of dust whirled through southern Saskatchewan, southern Alberta and south-western Manitoba bearing away the topsoil that had once yielded thirty bushels of wheat per acre. The drought was in its third year. Nothing grew but the once-despised weed, Russian thistle. Starving cattle were eating it as starving workers sampled the once-despised Russian bolshevism.

Nature had failed the farmers. The drought joined the Depression to complete the misery that had begun in the cities. In four years Canada's national income had gone down by fifty percent. Of ten million Canadians, a million and a half were on relief. An army of hoboes, the pride of the nation's young manhood, bummed its way across the continent looking for work and, failing that, a meal. Any job could be filled at below a living wage. Said a skilled tradesman, "if I don't work for a dollar a day they'll find a man on relief who'll do it for fifty cents."

"Hell, man," said a western farmer, "even a jackrabbit wouldn't dare start across my farm without packing a lunch."

To this desperate country came the Prime Minister's Thanksgiving message, cabled from London: "Canadians should be especially thankful for the manifold blessings that Providence has bestowed upon them. Notwithstanding trials and tribulations they have abundant reasons for thanksgiving. Not the least of the ways by which they can show their thankfulness is by using their savings to preserve the financial integrity of their Dominion, by renewing at a lesser rate of interest the loans that they made to their country in other days, not only continuing a safe investment but also rendering a real service to Canada."

What man could be so completely out of touch as to send such a message? Who could tell a bunch of down-at-heel travelling salesmen: "Sound a note of confidence in all your contacts"?

Only Richard Bedford Bennett, the archetypical Tory whose shoes, a reporter wrote, "not only glisten but gloat." Bennett inherited the Canadian Depression the way the U.S. President Herbert Hoover was endowed with the bigger American version. Neither deserved it, but neither was guiltless. Bennett was the perfect cartoon capitalist — a top-hatted, carnationed exploiter of the masses — a Marxist's dream villain. He had made millions defending big corporations and investing his fees. As Prime Minister he hoarded the public's money while the public clamored for it. As leader, keeping to himself the important jobs of Finance and External Affairs, he ran a one-man show. A popular story had Bennett alone at his club muttering to himself. Question: "What's he doing?" Answer: "He's holding a Cabinet meeting."

No Canadian prime minister has had such a one-dimensional treatment from historians as Bennett. His one defender has been Lord Beaverbrook, who knew him from boyhood and wrote a touching little book about him called *Friends*. Bennett was not an approachable man. Like King, he remained a bachelor, although he was not afraid of women and Beaver-brook catalogues his girl friends. He leaves behind the impression of a towering, valiant, but misguided prig.

If greatness lies in the ability to confess that one has been totally wrong and to try to reverse the course of a lifetime, then Bennett showed greatness. But by the time he got around to that it was too late; it can be written off as inconsistency. He had been accused already of so many worse things — conceit, intolerance, blindness, stupidity — everything but lack of courage. A Liberal Cabinet minister said, "he has the manners of a Chicago policeman and the temperament of a Hollywood film star."

Bennett's character was shaped amid the tall, straight spruce trees of New Brunswick, a province with a distinct, hard nature. Twelve thousand defeated Loyalists came there after the American War of Independence and set up a tightly-knit, defiantly British colony. "Just as the first British Empire in America had fallen, a second rose in its place," wrote Prof. W. Stewart McNutt. "Symbolic of this was the appearance on the walls of the new Trinity Church at Saint John of the Royal Coat of Arms. It had been removed from its former place in the council chamber of the old colony of Massachusetts at Boston." The new colony, which had been part of Nova Scotia, was named after the German home of the Royal Family. That was the only non-British thing about it, apart from the wonderful Indian names of the rivers:

> Sweet maiden of Passamaquoddy
> Shall we seek for communion of souls
> Where the deep Mississippi meanders
> Or the distant Saskatchewan rolls?
> Ah, no. In New Brunswick we'll find it
> A sweetly sequestered nook —
> Where the smooth-gliding Skookawaskooksis
> Unites with the Skoodawabskook
>
> (Prof. deMille)

In the Napoleonic wars, the British navy was cut off from its supply of Scandinavian timber for ships' masts and New Brunswick supplied the need. When the wars ended, Britain protected the New Brunswick industry by slapping a prohibitive tariff on timber imports from Scandinavia. In 1831 some British nobles tried to restore free trade. Parliament rejected the move, and the New Brunswickers celebrated by roasting oxen in the streets and burning the free-traders in effigy. Later in the century, Bennett's father Henry, a former sea-captain, prospered as a builder of wooden ships. Such were the historical roots of Bennett, the high-tariff Tory whose eyes moistened at the sound of "Land of Hope and Glory."

He was born on a seaside farm, not in poverty as he once claimed, but in what the Victorian middle-class would call "reduced circumstances." Henry Bennett's shipyard had gone broke with the advent of steam. Like King, young Richard had an adoring mother, Henrietta. She introduced him to books and encouraged his conviction that he would be a great man some day. In his early twenties he told friends he would become Prime Minister of Canada and then sit in the British Parliament at Westminster. He did both.

Like Meighen he began as a schoolteacher, then moved to law. He taught Methodist Sunday school and blasted the Demon Rum at temperance meetings. (He never drank, apart from the odd sip of creme-de-menthe which he believed was non-alcoholic; but he was to make a lot of money out of the Calgary Brewing Company.)

Beaverbrook described the young Bennett as "tall, austere, forbidding, conscious of coming greatness." He had a streak of egotism and a habit of dramatizing himself — qualities which Beaverbrook, predictably, admired. He also had an uncontrollable temper. At these times, Beaverbrook wrote, "his face would turn pale and his eyes would change in color. His neck visibly swelled."

The two met on a steamer on the Miramichi River when Max Aitken, the future Beaverbrook, was an irreverent, impish lad of ten and Bennett a freckled nineteen-year-old in a too-big bowler hat. They were to lead and follow each other, quarrel and make up for sixty years. Bennett had the great presence, the shattering machine-gun oratory; Beaverbrook had guile and a sense of humor. He was there at the start of Bennett's political career, delivering leaflets on his bicycle in Chatham, New Brunswick, when Bennett ran for the local council. He was there at the end, wangling him a seat in the House of Lords as Viscount Bennett of Mickleham, Calgary and Hopewell.

Along the way both men made a great deal of money. Bennett founded his fortune in Calgary on legal fees from the CPR and the Hudson's Bay Company and built it into his first million through real estate investments. He worked with Beaverbrook to corner the cement market and later to organize the Calgary Power Company, the Calgary Brewing Company, and in building grain elevators and a flour mill.

Out of the blue he acquired control of the large E. B. Eddy match and toilet-paper plant that still beclouds the view across the Ottawa River from Parliament Hill. It was bequeathed to him by Eddy's widow with whom he was friendly but not, according to Beaverbrook, romantically involved.

He was the richest Prime Minister and the only millionaire to hold the office before Pierre Trudeau. His money obviously colored his thinking — colored it true blue — but he did not consider it a political drawback. No leader, he said, could serve the public properly if he was constantly looking over his shoulder at the shadow of debts. This theory is now widely accepted in the United States where it has become practically impossible for a non-millionaire to run for high office without selling pieces of himself like a prize-fighter. Yet the public still suspects a self-made millionaire like Lyndon Johnson while revering the much-richer John F. Kennedy, who got it all from his father.

Bennett was indisputably the man of business and at the onset of the Depression he, the voters, and even King believed that a good business brain could soon sort the thing out. For all his legal skills and his marvellous grasp of detail, Bennett's answer was simple, crude and unworkable: Canada must retire behind a tariff wall and its ten million souls must take in each other's washing.

"We have been content since 1922 to send out of Canada into other lands, free, the resources of this country and buy back from them the manufactured materials," he said. "Thousands in the United States have been given employment fabricating Canadian goods. They've got the jobs and we've got the soup kitchens."

All that was needed, he said, was "individual initiative coupled with the desire to achieve and succeed." This had worked for Bennett and Beaverbrook. It had worked for sturdy Empire Loyalists in New Brunswick. The system was good; only faith and steadfastness and British pluck were needed to make it work. King had begun to query the system, declaring that capitalism was under fire, but he had no answer. The idea of government spending to cure depression was outrageous to both men. It had not yet occurred to Franklin D. Roosevelt, who was then campaigning for the White House on a promise to balance the U.S. budget.

In his suite at the Chateau Laurier hotel — he never had a home until he moved permanently to England — Bennett seemed as remote from the rest of Canada as he could possibly be. "Nero fiddled while Rome burned. Bennett worked while Canada danced," he joked to his worshipful secretary, Andrew D. Maclean. It didn't seem to occur to him that much of Canada had no work and certainly wasn't dancing. "His personal generosity is enormous," records the ardent Maclean. "At Christmas time he mails as many as 25 dozen boxes of candies, more than 100 floral gifts and cheques totalling over one thousand dollars to those who need it."

The ragged men lining up for thin soup got no candy or flowers. They failed to see why the prospective viscount in the Chateau should choose this moment to restore the granting of titles to Canadians, abolished by King. Or how their leader, while working day and night to solve their problems, could still afford to honor his sabbatarian principles and take Sundays off.

Maclean explains: "Bennett is more of an aristocrat than a democrat. He believes in government by the ablest and best — not government necessarily by the will of the people — who are often wrong. King renders more than lip-service to democracy . . . he really seems to believe in its efficacy, even in crises."

While other prime ministers had gone to London, Bennett summoned London to him, and with it the rest of the Empire, for the 1932 Imperial Conference in Ottawa. His predecessors had to struggle to establish themselves as the leading spokesmen of the Dominions; Bennett took the role as by divine right. The majesty of his tail-coated presence and the weight of the words he rattled out at great speed assured that. Beside him the squat British Prime Minister Stanley Baldwin and his scrawny henchman Neville Chamberlain looked rather like seedy and second-rate politicians. The other Empire leaders were soon singed and charred by the blazing personality of "Bonfire" Bennett.

The conference failed to reach any significant agreement on Bennett's plan for an Empire trading bloc, partly because Bennett didn't seem to want it. He was all for Britain taking Empire products duty free and taxing foreign imports, but he was not ready to reciprocate. He was already pledged to tax all manufactured goods entering Canada, including those made in Britain. He fought with Chamberlain, and, Baldwin said later, "Bennett had a brainstorm every day which wiped out what he had agreed to the day before."

Lord Beaverbrook, whose violent crusade for an Empire customs union had split the British Conservative party, was not invited to Ottawa. His friend, "Dick," no longer answered his letters since the Beaver failed to support him in the 1930 elections.

The conference resulted in the raising of some tariffs against foreign imports, but there was no large-scale reduction of trade barriers between the Empire countries themselves. Beaverbrook's ideal of "Empire Free Trade" — an ingenious contradiction in terms — faded from the real world to live on only in the wondrous pages of his newspapers.

As the conference broke up, the Colonial Secretary, J. H. Thomas, said to Bennett: "R. B., the first thing the King will ask me is 'what does Bennett want?' " Bennett replied, "At this time, nothing, but later I may want to retire and live in England and would like a peerage." (By the time Bennett did move to England, Chamberlain was Prime Minister and, remembering him with deep distaste, refused to recommend the title. Bennett had to wait until Churchill took over and brought Beaverbrook into his Cabinet where the Beaver was in a position to arrange things.)

For all his air of confidence, Bennett must have suspected that the day would come when he'd have to bail out. His name was a wry joke. Western farmers drove Bennett Buggies, an engineless or gasless automobile hitched to a horse. An abandoned farm was a Bennett Barnyard, and hoboes brewed Bennett coffee by boiling up barley or wheat. Newspapers wrapping the bodies of men sleeping by the railway tracks carried Bennett messages like this one — "There has never been a time in recent years in Canada when there was so much money available in banks and financial institutions. . . . No, there is no shortage of currency."

The *Winnipeg Free Press* of December 18, 1934 carried a front-page story:

VALOUR ROAD MAN RETURNS HOME TO FIND
BABY BOY DROWNED IN BATHTUB, FIVE-YEAR-OLD
DAUGHTER STRANGLED AND WIFE POISONED.

With thoughts of a poverty-stricken Christmas gnawing at her mind, a 28-year-old Winnipeg mother Monday afternoon took the lives of her two little children aged 18 months and five years and then committed suicide.

She had just completed the hanging of Christmas decorations in her little home.

Then, with the home bravely adorned and spotlessly clean she strangled one child, drowned the other in the bath and killed herself by drinking a powerful germicide. There had not even been enough money in the house to buy the poison that killed her.

She left a farewell note on the kitchen table bearing this out. "I owe the drugstore 44 cents. Farewell," it said.

A coroner's jury recommended that such powerful disinfectants be placed on the poison list.

While Bennett stuffed down chocolates (his only weakness) in the Chateau, flags of revolt appeared in the west. Tim Buck's Canadian Communist Party, formed in 1921 on three thousand dollars sent from Moscow, was at last getting somewhere.

In 1931 it had been outlawed and Buck and five others jailed for five years for seditious conspiracy. Buck went to Kingston Penitentiary and began organizing the inmates. There followed a prison riot which he may or may not have inspired. During it, while he was safely locked in his cell, two prison guards fired five shots into it apparently to frighten him. He was not hit.

Public feeling mounted in favor of the Communists and against the law which put people away for their political beliefs. When Buck was paroled in November, 1934, 17,000 people packed Toronto's Maple Leaf Gardens to welcome the wiry little Englishman back. Blairmore, Alberta declared a public holiday and renamed its desolate main street Tim Buck Boulevard.

His henchmen organized a march on Ottawa by two thousand of the hopelessly unemployed who had been cooped up in squalid western relief camps and bossed by Army sergeant-majors for four years. The movement had begun spontaneously in British Columbia, but by the time the men had ridden the rails to Calgary, Communist agitators were in command. The march was broken up by the Mounties when it reached Regina. There was a four-hour fight in which more than 100 were injured and one city policeman was beaten to death. The camps were disbanded. Now the homeless had nowhere to go.

While the Communists hoped for violent change, a more moderate attempt to clean up the dusty ruins of capitalism began in Regina. A mixed bag of farmers, trade unionists, clergymen and assorted leftist reformers founded the Cooperative Commonwealth Federation under the leadership of the gentle socialist J. S. Woodsworth.

Its Regina Manifesto of 1933 demanded nationalization of banks, insurance companies, transportation, mines, power utilities — everything to bread and milk. A small group of experts would plan every facet of Canadian society; and "no CCF government will rest content until it has eradicated capitalism." It read like Marxism without revolution — a dictatorship of bureaucrats. Unlike the British Labour Party it had no direct affiliation with the trade unions. It was too far left for most of the discontented from the old parties whom the CCF hoped to attract. Still, party platforms are built to be abandoned and many moderates put aside their dislike of complete socialization, reassuring themselves that the soup is never eaten quite as hot as it is cooked. Woodsworth was not the stuff of which dictators are made and he had rejected all overtures from Tim Buck's Communists. The CCF won only seven seats in Ottawa at its first try but it became the official opposition party in the legislatures of British Columbia and Saskatchewan. Later it was to take and hold Saskatchewan for a generation.

Just across the unmarked prairie border the same type of dour and leathery farmer who voted CCF in Saskatchewan would vote for the radical rightwing notions of Social Credit in Alberta. Provincially the Prairies were abandoning the old parties. Ottawa had failed them and what went on there no longer even interested them. King and Bennett could wrangle and wrestle all they wanted. They were so far from the western grassroots they didn't even realize there were no more grass-roots — only blowing dust and Russian thistle. If either of those retiring bachelors had dreamed that a sex scandal in Alberta, of all places, would put "Bible Bill" Aberhart in the Premier's office, he would have wakened screaming and taken a cold bath.

In the great days of radio more than 250,000 westerners received the word of God each Sunday night through the crackling voice of the Rev. William Aberhart. In some areas his audience was even bigger than Jack Benny's, for gospelling was more appropriate than wise-cracks in those times of biblical plague and trial. For Aberhart all truth was contained in the Bible and he preached it straight, letter for letter and word for word — until 1932. Then he discovered a second book — by Major C. H. Douglas, a Scots engineer who claimed to have found the secret of money. It was, and remains, very simple or forever obscure. Social Crediters say it comes to you in a blinding flash or not at all. As Aberhart adapted it from Douglas' book, the trouble with money is that most people don't have enough of it. So what do you do — print more? No, because that causes inflation. You create a new kind of money — vouchers issued by the provincial government to cover the gap between the amount people have to spend and the (always greater) cost of the goods they need. It was Lenin's idea plus gift coupons.

The Social Credit platform explained:—

"The shortage of purchasing power which results from the operation of the money system would be made good by putting new money directly into the hands of the people . . . it can be shown thus:—

Price of the goods for sale     — $2400
The people have     — $1400
<hr>
To buy the goods the people need — $1000."

Aberhart proposed to set up a separate banking system in

Alberta and hand out $25 worth of his vouchers — "funny money" — to each resident each month to make up this difference. It was all very strange, but no stranger than the miracles from the real Bible that Aberhart preached on Sundays. It was no stranger than the idiocies of the system which had brought disaster to his listeners, as epitomized by the Bennett Thanksgiving message, or by the Winnipeg coroner's jury's recommendation in the case of the woman who murdered her family because there was no money. The words of God, Major Douglas and Aberhart mingled into the powerful faith of Social Credit, and the people lined up to vote for it (plus $25 a month) in August, 1935.

As God-fearing people they had no choice. For the Premier of the ruling United Farmers' Party had been caught sleeping with a young girl secretary, and one of his ministers was divorcing his wife. "Rats, sons of Satan, liars, fornicators," cried Bible Bill as he drove the changers of old style money out of the provincial temple. (Social Credit governed Alberta until 1971. Although its attempts to introduce "funny money" were blocked by Ottawa, a new kind of wealth was found — oil.) At the time of his Alberta victory Aberhart launched a national Social Credit party that carried 17 federal seats, two of them outside Alberta.

By this time the king of all the money-changers, man of business and lord of the old order had seen the light. Bennett, of all men, had come out against capitalism. In a series of CBC radio broadcasts in early 1935 he declared: "The old order is gone. It will not return."

The economic system must be reformed through government intervention. "Canada on the dole is like a young and vigorous man in the poorhouse. The dole is condemnation, final and complete, of our economic system. If we cannot abolish the dole, we should abolish the system."

What was all this? "Is Mr. Bennett endeavoring to humbug himself, or the people of Canada?" asked the Tory Montreal *Gazette*. It is still a good question. Bennett's "New Deal" was light-years removed from the old Bennett policies. But while propounding these remarkable new ideas — unemployment insurance, price controls, regulation of hours and wages, marketing laws and a privately-owned central bank — Bennett gave the impression that he had planned his apostasy from the start. He accused King of wanting to carry Canada back to the days of sailing ships, coaches and crinolines. King could not see, the enlightened Bennett proclaimed, that "when capitalism controlled the modern state, the result was fascism."

King, the master of the sly about-face, couldn't match this one. He didn't even try. He simply agreed with Woodsworth that Bennett had undergone a "deathbed conversion" a few months before the election which had to be called in the fall. In the Commons he taunted Bennett as a Johnny-come-lately reformer. Possibly the Prime Minister had just discovered King's book *Industry and Humanity?*

(No, no, cried Bennett.)

If the Right Honorable gentleman had not read it, he revealed how slight his interest in reform really was. . . . And so on and on went King, interrupting himself to complain mildly: "It would be better if the Minister of Railways (Mr. Manion) would not say 'all poppycock' quite so loudly."

Bennett's conversion had begun with a Parliamentary Inquiry into the ways of business, sparked by a maverick free-enterpriser Harry Stevens, his Minister of Trade. Long before the inquiry was over, its shocking secrets were leaked to the press. Tales of sweatshops paying starvation wages, of brutal exploitation of farmers, and of the rigging of prices and watering of stocks inflamed the already suspicious public. For a time the secretary of the Inquiry, Lester B. Pearson, was suspected of leaking the evidence. But he was cleared when Bennett found the real culprit, Stevens, and accused him of slandering business. Stevens resigned, calling Bennett a liar and founded his own "Reconstruction" party which elected one candidate — himself.

This rupture in the party helped Bennett's conversion, but

not so much as the obvious truth that he was doomed unless he did something dramatic. The aristocratic Roosevelt had contrived a "New Deal." Why not the aristocratic Bennett? Most of Bennett's New Deal statutes were beyond the constitutional powers of the federal government to enforce as they encroached upon the rights of the provinces. Five of them were struck down by the Judicial Committee of the Privy Council in London. Yet much of the New Deal was later adopted by King as his own. And today government controls business to an extent undreamed-of by the late-blooming revolutionary of the Chateau, or by the middle-aged King.

The voters of 1935 were offered the choice of a very tired Bennett or a refurbished, slimmer and cheerier Mackenzie King. Both offered reforms. Although King's promises were characteristically vague, he, too, had come around to the idea of a central bank (state-owned) to control the money system in the public interest. He offered the simple choice: "King or Chaos" and declared that what the country needed was not "the fist of the pugilist but the hand of the physician." He attacked not Bennett, but business, knowing that the two were by now inseparable.

"Business," he said, "is concerned with money; government is concerned with men . . . many so-called business successes have been due to a ruthless disregard of humanitarian considerations. . . . Until industry is regarded in the nature of a social service . . . there will be, and there should be, social unrest." King had gone back to his own textbook.

The country voted overwhelmingly against chaos and Bennett, if not for King. The Liberals took 171 seats out of 245, and the Conservatives a mere 39.

Beaverbrook described his friend as "humbled, lonely, sad, hurt — the mighty, powerful and slightly arrogant R. B. Bennett had fallen. An ungrateful people rejoiced in his martyrdom. Some friends fell away and many flatterers were silent."

In 1938 Bennett left Canada for good. He bought a mansion in Surrey beside Beaverbrook's and pottered around buying furniture and planting shrubs. He had never lived in a house since he left the family home in New Brunswick. He waited for his peerage but it was long in coming. Alone in the big country house he dressed meticulously in black morning coat, grey striped trousers, wing collar, and silk tie with pearl pin. He could not unbend. When war came and German bombers were overhead, he was asked why he did not go back to the safety of Canada. He replied, "I would not leave this house for anywhere else in the world."

Beaverbrook brought him into his hectic wartime Ministry of Aircraft Production. Fur was flying, industrialists were furious, the Beaver was eating bureaucrats for breakfast but the planes were being built. Beaverbrook fell foul of the police. He had recruited German engineers from internment camps to speed up production—most of them, he insisted, were Jewish refugees from the Nazis — but it was against regulations.

To satisfy Churchill and get the police off his neck he asked Bennett to hold an impartial investigation and decide whether the Germans should continue working or go back to their camps. He had no doubt of the verdict; he had just arranged a viscountcy for his old friend.

It was R. B. Bennett's last important decision. He reviewed the evidence with his fine legal mind, dominated the witnesses with his massive presence, and reached a decision that was typical of the big prickly man: put the Germans back in custody.

The two New Brunswickers had their last mighty row and when it was spent, Bennett slid slowly downhill. He dozed in the House of Lords, growing ever lonelier in the seat which, as a young man, he had been determined to achieve.

On the night of June 26, 1947, his butler said, "goodnight, my lord," and closed the bedroom door as Bennett opened his Bible to read his nightly chapter.

Next morning he was found dead in the bathtub. His terrier Bill was still asleep beside the empty bed.

# X.  *Riddle of the Ruins*

Mackenzie King welcomed himself back to power in October 1935. "A new era dawns today," he rejoiced. "We take up at once our supreme task to endeavor to end poverty in the midst of plenty."

As it turned out this was not to be the supreme task of the second King era. Events abroad soon overshadowed the Depression and finally obliterated it by war, just as the young King had foreseen and the old King forgot. His supreme task and supreme achievement was to bring Canada through the Second World War in one piece.

In 1935, as King was happily putting his new Cabinet together, Mussolini's armies were tramping over Ethiopia and his shiny new planes bombing African natives in their grass huts. This savagery shocked the League of Nations into a mild form of action. Some, at least, of its members realized that, unless the Italian dictator was stopped, the dream that peace could be maintained by a committee of nations would be at an end.

Canada's record at the League had been feeble. Both Liberal and Conservative governments had tried to water down the League's key function — to use force when it was needed to put down an aggressor. After all, nobody was likely to invade Canada. "We live in a fireproof house," said an early Canadian delegate to Geneva.

Now the time had come to use that independent voice in world affairs which Canadian leaders had struggled so long to acquire. The League had condemned Mussolini as an aggressor and proposed limited economic sanctions against him. Members would be asked to stop sending certain war materials to Italy. But what materials? The Europeans searched their consciences. How much trade could they afford to lose? Would the United States, which was not a member of the League, move in on the Italian market?

Canada's man in Geneva was a civil servant, Dr. Walter Riddell. The official delegate, a politician, had left with the fall of the Bennett government and had not been replaced. Riddell had no clear instructions from Ottawa. His cables went unanswered. But he thought he knew the mood of the King government so he took bold action, proposing a tough embargo on iron, steel, coal and oil. The League cheered the Canadian resolution and accepted it. Mussolini wavered.

The new independent voice had spoken; the world had listened and turned to the path of peace. Or so it seemed.

Back in Ottawa, Ernest Lapointe was running foreign policy while King holidayed in Georgia. At first he supported Riddell's action, brushing off complaints by the Italian consul. Then the full force of French-Canadian opinion turned on him. The Quebec press said Canada was getting itself into another war. Catholic Quebec had always been friendly towards Italy. The province's Conservative leader, Camillien Houde, proclaimed: "If war should come between Britain and Italy, French-Canadian sympathies will be with Italy." Lapointe caved in and repudiated the man in Geneva. Riddell had acted on his own, he said. His views were not those of the government.

The oil embargo collapsed. Britain and France welcomed Canada's defection as an excuse to duck out of their earlier promises. Mussolini proceeded with his conquest, and the League of Nations became an empty and useless marble hall. Later Mussolini was to admit that if his oil supplies had been cut off he would have been out of Ethiopia within a week.

Thus Canada's first foray into international peacemaking turned into a humiliating disaster. King defended it as best he could. "I am not at all sure," he ruminated, "that when the whole story comes to be told it may not be discovered that but for the action of the government of Canada in this particular matter, the whole of Europe might be aflame today."

The story was soon told. Europe *was* aflame three years later because men like King in Canada, and Baldwin and Chamberlain in Britain, misjudged the dictators and opted for peace at any price. King visited Hitler in 1937 when he had digested the Rhineland and was preparing to swallow Austria and the Sudetenland. He was relieved to find him no serious danger to anyone. The Fuehrer, he told Bruce Hutchison, was "a simple sort of peasant."

When Chamberlain returned from Munich, waving the worthless piece of paper that was Hitler's pledge of peace in our time, King was among the first to cheer. He cabled Chamberlain: "The heart of Canada is rejoicing tonight . . . the voice of reason has found a way out of the conflict."

Reading this today, it would appear that King was an even simpler of peasant than he imagined Hitler to be. But the great majority of Canadians did rejoice. They had enough to do in surviving the Depression without poking into the powder kegs of Europe: it was just too bad about the Czechs, Albanians, Austrians and Ethiopians.

In 1936 the Canadian Army Chief of Staff, General Andrew McNaughton, reported that Canada had no operational military aircraft, no bombs, no anti-aircraft guns and only sufficient shells for 90 minutes' fire from the few old fieldguns left over from the Great War. "About the only article of which stocks are held," he concluded, "is harness. The composition of a modern land force will include very little horsed transport."

This position had improved only slightly when war came in 1939. There were just over 4,000 officers and men in the Regular army, equipped with 29 Bren guns, 23 antitank rifles and 5 three-inch mortars.

In the last years of peace King rejected all the alternatives offered him to cope with a European war. He dismissed J. S. Woodsworth's appeal for a declaration of neutrality. He rejected combined military action through the League of Nations. He would not commit Canada in advance to any imperial defence policy made in London. He obtained from his new friend, Roosevelt, a guarantee that the United States would not "stand idly by" if Canada were threatened by invasion. However, Canada was not directly threatened, and the United States was bound by Congress to stay neutral when Europe erupted.

In a fine ambidextrous speech in May, 1938, King summarized the alternatives, without committing himself to any. Canada was not inclined to join crusades in other continents; on the other hand Canada could not be indifferent to the fate of democratic institutions and the suffering of minorities. Canadians might find an emotional outlet in passing resolutions on this and that foreign crisis but that did not give them any power to shape the destinies of other nations.

It was, he cried, "nightmare and sheer madness" to think that Canada should automatically go to war to save Europe every twenty years.

Yet when the talking was done, King led Canada to war. He was the most unlikely warrior — small, plump and mild-looking. He had never worn a uniform or touched a rifle. The nation didn't want a man on horseback. A large part of it didn't want to go to war at all, and the rest entered the battle with none of the trumpeting of 1914. The country had to be manipulated, manoeuvred and massaged by Mackenzie King. He gave forth no Churchillian battlecries, but in his strange way he was one of the great war leaders.

At the start he laid down two conditions. Canada must declare war of its own free will through Parliament. And conscription of men for overseas service would not be needed although men would be called up for home defence. He was determined not to have a repetition of the 1917 conscription debacle.

Parliament was summoned, and the declaration of war was debated and approved. Canada was officially at war with Germany on Sunday, September 10, nine days after the Nazis invaded Poland. Woodsworth alone voted against the declaration, following his conscience to the end. His six CCF followers deserted him. King, ever respectful of principles in others, said, "I admire him in my heart." Lapointe and King's up-and-coming Quebec lieutenant, Charles Gavan "Chubby" Power, kept down French-Canadian opposition — always on the understanding that no Quebecker would be sent to fight overseas against his will. Maurice Duplessis, the Conservative ward-boss of Quebec, rose up to challenge the federal government's right to make war, and was squelched in a provincial election. One enemy down — one to go. The Liberal Premier of Ontario, a gallus-snapping onion farmer called Mitch Hepburn, tried to outflank King on the right. Three months after Duplessis was overthrown, Hepburn put a motion before his Ontario Legislature regretting that Ottawa wasn't pushing the war hard enough. In his reckless ambition, poor Mitch didn't know he was giving King the chance he wanted — to spring an election in the calm of the phony war period and clear the decks for the real war that lay ahead.

On January 25, 1940, the first day of the new Parliamentary session, the Prime Minister smiled benevolently upon some new Members, shook their hands and welcomed them to the House. He gave no hint that he was about to send them

straight home again. With the air of fussy confusion that concealed his lethal master-strokes, he read Hepburn's Ontario
resolution. For a moment Hepburn soared in stature. Here,
said King, was the biggest province in Canada challenging his
conduct of the war. He could not carry on under such circumstances. The people must decide if he was fit to govern —
decide immediately. He moved the adjournment of Parliament
and called an election. The furious Tory leader, Robert
Manion, whose party was in no way prepared to fight a campaign, accused him of gagging Parliament and proving himself
unfit to govern. Well, King smiled, that settled it. The people
must decide upon his fitness. Manion had completed what the
ambitious Hepburn had begun.

In the election that followed, Manion lost his seat and the
Tory leadership passed to R. B. Hanson. Hepburn's anti-King
movement collapsed and he soon retired to his onion patch.
King had 178 seats to 39 for the Tories. The decks were clear,
if slightly bloodstained.

In the black summer of 1940, France fell and the remnants
of the British Expeditionary Force were scooped up and ferried
home from Dunkirk. Hitler was poised to invade England, and
there wasn't much there to stop him.

While Churchill growled magnificent defiance, secret plans
were made to ship King George VI and the British government
over to Canada. If the worst happened the war would be car-
ried on from there. As Churchill promised, the new world
would rescue the old. The new world meant America, and
King worked to bring the United States into the war. In the
first two years of war he at last fulfilled what he called *Canada's*
Manifest Destiny — to be the missing link between the
United States and Britain, an independent voice loyal to the
Mother country but bound up with big Daddy. Succeeding
Liberal prime ministers tried to play this role, but by then
Canada had moved too far into the American orbit for them
to succeed. The bargains King made with Roosevelt began
this process, but at the time they helped save Britain. They

were to bring undreamed-of prosperity to Canada, along with undreamed-of dependence on the United States.

Ogdensburg was the first. Parked in the President's private railway car in a siding in that New York State town, in August, 1940, King and Roosevelt quickly arranged the first across-the-border military alliance. Written out by FDR on a piece of paper salvaged from a waste-basket, it set up a permanent joint defence board for continental defence. It was the forerunner of NORAD, the alliance that brought H-Bombs airborne over Canada and the screaming match over the unfortunate Bomarc missile. It prepared the way for the first major transfer of American weapons to Britain — the swapping of fifty over-age U.S. destroyers for British bases in the West Indies, Bermuda and Newfoundland. Warships lose their value rapidly, while real estate increases in price with the years, so from a book-keeping point of view, that deal was a loss for Britain. But it got America deeper into the fringe of war, so it was a tremendous gain.

King wrote in his diary: "I had explained that we would not wish to sell or lease any sites in Canada but would be ready to work out matters of facilities. The President said he had mostly in mind the need, if Canada were invaded, for getting troops quickly into Canada . . . that similarly if the U.S. should engage in conflict in the South or around the Panama Canal, or had its men concentrated there, that it might help for us to be able to move men immediately through Maine to Portland. . . . He thought we might have to arrange for annual manoeuvres of troops on our respective soils. I said that would be all right."

At that time there was a real possibility, even a likelihood, that Britain would go down. Canada had sent what navy it possessed across the Atlantic and was defenseless against the U-boats reported to be off its shores. King needed some form of insurance and Roosevelt offered it, apparently free of charge.

As go-between, King knew secrets neither Roosevelt nor

Churchill could tell their peoples, or even their Cabinets. As France was about to collapse, Roosevelt suggested that King, with the other Dominions, try to persuade Britain to turn the Royal Navy over to the United States. King wrote: "For a moment it seemed that the United States was trying to save itself at the expense of Britain. That it was an appeal to the selfishness of the Dominions at the expense of the British Isles, each of them being secure by the arrangement. I instinctively revolted against such a thought. My reaction was that I would rather die than do aught to save ourselves or any part of this continent at the expense of Britain."

This instinctive feeling was part of the Canadian Prime Minister's heritage — something the U.S. President could not be expected to understand. In his rambling way, King was to explain it to him in the war years ahead. He would also soothe Churchill, who suspected that the U.S. was about to grab the British Empire, minus Britain, just as soon as the Nazis had done the dirty work.

For thanks, King received cables from Churchill that described him as "the link which, spanning the oceans, brings the continents into their true relation." But his own Canadian troops booed him when he went to review them in the south of England. Perhaps there was nothing personal in it. They had been waiting an hour in bone-chilling rain for his appearance and might have booed anyone. Perhaps it was a hint of the coming conscription crisis which was to rack Canada in the second war the way it had in the first.

It began as a cloud no bigger than Arthur Meighen, whom King had shrunk so long ago. The old Tory demanded all-out conscription. He had taken back his party's leadership and was running for a Commons seat in South York. If he got in, King reasoned, he would split the country, drive the Quebeckers into the hills again and demolish the war effort. And — King abandoned reason — he couldn't stand that abominable, self-righteous face staring at him once again, day after day, across the Commons floor. Enemies King had slaughtered must stay that way. Once one came back to life a whole political graveyard might open up. To cope with Meighen he took the first step that would lead to overseas conscription. He adopted a famous phrase "not necessarily conscription, but conscription if necessary." He would ask the people, in a national plebiscite, to release him from his pledge never to introduce conscription for service overseas; it would be introduced if needed, but it wasn't needed then. That, plus King's support of the CCF candidate, defeated Meighen in South York.

The plebiscite showed the English provinces to be four-to-one in favor of conscription and French Canada three-to-one against. King was now empowered to change his no-conscription policy if he had to.

His diary reveals two rather negative principles: "In politics one has to do as one at sea in a sailing ship; not try to go straight ahead but reach one's course having regard to the prevailing winds"; and "I really believe my greatest service is in the many unwise steps I prevent." Conscription would be an unwise step, but the prevailing winds were for it. His Defence Minister, Colonel Layton Ralston, interpreted the plebiscite as a clear order to send the boys abroad, and when he realized that King had no intention of doing so he offered his resignation. King refused it, for the time being, knowing that if Ralston walked out waving the flag, half the English-speaking Cabinet members would follow him.

The Opposition constantly criticized Canada's war effort as inadequate. In fact it was staggering. In two years the depressed, largely rural nation went through an industrial revolution, driven by C. D. Howe, the remarkable Minister of Munitions and Supply. By the end of 1941 he could report that every six weeks Canada was producing enough of the 2,000 different pieces of equipment needed to supply an infantry division. Factories were sprouting and American tools and parts were flooding across the border. Canada had suddenly become an arsenal, but the arsenal was in debt. The trading deficit with the United States soared to half a billion dollars. In 1941 King met Roosevelt at his Hyde Park, New York mansion and told him production would have to be cut back for lack of U.S. currency. The U.S. was supplying war materials to Britain under Roosevelt's Lend-Lease plan — a form of fight now, pay later — but this didn't help Canada's dollar drain.

In the President's small, paper-strewn study, King handed him a draft agreement which solved the immediate dollar problem and laid the foundations of future industrial cooperation, Canadian prosperity, and U.S. economic domination. Each country would supply the weapons it could best produce, and the American parts Canada needed to make arms for Britain would be paid for in Lend-Lease dollars. Roosevelt said it was a "swell idea" and signed. He scribbled, "Done by Mackenzie and FDR on a grand Sunday in April." Nobody else ever called King "Mackenzie."

The deal was a temporary wartime arrangement but it endured and spawned more agreements. Without them Canada's industrial expansion would have been a temporary wartime thing, too. The integration of defence forces begun at Ogdensburg and the integration of production begun at Hyde Park were to bring Canadians a higher standard of living and a lower standard of independence. There could be integration but no equality between partners, one of whom happened to be ten times bigger than the other. Prime Minister Trudeau was to compare the relationship to sleeping with an elephant.

For good or ill, these deals with Roosevelt were to have greater effect on Canada than the conscription crisis which loomed so large at the time.

On the battlefronts, King's problem was different from Borden's. The Canadians were not being slaughtered wholesale as in World War I. With notable exceptions, they were left hanging around on guard duty in England. The exceptions were the hopeless Canadian defenders of indefensible Hong Kong and those massacred in the Dieppe raid, the survivors of which felt that they had been used as guinea pigs. When the invasion of

Europe was postponed until 1944, King worried about the morale of his troops. He could see the gloom of history descending on Canada if its men were not given a more active part in the war. So he asked Churchill to send Canadian units to fight in North Africa. General McNaughton had made a similar request to the British general staff, but he insisted his army be kept together and deployed as one force. For the overall planners this was a nuisance.

Rows broke out between Ottawa, which wanted the men in action somewhere; McNaughton, who wanted them under his control; and the Allied High Command, which wanted to use them as it saw fit. As a result, many of the Canadian troops remained on fatigues.

The infantry division and tank brigade sent to invade Sicily were taken out of McNaughton's command, and when he tried to visit them the British commander, General Montgomery, threatened to arrest him. The Canadians who finally arrived in North Africa were shabbily shunted to the rear, given worn-out British tanks and generally made to feel unwelcome.

All this ill-feeling was repaired in the final assaults in Italy and France, when every man was needed. But by then McNaughton had been dumped by the British planners — with Ottawa's approval. Canadians were told that their military hero was sick and retiring from the battle. In fact, he was fit and soon to be thrown into a political battle as nasty as anything he had seen overseas.

The 1917 argument was back: did Canada have sufficient men abroad to play its part? After talking with Montgomery in early 1944, King was sure Canada did. The army of seventy thousand "Zombies," the conscripts dragged in for home defence, was an embarrassment as there was no longer any risk of invasion; but it was better to keep it idle than to stir up a racial holocaust. After D-Day, Ralston went to Europe and came back with a different story. His officers on the spot told him they were desperate for reinforcements. Men wounded two and three times were being sent back into action. The

upright colonel flew back to demand that fifteen thousand
Zombies be sent overseas at once.

As King saw it, the military mind was sabotaging the unity
he had maintained so precariously for three years. There were
two hundred thousand volunteers available in Canada and in
England, some fully-trained, some partly. If the generals
couldn't find fifteen thousand battle-ready men out of two hundred thousand they didn't know how to run an army. Germany
would be destroyed with or without the extra fifteen thousand
Canadians; Canada could be destroyed because of them. "Why
blame me for this mess?" he cried in despair.

He embarked on one of his obtuse but deadly missions.
Secretly, he recruited McNaughton, the deposed military hero,
to replace Ralston as Defence Minister. With his personality
and soldierly reputation, he would persuade fifteen thousand
Zombies to volunteer for the battle and conscription would not
be needed.

King reached into a desk drawer and produced Ralston's
three-year-old resignation letter. At the next Cabinet meeting,
he suddenly informed the Defence Minister that his resignation
was accepted and McNaughton would replace him. Military
discipline saved the King government. If Ralston had resisted
he could still have split the Cabinet. But the colonel knew his
firing-squad procedure. He bowed stiffly, shook hands all
round, and marched out to his political execution.

McNaughton began his recruiting mission. The pro-con-
scription faction booed him. The Zombies turned him down.
After three weeks only five hundred of them had volunteered
to go overseas. The rest said, in effect, if you want me, come
and get me. Worse, the Army Council, the senior brasshats
who had been McNaughton's comrades, informed him that
they would resign if the Zombies were not ordered abroad.

King was now convinced that conscription had to come.
The prevailing wind had become a hurricane. He saw in the
impending revolt of the generals the nearest thing to a military
coup that Canada had ever experienced, and he used this
threat to win over his new Quebec lieutenant, Louis St.

Laurent, to conscription. He may have exaggerated the danger. Probably he did. Most of his Cabinet members thought he went too far when he later hinted in Parliament at "the possibility of anarchy." They were never told of the Army Council's threat. King managed his about-face with loss of only one Cabinet minister — "Chubby" Power who resigned "in sorrow, not in anger." The calm chill of the now-indispensable St. Laurent cooled the French-Canadian Liberals and persuaded them to stick with King. (If they didn't, he told them, King would resign and hand the government over to an all-out conscriptionist prime minister.)

By order-in-council, sixteen thousand Zombies were sent overseas. King had dodged and prevaricated for four years. While he had not drawn the teeth of the issue he had so bored and exhausted both factions that they now fought limply. In Parliament, Ralston contented himself with a biting cross-examination of his successor McNaughton; he did not bolt to the Tories. St. Laurent declared he would stand or fall with the Prime Minister. The will of the majority must prevail, he said, and the majority was acting only after considering the feelings of the minority. The Liberals comfortably won the conscription debate.

As in 1918, mobs rioted in Montreal, smashing recruiting offices and burning Union Jacks. St. Laurent's Quebec City home suffered some broken windows. But the outbreaks were not on the scale of the First War. In 1942, King had confided to a Liberal caucus that if men were ordered overseas, "we would have to enlarge our jails and use our tanks and rifles against our own people."

It didn't come to that. King steered the nation through the conscription crisis by his political genius, knowing from the start that it was a political and emotional issue. There was no military need for the Zombies, as he saw it, and from the military point of view the whole crisis was phony. Of the first 10,000 Zombies ordered to sail, 8,200 disappeared at once and more than half were still missing when the ships weighed anchor. Nearly 13,000 eventually got overseas, about 2,500 reached the battlefront and 69 were killed. Those who fought, fought as well as the volunteers.

As the war ended, Roosevelt died and Churchill was pushed out of office. The iron dictators of Europe disappeared, but Canada's man of rubber wore on. In June, 1945, he won another election and a mandate to govern, seemingly forever. He was not loved nor particularly well liked. He wasn't even trusted by many of his supporters. But he was comfortable and capable. Behind his banner of inspired mediocrity the nation sauntered forward at a surprising rate.

The war had killed the Depression and the Liberals stamped on its grave. Tacitly, they admitted the justice of Quebec nationalist Maxime Raymond's charge — "They knew where to find the money for war. Why could it not be found for peace?" Plans were laid for old-age pensions, health insurance, subsidized housing, and medical insurance. It would take nearly a generation to achieve all these things, but the seeds of expectation had been planted in the prospective recipients and the politicians in Ottawa and the provincial capitals must eventually respond. And the economic thinking which produced and nurtured the Depression was changed. A White Paper tabled by C. D. Howe committed the government to the theory of spending to cure depression and maintain employment. The hell-for-leather capitalism which had built and nearly destroyed the country was out. King, grandson of the Rebel and author of *Industry and Humanity,* was developing the social revolution that had begun, almost unnoticed, during the war. Having broken Tory leader after Tory leader, he could set his sails to catch the prevailing wind from the left.

In the last three years of the King regime, the nation moved with deceptive ease from a pumped-up war economy to a peacetime boom, and prepared to embrace a new province, Newfoundland. The Prime Minister, now in his seventies and showing his age, reluctantly concluded that his work was done. His first choice of successor, Lester Pearson, refused, and he persuaded St. Laurent, a still reluctant statesman who had hoped to be released from duty at the end of the war, to offer himself at the party leadership convention. He cried as he resigned the leadership he had held for 29 years.

He paid a final visit to London, where he took ill. King George and Winston Churchill came to his bedside and, at King's request, Churchill stooped and kissed his old friend on the cheek. He had two other visitors, middle-aged women who were smuggled into his hotel by a back door. They were his favorite British mediums; through them he talked with those whom he expected to join, old Mackenzie, his mother, Laurier, Roosevelt, his dog Pat. Not until after his death were Canadians to learn that he had consulted the dead throughout his prime ministership. Two of his mediums, questioned by Blair Fraser of *Maclean's Magazine,* insisted that he talked with the departed about trivial, personal matters, not affairs of state. Yet one of them revealed that the ghost of President Roosevelt warned him to beware of the Far East, because the next war would break out there in 1947. King apparently acted on this information, demanding that Canada withdraw its delegate from a United Nations Commission in Korea. St. Laurent and the rest of the Cabinet disagreed, and successfully defied their leader for the first time.

King lived in several worlds. He believed that God directly guided his decisions, and, as he readily accepted His advice, it is hard to believe he ignored the messages from the dead which he so eagerly sought.

He returned to Canada for the last time, resigned his prime ministership and went to Kingsmere to wait out his last years of loneliness. There stood his piles of souvenirs in old scrapbooks — programs of long-forgotten meetings, pieces of ribbon, coins, the rose petals he was given to throw at Princess Elizabeth's wedding but pocketed instead, a selection of stones from the bombed British House of Commons.

And there were his ruins — strange, contradictory and unfinished, like his Canada. If the ancient secrets of the universe lie in the mystery of Stonehenge, the secret of Mackenzie King lies somewhere in these weird relics. He died in the farmhouse beside them on July 22, 1950.

**ST. LAURENT**
1948-57

# XI.   *"We stayed — and look what happened!"*

No, said Quebec's leading lawyer. Regretfully, he must refuse. He lacked, you see, that spirit of *noblesse* necessary to give up one's profitable practice and sacrifice oneself on the altar of politics. But there was Louis St. Laurent — a man without political experience, but the poor devil had a streak of nobility in him that might make him fall for it.

Thus Aimé Geoffrion passed the buck, as did other prominent French-Canadians, when offered the job of managing Quebec for Mackenzie King. It was 1941 and the great Ernest Lapointe was dead. As his funeral train wound along the St. Lawrence from Quebec City to Rivière-du-Loup, the search for a successor went on. The Prime Minister began a letter.

"If ever the finger of destiny pointed to man who was meant to succeed Laurier and Lapointe in the representation of Quebec East and of his province in the Federal arena, that man is . . . yourself."

It was addressed to Adele Godbout, Premier of Quebec. But Godbout preferred to stay where he was. King flicked down his list of prospects and found St. Laurent. He was half-French, half-Irish. As a lawyer, he had represented "Les Anglais," the English financial brains of Montreal. He supported a strong war effort which put him in line with the King government but out of line with the mood of Quebec nationalists. He was no politician — King had just discovered he was a Liberal. Still, he had a first-class mind and obviously commanded respect in the province. With Godbout out, he seemed the best man available.

King phoned him at his Quebec City home at dinnertime on December 4. The scene at the other end was a model of comfortable Quebec family life. Madame St. Laurent was directing the cook and maid as dinner took shape. Two of the five grownup children were visiting home — Jean-Paul, whose wife was in hospital, and Renault, a lieutenant in the Royal Canadian Navy stationed at the local base. And Aunt Lora was in from the country to do her Christmas shopping.

The St. Laurents were well-to-do. The head of the family, now nearing sixty, had built his law practice up from fifty dollars a month to over fifty thousand a year and was just getting into the fat directorships belt. The family had servants and a chauffeur, belonged to the best clubs and took their holidays abroad. It was a good life, created by a village storekeeper's son.

The phone call wrecked it. Madame St. Laurent wept. Aunt Lora reminded Louis that their mother had taught them to put family life first. The sons were enthusiastic. Jean-Paul could see his father becoming the greatest man in Canada. Renault, in uniform, reminded his father where duty lay. "Don't forget," their father told them, "if I accept, you will suffer enormously and will certainly not benefit from the move." A Cabinet minister was then entitled to twelve thousand dollars a year. He took the train to Ottawa that night, after promising his wife he would tell Mr. King he was too old to go into politics.

No Canadian leader had greatness thrust upon him so suddenly. When Abbott was pushed into the prime minister's office he had been a politician for 42 years. St. Laurent was plucked late in life from his law office and installed as Number Two man in the government. There was no question of his making a modest entry into Ottawa. The mantle of Lapointe and Laurier awaited him and he must wear it nobly or shatter himself and King. No English-speaking prime minister could survive without a strong French-Canadian. Meighen and Bennett had proved this and John Diefenbaker was to demonstrate that the rule still applied in the sixties. The mantle was a deadly garment — everyone who wore it would be accused of selling out his race to the English and would know in his heart that the accusation was sometimes true. Laurier had tortured himself with doubts. Lapointe had listened to village voices from Quebec and helped to destroy the League of Nations.

That night St. Laurent agonized between the calls of home and duty. Canada was at war to prevent enslavement by dictators — not meddling needlessly in a European quarrel, as St. Laurent had viewed her participation in the 1914–18 bloodletting. If he had to serve — and King, Godbout and Cardinal Villeneuve soon convinced him of that — it would be for the duration of the war only. If this calm, grey man burned with ambition to lead he concealed it better than any other Canadian leader.

From boyhood he had been remarkably free of prejudice, political or racial. His father's family came from France 300 years previously and took the name of the great river beside which they settled. His mother, Mary Broderick, was Irish. Young Louis addressed his father in French and his mother in English and assumed that everybody else did the same. There was no trace of French in his English, only a tinge of the Irish. He was brought up in the Eastern Townships where both cultures flourished side by side and even his middle name was adaptable to both languages. It was Etienne on his birth certificate but became Stephen. If ever there was a balanced Canadian it was he.

At the seminary in Sherbrooke where he was prepared for

the priesthood he wrote wryly: "We should be thankful that
we are closeted out of harm's way where we are not tempted
to meddle in politics, steal apples or kiss or commit any of
those petty crimes of youth. We should be thankful that we
have someone to wake us up at twenty minutes past five in the
morning."

As a resident, young Louis was not allowed out to hear
Prime Minister Laurier when he spoke in Sherbrooke in 1900.
Nor was he allowed to read newspapers. So the effect of
Laurier's speech, in accounts smuggled in by day pupils, was
heightened and remembered. The great Liberal said: "In
Ontario and the other English provinces they say Laurier has
not done this or that — he is a Frenchman. In Quebec they
say Laurier does too much — he is *un anglais*, an Englishman. Because I do my duty, placing myself above considerations of race, party or faith, I am exposed to attack on the
basis of every prejudice from either side."

The seminarians, forbidden to "meddle in politics," came to
blows over political arguments in the dormitory. On election
night St. Laurent lowered a bucket on a rope from an upstairs
window and hauled up the results, on bits of paper placed
there by a day pupil. Laurier was ahead. "We're winning," he
whispered.

The priests soon recognized that St. Laurent did not have the
single-mindedness demanded by the Church, and he left the
seminary to study law.

When, after his successful law career, he arrived in Ottawa
as King's Minister of Justice he brought an impartiality that
was new to that hot-house of ambition and intrigue. He could
assess a problem coldly, decide what should be done, and
explain it crisply to Parliament. The House found this refresh-
ing after King's verbal voodoo dancing. If inexperience brought
clarity, perhaps it was a good thing. The quiet man with the
face of a well-bred fox-terrier was not ambitious enough to be
dangerous. He was a technician, a war-time conscript.

King had hoped to bring him into Parliament unopposed in

Quebec East, but a right-wing nationalist candidate appeared, supported by Duplessis forces and Liberal rebels. The plebiscite on conscription had been announced and St. Laurent defended it as a lesser evil. He faced a tough workers' audience in Lower Town. His reasoned, lawyer's speech met with surly silence. This was no courtroom. Carefully he removed his pince-nez and tucked away his text. "Now," he barked, "I want you to know what Louis St. Laurent is made of." He conjured up the riots of 1917 — machine-guns chattering in Quebec streets, mobs screaming, troops charging. That was the kind of conscription he was against. That was what Arthur Meighen and his Tories would bring if they got in. But St. Laurent was in favor of French-Canadians doing their bit to defend their country. He went on bravely: "For my part I will probably come to you and ask you to vote 'yes' on the plebiscite. You can listen to me or not. You will be free to do what you want."

There was a hush. The crowd looked up with a new respect. This man, at least, was giving it to them straight. They clapped, then cheered, then roared and sang *"Il a gagné ses épaulettes"* — the French equivalent of "For he's a jolly good fellow." St. Laurent listened and was never quite the same again. He *had* won his epaulettes.

Three years later he made his decision to stand by King in the conscription crisis, and that led him to the party leadership and the prime ministership. "The more I see of St. Laurent," King wrote, "the nobler soul I believe him to be. One of God's gentlemen if ever there was one." He admitted later that if St. Laurent had wavered on conscription he would have been forced to resign as Prime Minister.

In the high, hopeful summer of 1945, King and St. Laurent won an election and flew together to San Francisco to sign the Charter of the United Nations.

A new era of peace had arrived, and the wartime conscript was persuaded to stay on for a while and help it along. So he was at his desk in the Justice building on Wellington Street the day the Cold War began.

For two years a mousy little cipher clerk called Igor Gouzenko had worked behind the steel bars of the Soviet embassy on Charlotte Street, decoding messages to and from Moscow and filing them away. They told of the existence of a large Soviet spy ring working in the middle levels of the Canadian government. Agents had penetrated the cipher room of the External Affairs department, the secret laboratories of the National Research Council, and the closed sessions of the wartime Parliament. Canada, as Churchill proclaimed, had been the linchpin between Britain and the United States, so the Russians worked on the linchpin to tap the secrets of both big powers, including the biggest secret of all: how to build an atom-bomb. The documents Gouzenko read were so confidential that even the Soviet Ambassador Zaroubin was kept from them. They were the property of Colonel Zabotin, military attaché and head of the Soviet army spy ring, and his deputies, who were officially listed as a chauffeur and a doorman.

On September 5, 1945, Gouzenko stuffed a bundle of these confidential papers under his shirt and left the embassy for the last time. The protection of a free society, as he saw it, lay in publicity. Once his story was told in the newspapers Colonel Zabotin wouldn't dare to kill him.

So he hurried through the dark streets to the Ottawa *Journal's* office, carrying the biggest story of the decade. It was too big for the Ottawa *Journal*. Gouzenko understood the ways of a controlled press in a police state; he didn't grasp the lackadaisical mood of a free newspaper with no free competition worth bothering about. It printed what its staff thought people wanted to read, and at that time the people didn't want to read anything nasty about Stalin, their glorious wartime ally. The night editor in charge sent Gouzenko out into the terror-filled darkness, suggesting he talk to the RCMP.

At the RCMP office he asked to see the Minister of Justice, Louis St. Laurent, and was told to come back in the morning. The next day the Minister was in Parliament and unavailable.

A secretary had told him about the strange Russian visitor and he decided to stall. As Canada had diplomatic relations with Stalin, it would be a dreadful breach of protocol to receive a defector laden with stolen documents. The glum news was passed to the External Affairs Department's Norman Robertson, a veteran who understood every nicety of diplomacy except this one.

That afternoon St. Laurent ran into Ambassador Zaroubin at a reception. The subject of fishing came up. "Has your Excellency found the fishing good today?" asked the Russian. St. Laurent stammered something innocuous, and moved away.

Gouzenko tried the Ottawa *Journal* again. This time he got a hearing, but the *Journal* decided the story was not its cup of tea.

To Gouzenko, the bland bureaucracy of the free society seemed just as stony as the one he had deserted. He went back to his wife and child in his apartment, talking of suicide. That night there came the expected knock on the door. He recognized the voice of Zabotin's deputy calling his name. The Gouzenkos crouched in silent terror. The visitors left, the sound of their footsteps dying away in the distance.

After the newspapers, the government and the police had failed Gouzenko, a neighbor rescued him. An RCAF sergeant living next door took him into his apartment and listened to his story. Later, when four Russians arrived, smashed in Gouzenko's door, and began searching his belongings, the sergeant called the Ottawa city police. There was no bashfulness about the city cops; they simply arrested the intruders as housebreakers.

That broke the Gouzenko case. Although Zabotin's men were swiftly released under diplomatic immunity, the cipher clerk and his family were taken under the wing of the Mounties, and an investigation began.

There had been nothing like it in Canada before. The modest nation had never considered its secrets worthy of such professional spy work. The international implications were enormous. The case could wreck the rapport with the Soviet Union built with countless corpses spread from Stalingrad to Normandy. It threatened the new United Nations. And what if Russia had the Bomb?

Mackenzie King wanted the affair hushed up or, failing that, handled in a way that did not incriminate Moscow in the doings of its underlings in Ottawa.

St. Laurent handled it by tough, secretive and underhand means. Spying, after all, was a dirty business. The investigation reflected little credit on anyone, including the Canadian press which was scooped on its own story, months later, by an American reporter.

After weeks of secret examinations of witnesses by a secret Royal Commission, two women and twelve men, all civil servants, were arrested in Ottawa, held incommunicado, and interrogated before they could call their lawyers. This questioning led to the arrest of Fred Rose, a Communist M.P.

St. Laurent was accused in Parliament of using Star Chamber methods. He was caught out in his denial that a secret order-in-council had been issued for the clandestine detention of suspected spies. The evidence was tabled in the House. A back-bench Conservative, John Diefenbaker, stormed at him for forgetting an order that "swept aside Magna Carta and the Bill of Rights." St. Laurent had to agree that people should not be secretly held and questioned in peacetime, but argued that the national security demanded it. It was a bad time for justice and her minister.

The spy revelations reverberated around the world. Churchill made his first post-war anti-Communist speech at Fulton, Missouri, predicting that an "iron curtain" would fall across Europe. The U.S. was still prepared to give Stalin the benefit of the doubt, but when its own spy revelations began, that volatile nation plunged more deeply into the negative religion of anti-Communism than anyone else.

In Ottawa, twenty people were charged with spying; fourteen were convicted and given sentences of up to five years.

Gouzenko still lives in Canada, under another name. For years the RCMP provided a guard who lived in the cottage behind his house. He believes that Soviet spy-rings other than the one he smashed were operating in Canada in 1945 and are still operating, and he campaigns for government pensions for future Soviet defectors who may break these rings. Life in Canada has brought him freedom from oppression but not from fear. For him, the night of September 5, 1945 goes on forever.

In 1946, St. Laurent still planned to get out of politics. King took him to Kingsmere for a quiet talk. The comforts of home and the profitable law practice faded farther away. St. Laurent agreed to take over External Affairs — a new interest that was to end his days as King's loyal conscript and to begin his career as an independent statesman. He set a course for Canada far different from what King had imagined.

No previous Canadian foreign minister had such opportunity before him. The bungling of the thirties was still fresh in mind. The new titans of the post war era were eyeing each other suspiciously but had not yet frozen into fixed poses of hostility. The new peace organization just might work. St. Laurent brought his calm legal eye to these larger problems and for a time he was hopeful. He shook hands with the inscrutable Mr. Molotov, Soviet Foreign Minister, and told him there was no reason why Canada should not be on as good terms with Russia as with America. He offered Canadian troops to a future U.N. peace-keeping force. He opposed a move to censure South Africa for its racial policies, and Franco's Spain for its dictatorial repression. Everyone could get along, he thought, if reason replaced passion.

The U.N. represented reason, and St. Laurent, with his under-secretary, Lester Pearson, determined to lead Canada in that direction and away from the dissolving British Empire. While King still looked back to the old ties, the new men at External Affairs headed for the unplowed pastures of internationalism. Canada's influence in the world was to flower with the United Nations, reaching full bloom in the Suez crisis of 1956, when Pearson earned his Nobel Peace Prize. (It would wither, too, as the United Nations withered.)

At the same time, St. Laurent found a second club to join. He was one of the first to suggest the regional defence grouping that became the North Atlantic Treaty Organization. Although he and Pearson inserted a clause in the NATO treaty providing for economic cooperation between members, this was never used. No peaceful purpose was devised for NATO. It remained a purely military alliance run by the United States under stricter discipline than the old Empire had imposed upon its Dominions.

Within the frameworks of these two clubs, St. Laurent, the reasonable French-Canadian, managed what Borden or King would never have attempted. He sent troops abroad, ready for battle at a moment's notice, without a declaration of war or even a declared enemy. Reason succeeded where passion had failed, but the result, at times, seemed totally unreasonable.

Mackenzie King dragged against this rush toward involvement in the world's distant troubles. He had turned more and more of international policy-making over to the External Affairs team, but occasionally he asserted himself. In December, 1947, he returned from London to find that in his absence Canada had joined the United Nations' commission in Korea. Angry and alarmed, he demanded that the delegates be withdrawn. St. Laurent dug his heels in; Canada stayed on the commission for a year, then dropped out. King, helped by his ghostly warning from Roosevelt, had foreseen that the Korean situation would lead to war and he thought that by taking no official role there Canada could stay out of it.

(When the war did come he was dying. The Cabinet decision to send troops was taken, appropriately, on his funeral train.)

The row over the Korean commission was hushed up and smoothed over so that King could hand over to his successor.

Having finally decided on St. Laurent, he manipulated the Liberal leadership convention so that the successor was chosen according to plan. Then he left St. Laurent dangling for three months, power just beyond his grasp, before he handed over the prime ministership. When St. Laurent got it, on November 15, 1948, it was a magnificent inheritance — a booming country, a wonderful party machine built to last forever and an able, if complacent Cabinet. He brought to it, at sixty-seven, an impeccable reputation as statesman and gentleman. If few Canadians really thought of him as their "Uncle Louis" — he was too distant for that press nickname — he was the kind of uncle everyone *ought* to have had.

With C. D. Howe as his English-Canadian strongman and Pearson, inveigled in from the security of the civil service, as his External and U.N. handyman, he offered the country everything it wished — unity and cash to spend at home, and a clear conscience abroad. After six months in office he called an election and won what was then the biggest majority in Canadian history — 194 seats to 41 for the dejected Tories. Liberalism rolled on like a mighty river, changeless and eternal. The eye could not detect that it was changing all the time; the same drop of water never passed twice. And the wildest Tory could not imagine that it would all flow down the drain in nine years.

St. Laurent ruled with the quiet confidence of the chairman of the board. He saw no need to set up scarecrows and demolish them as in King's mumbo-jumbo rites. No feints were needed to distract the foe, for he was impotent.

Diehards would have screamed treason if some earlier Grit had attacked the foundations of the legal system by abolishing the final appeal to the Privy Council in London. St. Laurent went ahead and did it. It was simply a matter of accepting responsibility for one's own laws, and thus relieving Britain of a tiresome burden. Perfectly reasonable.

All Canada's governors-general had come from Britain, pre-packaged in gold braid and supplied with cocked hats and clipped military accents. St. Laurent appointed a Canadian, Vincent Massey, to represent the Queen of Canada. "I would not like to think," he said, "that a Canadian, alone of the Queen's subjects would not be considered fit to represent her in Canada." Older Tories felt instinctively that there was a hole in this reasoning, but they couldn't find it.

The ultimate challenge was the Canadian constitution — the British North America Act — which could only be amended in Westminster. Why not change it in Canada? St. Laurent boldly asked Parliament to take that power into its own hands, as it affected federal authority. He hoped the provinces would agree, too, and complete the Canadianization of the constitution; but they didn't. The problem of repatriating the BNA act is still unsolved, but at least St. Laurent had the guts to try.

As the product of eight generations of *habitants*, he might have been expected to frown upon immigrants. However, his mother's family came from Ireland. Louis Stephen re-opened the doors that had been closed during the Depression, and a new kind of immigrant arrived from Europe. They did not all come as in days of yore "from Britain's shore," nor were they bundled in sheepskins like the peasants Clifford Sifton lured over at the turn of the century. Germans and Italians soon outnumbered the British, and refugees swarmed in from the Communist East.

Most of them went to the cities where they found no melting pots — only individual frying-pans prepared for them by those of their countrymen who had arrived on earlier boats. Each ethnic group assisted and exploited its own immigrants until they found their feet and could do the same for or to the next wave. The elders nurtured the ways and the ancient hatreds they brought from the old lands, but the sons and daughters usually drifted off into the mainstream of North American life. They were English speakers by this time and they resented, even more than the Anglo-Saxons, the emphasis on French as a second language. "Already I speak the both languages," said the New Canadian, "English and Ukrainian."

Like Laurier before him and Trudeau after, St. Laurent undertook to tell his own people the facts of life. In one of his first speeches as a politician he had told Quebec to give up the "illusive dream of a French-Canadian state in North America." But in the 1950s it was no longer just a dream. While the rest of the nation surged ahead, getting richer, busier, and more antiseptically American, Quebec stagnated under Maurice Duplessis.

Graft, bribery and looting of the treasury were not new to the province; the Duplessis machine merely organized them to a high degree of efficiency. His Union Nationale ran French Canada like a perpetual Mafia Christmas party with gifts for all members of the family and the occasional penny thrown to the poor in the snow outside. "Le Chef" milked Ottawa for what he could get. He collected the loot at his border and locked the gates before the donors could see what became of it. There was no need for a separatist movement, as Quebec was already quite separate in its ways.

In the fall of 1954, Uncle Louis declared war on Le Chef. He told the Quebec Reform Club the province must become a province like the other nine. Duplessis argued that federal tax-sharing agreements were undermining Quebec and its Roman Catholic school system. This, said St. Laurent, was a smokescreen to hide the misdeeds of the Union Nationale. He offered to pay half the cost of Quebec's part of the trans-Canada highway, providing Ottawa could examine the accounts. (Duplessis' building contracts were notorious.) "After all," he sneered, "even the Union Nationale must be honest about it." He even allowed himself a chuckle at the expense of the priesthood. He recalled the question he had put to a priest who called the federal baby-bonus an invasion of Quebec's rights — "How many children have you?"

Le Chef was incensed. He could not understand how a man could lose his self-control to the point of disowning his race, his province, his rights. No English politician had dared to say that Quebec was a province like the others. It was against the facts and the law. Quebec would never surrender the mastery of its own house for a federal pension. And so on. . . . The row, which began over money, degenerated into the familiar racial shouting match in which one French-Canadian calls another a *"vendu"* or sell-out to the English.

St. Laurent's legal mind took over. Perhaps he had lost his self-control. It was not worth fracturing Canada to put down a provincial demagogue. He met Duplessis in the neutral halls of the Windsor Hotel in Montreal and settled on a tax compromise. His Reform Club speech made him a hero in English Canada but had neither dented the Duplessis regime nor improved prospects of a détente between Quebec City and Ottawa. Canada's second French Prime Minister, like the first, was to leave relations between the two Canadas no better than he found them. By the time the third came along they were worse.

The Duplessis affair was St. Laurent's personal battle, one of the few occasions when he descended from the aloofness of the chairman of the board. Mostly he let his capable ministers, supported by a generation of loyal Liberal-minded civil servants, run their own shows. They supplied sound business-like government, unbothered by squeaks from the tiny Opposition. The voters were content. They returned the Liberals with a reduced but still huge majority in 1953. Uncle Louis was getting on in years, but seldom talked of returning to his blissful family life. He heeded Churchill's advice — don't walk when you can ride, don't sit when you can lie down and, on official occasions, use the washroom at every opportunity.

This orderly existence was shattered by C. D. Howe and the great pipeline debate. It brought Parliament into a state of revolt bordering on anarchy and changed the image of the ruling Liberals from competent managers to grinding despots. It was silly and useless but inevitable. If it hadn't come over Howe's ridiculous schedule for the building of his hollow pipeline, it would have come over something else. For the Liberals had grown so accustomed to power that they had forgotten whence the power came.

Howe had been a Cabinet minister since 1935 when King brought him in for his executive drive, fully aware that he was a political ignoramus. Howe got things done. He set up the British Commonwealth Air Training scheme, creating 126 airfields. He started Trans-Canada Airlines from nothing. He founded the Canadian aircraft industry, built the Canadian war machine, and converted it to peacetime production. He made the economy boom and guarded the boom like his own child. Under King and now St. Laurent he was an independent, unchallengeable force. He knew best.

The "extraordinary powers" given him in wartime had been extended to cover postwar reconstruction, then renewed for another three years during the Korean War. He then demanded that they be extended indefinitely. He admitted that they were absolute powers, but he was used to having them. When it was suggested they be extended only for a further three years, Howe snapped, "that would mean coming back to Parliament every three years and I've more to do than spend my time amusing Parliament."

Parliament heard this and remembered. The Opposition lay in wait for Howe; in 1956 they got him.

The Trans-Canada Pipelines scheme was praised, reviled, and fought over until it assumed the proportions of another CPR. In retrospect there seems nothing remarkable about it. Howe made a deal with an American-controlled firm to build a pipe along an all-Canadian route bringing natural gas from the oilfields of Alberta to the cities of the east. The government of Canada would underwrite the project. The Conservatives wanted an all-Canadian company to do the job; the CCF thought the pipe should be publicly owned, but all sides wanted it built. After six months of wrangling Howe failed to get the government guarantee that he wanted but he agreed on a compromise — Ottawa and Ontario between them would lay the pipe along the least profitable part of the route, the wilderness between the Manitoba border and Kapuskasing in northern Ontario. The pipeline company would build the rest but, its promoters announced, they needed an eighty million dollar loan immediately if they were to start work on the western section in 1956. By the time Howe had arranged the loan it was May and he had only three weeks to get the pipeline bill through Parliament before the deadline for the start of construction.

The company had to have the money by June 7 to buy its steel pipe. Tory leader George Drew planned a filibuster, which the government could stop by imposing closure to cut off the debate. But Howe was in too much of a hurry for this. He served notice of closure before the debate even began.

The Opposition howled "guillotine" and "dictatorship." That was only the start. During the fifteen days of vituperation that followed, Hansard recorded "meathead," "jackals," "magpies," "Hitlerism" and "trained seals." Howe was accused of selling out to the Americans and of being one himself. (He was born in Massachusetts but had been a Canadian citizen for forty-two years.) M.P.s sang, whistled, jeered and shook their fists. Never in Parliament's history had such emotions been aroused by a debate that had nothing to do with the French-English problem. As the turmoil mounted, the Prime Minister sat reading a book.

The Liberals used closure motions to cut off every stage of debate. After two weeks the Liberal Speaker of the House, Réné Beaudoin, slipped up. Distracted by a trivial question of privilege he allowed the House to adjourn for the night without considering that day's closure motion. The debate was to resume the next day; Howe would miss his deadline.

Here the question arises: so what? The city people could survive another year without natural gas. The government could survive, and so (as it turned out) could the pipeline company. Missing the deadline would hurt only the enormous ego of C. D. Howe and the mountainous conceit of the Liberals. The public didn't particularly care about the pipeline.

But watching the incredible performance in the Commons it was beginning to care about the future of the parliamentary system. It looked on, at first amused, and then repelled as Parliament utterly lost its head.

Next day Speaker Beaudoin rose to announce that he had made "a serious mistake." He suggested the House forget everything that had occurred since 2:15 the previous afternoon, return to square one, and finish the pipeline business forthwith.

The House exploded. Opposition M.P.s tumbled out from their desks and on to the sacrosanct carpet of the center aisle, shouting and cursing the Speaker. The schoolmasterly CCF leader, M. J. Coldwell, climbed the Speaker's dais and shook his fist in Beaudoin's face. Parliamentarian John Diefenbaker slumped in his seat muttering "I'm choking." St. Laurent stared emptily at the tumult and Howe looked straight ahead, seeing nothing but his deadline, and beyond it miles and miles of hollow steel pipe.

The Speaker's unparliamentary suggestion was endorsed after the Opposition refused to vote on it — the pipeline bill went through and the deadline was met.

But the pipeline was not built that year. The factory producing the pipe went on strike, and the contractors couldn't get their materials.

Nothing had been accomplished by the destruction of parliamentary procedure and the demeaning of the Speaker. The government failed even to take a lesson from it. They didn't realize what resentment had been aroused in the country by the mob scene in the House. To them it was only a scuffle in a locker-room. The cosy Cabinet club-house was as calm as ever. There the real decisions were made.

A year later, when this arrogance had laid them low, C. D. Howe told Blair Fraser: "We were too old. I was too old. I didn't have the patience any more that it takes to deal with Parliament. You know, over a year ago I went to the Prime Minister and suggested that he and I ought to retire. He

wouldn't hear of it — I guess he'd decided he was going to
live forever and everything was to go on as it was going. So he
said nonsense, we must both stay. So we did — and look what
happened!"

The St. Laurent government's handling of the 1956 Suez
crisis has been justified by time and internationally acclaimed.
It now stands out as a masterstroke of Canadian diplomacy,
the ultimate victory of postwar reason over passion. At the
time, however, it was a domestic disaster, a political atrocity
comparable to the pipeline debacle. Never before had Canada
turned on Britain, not only refusing support but conspiring
with the United States to defeat her.

When Britain's Prime Minister Anthony Eden hinted that
he would use force to get back the Suez Canal which had been
seized by Egypt, St. Laurent and Pearson, the lawyer and the
diplomat, thought with their passionless apolitical heads.
Finance Minister Walter Harris warned them that to desert
Britain would cost the Liberals forty seats in the House. St.
Laurent replied, "you're thinking with your blood."

The lawyer and the diplomat coldly assessed the effects of
the lion's roar upon the ex-colonies at the U.N. Both were irritated by Eden's assumption that Canada would offer at least
verbal support to action against Egypt's President Nasser. The
U.S. State Department had warned them that Eden meant business and had asked them to help calm him down. Canada was
back in the job of mediator between the two big English-speaking powers — only one was now a super-power and the other
a feeble relic about to issue its last imperialist gasp.

When the gasp came — the joint Anglo-French attack on
Egypt, launched on the pretext of stopping a previously-
arranged Israeli invasion of Suez — St. Laurent sent Eden a
telegram. Outraged Tories were to describe it as a "blistering
rebuke," but actually it was quite mild. Canada "regretted"
Britain's action and could not endorse it. The telegram mentioned Canada's "close friendship and intimate association"
with Britain but worried about the effects of the invasion on

Commonwealth unity and Anglo-American co-operation, the latter being the most important.

While Pearson manoeuvred brilliantly in the airy halls of the U.N., the voters of Canada were thinking with their blood. A Gallup poll showed forty-three percent of Canadians supported the invasion; forty percent were against. Both sides were vehement. St. Laurent was besieged by packs of reporters in the corridors of the East Block. Australia was supporting Britain. What was Canada doing? The harried Prime Minister shouted from the door of the Privy Council chamber: "It's too bad you can't come in and tell us how to do it, but we are the ones responsible to Parliament and the Canadian public."

When the crisis was over, cooled by Pearson's U.N. police force proposal, the External Affairs Minister emerged smelling of laurel leaves; the Prime Minister was branded as the man who stabbed Britain in the back. (Pearson's work will be described in his chapter; let it be said now that St. Laurent was constantly in touch with him and supported him all the way.)

During the furious post-mortem Commons debate, St. Laurent was goaded into attacking "the big powers" for using the United Nations to regiment small countries and ignoring it when their own interests were at stake. (An unremarkable statement. The Soviet Union, Britain and France had all flouted the U.N. Charter. The United States was to do the same in its military adventures in Lebanon, Cuba, Santo Domingo and South East Asia.)

"Why not?" somebody shouted.

St. Laurent retorted: "Because the members of smaller nations are human beings just as are other people; because the era when the supermen of Europe could govern the whole world is coming pretty close to an end." Out of temper, he, too, had "spoken with his blood." He had damned the mother country and given substance to the Conservative charge that his handling of Suez was ordained by Washington. Howard

Green, the finger-wagging Tory from Vancouver proceeded to lash him into a fury. Green supposed, he said, that all the "supermen" were either in the St. Laurent government or in Washington. He assumed the Prime Minister included Sir Winston Churchill in his "nasty biting remarks."

"The Uncle Louis kissing babies went out of the window this afternoon," said Green. "So smug. So full of self-righteousness. So hypocritical." He went on to lay the foundations of the Conservative campaign in the 1957 election:—

Canada had acted as the chore-boy of the United States. The Prime Minister had been a better friend to Nasser, the tin-pot dictator, than to Britain and France. He had knifed Canada's best friends in the back.

By the time the debate ended, St. Laurent had two knives in his back — the pipeline debate and Suez. It remained for that glittering toreador, John Diefenbaker, to deliver the final thrust.

In 1957 the Liberals marched into the June election with the cheery tread of lemmings off to the seaside. The boom that had borne them along since the war was fading. The government had worked so many miracles that it had none left to perform. The party had even run out of promises. Diefenbaker, the new Conservative leader, offered the sun, moon and stars but, more than that, he offered a change. The Liberals had been in office for twenty-two years and were not only overbearing, irresponsible — almost dictatorial — but also bloodless and bureaucratic. The country craved excitement and Diefenbaker offered it. He had passion. It was not yet apparent that he was short on reason.

On June 10, Louis St. Laurent sat in his Quebec City home, manfully concealing his amazement as the returns piled in. The Conservatives swept across the Maritimes, Ontario and the West, gaining 112 seats to the Liberals' 105, with 25 CCFers and 19 Social Crediters. Diefenbaker had won the right to form a minority government. St. Laurent could have clung to office but that was not his nature. He stepped aside with dignity and, seven months later, gave up the Liberal leadership and returned home. The war and its aftermath were over. The conscript could go back to his family and his law firm, knowing he had done his duty to the best of his ability. He lived until 1973—with no complaints or recriminations to sour his old age. He was a gentleman. Never truly a politician.

**DIEFENBAKER**
1957-63

# XII.  *The Wind from the Wilderness*

John George Diefenbaker had Sir John A. Macdonald's old bed enlarged to accommodate him. He sat in Macdonald's chair, watched his clock, looked in his mirror. He chortled over his repertoire of Macdonald stories, rumbling his respect for the Old Chieftain's love of humanity and winking forgiveness for his hero's love of the bottle. In everything but accomplishment, Diefenbaker was the most outstanding Prime Minister since Macdonald.

He was large, loud and rambunctious, humorous and churlish, sanctimonious and savage, magnificently obtuse and devastatingly incisive. His worst enemies never called Diefenbaker a small man.

He was an actor of the old school, towering over his audience and commanding them to laugh or cry. As Bruce Hutchison said, he mistook acting for action and came to believe in his own act. He burned Canada's economic candle at both

ends, giving forth a lovely light but consuming the fat left by
the Liberals. Abroad, he maintained Canada's balanced position between the United Kingdom and the United States by
enraging the leaders of both countries. John F. Kennedy's
lasting memories of Ottawa were a chronic pain in the back
(he strained it there planting an official tree) and its Prime
Minister (whom he described as a son-of-a-bitch).

The Diefenbaker years now seem like an interlude, a light
diversion from the sober task of nation-building, a national
fishing trip to a wild, northern lake, where tales of the rude,
hilarious past were told and fantasies of the future took shape
in the flickering firelight. No fish were caught, and we awoke,
shivering in the morning.

Those years were an interlude, too, in the long career of
Diefenbaker himself. From 1925, when he first ran for Parliament, until 1940, when he got in, almost by chance, his record
of political failure was perfect. He was defeated twice in
federal contests (once by Mackenzie King), twice for provincial office in Saskatchewan and once for mayor of Prince
Albert. He spent sixteen years on the dreary backbenches of
Opposition before he captured the Conservative leadership.

He was dogged by his German name and his radical Prairie
outlook. The Tory establishment in Toronto had no time for
"foreigners" and less for wild western prophets.

The *Diefenbacker* family came from southern Germany,
via Holland, in 1816. His mother's forbears, the Bannermans,
came over from the Scottish Highlands with Lord Selkirk's
immigrants in 1812. John George was born in tiny Neustadt,
Ontario, forty-four miles south of Owen Sound; he took the
wooden-seated settlers' train west at the age of eight when his
schoolmaster father decided to try homesteading in the Saskatchewan wilderness. The land cost ten dollars, plus the
promise to work it for three years, and the house, the size of a
big toolshed, was hammered together board by board by
father Diefenbaker and sons John and Elmer.

He took the press to see it during the 1965 campaign and

reminisced sentimentally over the Forest Beauty kitchen stove, the parlor piano and the coal-oil lamps by which he read of the great world outside and so far away. A political joke (adapted from an earlier U.S. campaign) had him declaring: "Some compare me to Lincoln because I was born in a log cabin. In fact, it was a manger."

Young John was born an underdog and continued to regard himself as such even as he scaled the heights. He spent much of his life as a country lawyer, defending the downtrodden. In twenty murder cases he lost only two clients to the gallows. His courtroom trick was to fix his eye on one member of the jury at a time and attempt to convert him before moving on to' the next. He seldom called defence witnesses because this deprived him of the last word. And words, great suffocating swarms of them, were his soldiers. "The relationship between the Prime Minister and the cliché," a CCF M.P. once said, "is not that between master and servant; it is that of master and slave, because he beats these clichés and bruises them, sets them dangling before us and then, having bludgeoned them with such violence, he hurls their bleeding bodies in the pages of Hansard. If we want to find out what has been happening we have to disinter these victims of verbosity and when we conduct a post-mortem we find that nothing has been happening."

With the words came the punctuation — the distracting grunt, the terrible pause, the accusing finger, the massive head in disdainful profile. Diefenbaker once threw himself on the floor of the British Columbia Supreme Court, clutching his throat, to show how a murder had been committed.

He entered Parliament as an advocate, not as a party representative. He saw the Commons as an extension of the dusty prairie courtroom, wherein wrongs could be righted and liberties upheld. In one of his first speeches he urged the political parties to suspend politics for the duration of the war. "I care nothing for party name," he said, "I say forget about party in the greater danger that is facing our Empire."

He was appalled by the ruthless, needless uprooting of Canada's Japanese community from their west coast homes — the worst excess committed in the name of wartime security. He tried time and again to introduce a Canadian Bill of Rights. He condemned the American witchhunter, Senator Joseph McCarthy, and he managed to stop a Conservative party move to putsch the Canadian Communist party. When the Tory establishment blasted the Liberal plan for family allowances — "the baby bonus" — Diefenbaker said he would vote for it. In 1950, still a defence lawyer, he took on a case just as unpopular in its time as that of the Polish-Yankee invader, von Schoultz, whom Macdonald had represented. A railway telegrapher in British Columbia was charged with manslaughter in a train crash that killed twenty-one Canadian soldiers on their way to fight in Korea. Diefenbaker defended him and, unlike John A., Diefenbaker won his case.

He pursued the job of Conservative leader at the party conventions of 1942, 1948 and 1956 knowing that Conservatism was an unpopular cause. The party old guard provided a string of ineffectual or out-moded leaders — Meighen, Bracken and George Drew, the former Premier of Ontario. The party wallowed in genteel failure. Even in December, 1956, after the pipeline debate and the Suez affair, the convention saw no immediate prospect of power. Later, perhaps, when old Uncle Louis retired. . . . In the meantime, Drew had collapsed under the strain of hopeless battle. A replacement had to be found. And there was John, whose years of crying in the wilderness had given the old guard a pain in the neck but who had won over those other residents of the wilderness, the backbench Conservative M.P.s. Nominating him, the gallant Major General George Pearkes, V.C., fearlessly described him as "the greatest living Canadian — a cross between Simon de Montfort and Benjamin Disraeli." The old guard could well have done without a de Montfort to curb their feudal powers or a flashy ethnic like Disraeli, but the old guard knew it was finished. Diefenbaker was chosen on the first ballot.

He accepted humbly. "I know I will make mistakes but I hope it will be said of me when I give up the highest honor that you can confer on any man — 'He wasn't always right; sometimes he was on the wrong side, but never on the side of wrong'."

All the delegates cheered, including the men he had beaten. He would take them into his Cabinet but never trust them completely. He would always suspect those who had blocked his path for so many years and at the end, like Mackenzie Bowell, he would feel himself surrounded by a nest of traitors. Like King, whose agility he admired but could never emulate, Diefenbaker did not forgive. He, too, was a man of destiny.

Although more Canadians voted Liberal than Conservative in the 1957 election, there was never any doubt about Diefenbaker's mandate to govern. When the surprising results were in, lifelong Liberals seemed happy their party had lost. There was an infectious, naughty thrill in the air. In his incoherent way, Diefenbaker offered a taste of greatness. The nation had been through poverty, the torments of disunity and immaturity, and it now wore a cloak of second-hand prosperity, handed down from the United States. The new leader talked of vision, faith and spiritual springs, a "Canada First" policy that no one, himself included, understood; but that every man could interpret according to his secret yearnings. If there was, by the mid-twentieth century, a uniquely Canadian life-force, Diefenbaker had found and tapped it.

In the three Kennedy years, the United States was to experience that "one brief shining moment" that Mrs. Jacqueline Kennedy called Camelot. It was marred by military blunders, a narrow escape from World War Three, and stagnation in Congress.

It was, in many ways, a cardboard Camelot, glued and plastered by PR men. But John Kennedy challenged Americans to be somehow better and nobler than they were; and they were elevated and purified by the thought, even if they didn't make the effort. John Diefenbaker struck a similar chord in

Canada in 1957-58. That was The Chief's great accomplishment, and it still stands, although in retrospect the Diefenbaker era looks more like the Red Queen's court than
Camelot.

The champion of the underdog took office looking for
dragons to slay, not noticing that most of them lay dead at
his feet. He was 61, full of bounce and vigor; but a lifetime
on the losing side had taught him only how to attack, not how
to defend himself. He had stormed the ramparts of power;
now he didn't know how to work the drawbridge.

Peter Newman wrote (in *Renegade in Power*): "John Diefenbaker came to the toughest job in the country without having worked for anyone but himself, without ever having hired
or fired anyone, and without ever having administered anything more complicated than a walk-up law office."

As soon as his Cabinet was sworn in he flew to London,
ready for fresh conquests at his first Commonwealth Conference. He was an instant hit — a massive, self-confident Canadian who took his power for granted instead of whining for
more and instead of begging for trade, grandly offered some to
the mother country. On his return to Ottawa he told a press
conference that fifteen percent of Canadian import trade
should be shifted from the United States to the United
Kingdom.

Harold Macmillan's Conservative government promptly
took him up on the offer. As such a dramatic switch would
contravene GATT, the international agreement on tariffs and
trade which bound both nations, they devised a way around
it. Britain publicly offered a free trade agreement with Canada.

The proposal was greeted with blank horror in Ottawa. The
Prime Minister, it appeared, had no intention of giving Britain
anything but the opportunity to buy lots of Canadian goods.

The fifteen percent figure was never mentioned again.

There are two explanations for the British move. One is that
Macmillan believed Diefenbaker was sincere, if naive, and
jumped at his offer. The second is that he wanted to expose it

for all to see as a phony echo of Bennett's grandstand play at the 1932 Imperial Conference and demonstrate once again that "Empire Free Trade" could not work. For Beaverbrook was snapping at his heels, as he had at Baldwin's, demanding expanded Commonwealth deals as an alternative to Britain's joining the European Common Market.

Whatever the reason, relations between London and Ottawa got off to a bad start and were to get worse. At future conferences Diefenbaker harangued Britain for deserting the Commonwealth and turning towards Europe, forgetting that he had made the fifteen percent offer and then withdrawn it. He believed ardently that the Crown and the ever-loosening collection of monarchies and republics to which Canada belonged were needed to keep his nation from falling into the jaws of the United States. He followed Macdonald in his dependence on the Crown, which had now become the Commonwealth. The basic Canadian problem had not changed.

Where trade and the Common Market were concerned he had the rest of the Commonwealth behind him. Only Trinidad and Tobago supported Britain's (unsuccessful) attempt to join Europe.

On another vital Commonwealth question, Diefenbaker played a more decisive role. He amputated one chunk of the organization to save the rest. His revulsion against South Africa's iron policy of racial discrimination — apartheid — was real. He did not see how the association of mainly black and brown peoples could afford a member like that. While Britain tried to smooth things over, Diefenbaker promoted the set of rules against racial discrimination which drove South Africa out. This was supported by all sides in Canada's Parliament but did nothing to improve the relations between Canada and Britain which Diefenbaker had promised to "restore."

The arrogance of the Liberals in Parliament had prepared the way for Diefenbaker's minority win in 1957. Their utter idiocy rolled out a red carpet for him in 1958. Lester Pearson, the diplomat, was chosen to lead the party on January 16. Four days later this slight, un-political figure was thrust into the ring with Diefenbaker in the mismatch of the century. Pearson's craft was practised in chanceries and drawing-rooms — the shy smile, the deprecating gesture, the reasonable compromise settled over a sherry with reasonable men. He had never smelt the sawdust, the sweat and the horse-droppings of the big political arenas, or been deafened by the trumpets as the fools, the tumblers and the spangled high-wire acts rode in.

He rose with his smile and his bow-tie to make the silliest suggestion yet heard from an Opposition leader. The country was not ready for another election. So why didn't Mr. Diefenbaker simply resign and hand the government back to the Liberals? He, Pearson, was prepared to form a Cabinet and put the country back on the road to progress from which it had been temporarily diverted seven months before.

As he spoke, Pearson realized how childish he sounded. His first impulse had been to offer Diefenbaker his support for the time being to avoid any chance of bringing down his government and springing an election for which he was not prepared. St. Laurent, Jack Pickersgill and C. D. Howe talked him out of that and persuaded him to make this bumptious appeal to the Tories. Only men who had forgotten what parliamentary democracy was all about could have thought of it.

Pearson sat down and waited apprehensively for the thunder to roll. Slowly the Prime Minister ascended to his full height. Inaudible bands blared "The Entry of the Gladiators."

Tom van Dusen wrote in his biography *The Chief*: "I felt sorry for Lester Peason; his bow-tie seemed to wilt and his affable smile became painted on his features as the verbal hiding went on. It was a little like Rocky Marciano going to work on the block champion."

One rapier shaft would have disposed of Pearson that day. Diefenbaker used cudgels, bludgeons, bombards and boiling lead. He went on for two hours.

A year before, the Department of Trade and Commerce had

produced a gloomy report on the country's economic out-look. It was stamped *Confidential* on the fly-leaf and *Secret* on the blue outer cover. Liberal Cabinet ministers had a chance to read it three months before they went out on the hustings to tell the voters everything was dandy and they never had it so good.

Diefenbaker now brandished the document, shorn of its *Secret* blue cover and laid it naked before the House. "No renewed strengths in corporate profits are expected," he read. ". . . The possibility of a more pronounced decline cannot be ruled out. . . . The lower level of exports is likely to result in a decline of cash income on the prairies again. . . . A higher average level of unemployment seems likely. . . ."

"Why didn't you tell the people these things?" he roared. "What did you do about it?" The Liberals cringed. Diefenbaker had found an election issue in his "Hidden Report," and Pearson's petulant little speech asking for their ball back had given him an excuse to use it.

Within two weeks Diefenbaker had dissolved Parliament. He was bounding around the country laughing at the Grits and exulting in his new Vision.

"I see a new Canada," he proclaimed, "a Canada of the North!" The pale eyes glittered towards thousands of miles of barren muskeg and permafrost. "Jobs! Jobs for hundreds of thousands of Canadians. A new Vision, a new Hope. A new Soul for Canada . . . to the young men and women of this nation I say, Canada is within your hands. Adventure! Adventure to the nation's utmost boundaries, to strike, to seek, to find and not to yield!"

What did all this mean? The north was the symbol of things left undone. Untold riches were buried up there, but they were useless because there was no economical way of getting them out. Perhaps this reflected the general state of the economy — lots of money but no way to distribute it fairly. Perhaps there were hundreds of thousands of jobs if hundreds of thousands of adventurers went out to create them.

In his small, pragmatic way, Pearson mocked the Vision as "a scheme to build roads from igloo to igloo." He never grasped its mystic effect on the denizens of the empty continent. The Vision was vague but not phony; it was the kind of myth people live by.

It grew larger and more diffuse. It left the north and hung like a silver cloud over the prairies, leaving the farmers starry-eyed. It reflected vague hope on the disgruntled Maritimes. It even touched the cynical cities. It brought the Tories 208 of the 265 Commons seats.

Diefenbaker modestly described his great win as a victory for the democratic process, but he had done it alone. There had not been such a Conservative victor since Sir John A. And John G., surrounded by his Macdonald mementoes, began to believe the bright blue posters that hailed him as almost a reincarnation of his hero.

Yet the Old Chieftain was a Tory; Dief the Chief was a radical one-man band. He distrusted all that the old guard Tories stood for — money, tariffs, free enterprise and money. He hated big business and Toronto's Bay Street. By the time he brought a Bay Street mandarin, Wallace McCutcheon, into his Cabinet to placate the businessmen it was too late; they hated him. He was essentially a rural politician, and the "average Canadian" he invoked was a kind of farmer-fisherman-trapper who taught in a little red schoolhouse, cursing central government as he picked up his federal cheque. Statistically the real-life average Canadian of the period lived in the city or the suburbs and spent one-tenth of his time looking for work.

Diefenbaker confessed to "a sense of loneliness" as he returned to Ottawa with a bigger margin of support than any other leader of a western democracy. He could not share his power. He would not run his government like a corporation. He had no powerful Number Two man, like Macdonald's Cartier, King's Lapointe or St. Laurent's Howe. He had no French-Canadian of any stature. He knew hardly any French-Canadians.

He did not delegate authority, but neither did he exercise it himself; he seemed to squander it.

Peter Newman theorized: "Each unresolved national problem represented an addition to his power, since it left the advocates of alternative solutions at his mercy. A decision once taken, on the other hand, represented a dilution of that power, since it lined up the dissatisfied factions against him."

With some reason he distrusted the civil service bequeathed to him by a generation of Liberals. The top ones had a way of nipping into political jobs and sometimes back again. External Affairs, in particular, looked like a farm club for the professional Liberal team.

Diefenbaker's government failed and finally fell apart because Diefenbaker never really believed in it. He tried to reach beyond it and commune personally with the people. He would satisfy their various and contradictory wants because they, the average Canadians, knew best. The puffed-up Liberals had failed because they ignored the people. The Chief floundered trying to please them.

The unfortunate Finance Minister, Donald Fleming, would shudder as he read the latest Diefenbaker speech promising some new expenditure that the Chief had omitted to tell his Finance Minister about. Fleming was a model of frugality, a dumpy Toronto Sunday school teacher who quibbled over his staff's ten-dollar expense accounts. He had no time for Keynesian notions or creeping socialism. Budgets should be neat, round, orthodox and balanced, like Donald himself.

But while his visionary chief soared off on expensive adventures, Fleming was left to pass the plate. He produced seven budgets, all wildly unbalanced, and ran up a total deficit of two billion dollars. As a former candidate for the Conservative leadership, he was treated as a second-class Cabinet minister and seldom allowed into the Prime Minister's office. He had to swallow his pride as well as his principles while the Diefenbacchanalia of spending went on.

The man who spoke out and destroyed public confidence in Diefenbaker government's money policies was James Elliott

Coyne, the Governor of the Bank of Canada. He was more conceited and even stingier than Donald Fleming and a figure of icy terror when roused. A man who would, for entertainment, play tic-tac-toe with a computer had the guts to play politics with John Diefenbaker.

The Bank of Canada regulated the amount of money in circulation and the government controlled the bank. Or did it? As money ran short, Fleming and Diefenbaker disclaimed responsibility for the bank's doings. Diefenbaker had blamed the Liberals for the tight-money situation and had undertaken to end it. Two years later money was still tight and it was handy to have the arrogant tight-fisted Coyne around to take the blame.

After a time Coyne refused to take it any more. He decided to state the financial facts as he saw them, and that carried him out beyond banking into politics and one of the great Canadian dilemmas. Canada, he said, was living beyond its means and supporting itself by selling out its resources to the Americans. Unless there was a tightening of belts, and strict Canadian control of business and the economy, the Yanks would take over completely. This warning now sounds familiar and no longer alarming. The takeover has proceeded apace, despite occasional outbursts of economic nationalism from men like Walter Gordon and Eric Kierans. In the Diefenbaker era it was heresy; it clouded the Vision.

The government had perfectly sound reasons for getting rid of Coyne. He was sabotaging its policy and dabbling in politics. The mistake they made was in trying to smuggle him out the back door of his bank and smearing him for accepting a large increase in pension.

When he refused to resign, the government was forced to introduce a bill declaring his job vacant. Coyne fought back, grinding out press releases that screamed "smear," "blackmail" and called Diefenbaker "an evil genius" of "unbridled malice and vindictiveness." He demanded his day in court before he would quit and the Liberals supported him in this, although they didn't go along with his ideas — the "sell-out" of resources had taken place under Liberal auspices. Tories called him an anarchist and an odd-ball.

The dump-Coyne bill passed the House but Coyne had his hearing before the hoary old Liberals in the Senate. They gave him the Not Guilty verdict he passionately pleaded for, on the understanding that he would then go. And the man of ice, his honor vindicated, walked out into the sunset with his misty-eyed wife on his arm — a beautiful bit of theatre that upstaged the great tragedian in the East Block. Out in darkest British Columbia eleven Freedomite Doukhobors heeded Coyne's plea for austerity. They set fire to their cars in protest against a life of luxury.

Otherwise the plea was ignored. But the fact that the government had been declared financially irresponsible by its bank manager had a lasting impact on the nervous souls who invest money. Capital surged out of Canada, and Fleming was forced into what he himself had called "a gigantic financial speculation with no assurance of success." On May 2, 1962, he devalued the Canadian dollar to 92.5 cents U.S. and pegged it there.

The 1962 election campaign was starting up. Gleeful Liberals printed "Diefendollars" — flimsy bills bearing a manic face of the Tory leader and a dotted line showing where seven and a half cents had been cut off.

It was Diefenbaker's third national campaign. The grease-paint was cracking and the costumes were wearing thin. Some of the old props fell down on-stage, revealing their cardboard backs. The villainous, arrogant Liberals, for example, were the same unsavory, treacherous crew they had been in 1957; but they hadn't had a chance to do anything unsavory or treacherous for five years. And the Chief's "average Canadian" was still there, to be defended to the last gasp and quiver.

But against whom? Already he had his Bill of Rights (1960) which, the Prime Minister told him "assured equality to every Canadian whatever his race, color or religion." Illuminated

copies of the bill, signed by its creator, were handed out like
icons to the faithful. You could pray to them for justice but
they were no use in court. Judge after judge decided that the
rights incorporated in the bill — most of which had been
guaranteed previously — did not take precedence over existing laws.

Canadians, average and otherwise, turned out as before,
though not in the hordes of 1958. The fascination was still
there but not the rapport with the leader. When the Prime
Minister's caravan reached Edmonton, Southam's correspondent Charles King wrote: "In the same city where the Conservative campaign caught fire in 1958, the Diefenbaker
bubble burst Friday night."

Diefenbaker turned on reporter King, accusing him of
"diabolical concoctions" and declaring he would never again
answer his questions at press conferences. Charles King was
through, he said. When he reached Vancouver, hecklers waved
placards reading: "We Want Charlie King."

While the "Diefenbubble" popped, the financial crisis blew
up back east. The devaluation of the dollar should have
brought an immediate surge of funds back into Canada.
Instead the drain continued and grew worse; the country was
going bankrupt at a rate of $20 million a day.

Diefenbaker and his ministers maintained that all was well.
Four days before the election the Prime Minister told a
national television audience: "The truth has been on our side.
We have given you the facts. We have bared the record. We
have concealed nothing and shaded nothing."

Six days after the election he discovered that "emergent
action" was needed instantly in the shape of a billion dollar
loan from the U.S. and the International Monetary Fund,
austerity cuts in government spending à la Coyne, and taxes
to restrict imports. It was hard to believe all this had become
necessary in six days. Certainly little of the truth, few of the
facts, and only part of the record had been put before the
voters. Nevertheless, they showed their loss of faith. Diefen-

baker lost 92 seats, retaining 116. The Liberals climbed from 48 to 98. Social Credit came back from zero to 30 and the New Democratic Party (a revamped CCF) went from 8 to 19. Only the farmers and small-town folk clung to their Chief. They represented thirteen percent of the population.

If the financial crisis had been unearthed a week earlier, the Diefenbaker regime would have ended there and then, brought down by its poor housekeeping. Instead it staggered on, crumbling inside and out, shedding fragments as it went. It fell at last as a result of a long series of blunders that began with the cancellation of an airplane contract on February 29, 1959.

The Avro CF 105 "Arrow" interceptor was the ultimate triumph of the Canadian aircraft industry built up by C. D. Howe during and after World War Two. It was the fastest and most powerful fighter in the world when it first flew in March, 1958. Similar sinister-looking jets are now standard equipment in the American and Canadian air forces but they are all American planes. The Arrow, with its Iroquois engines, was all Canadian. It had taken ten years to build up a team of scientists and engineers capable of creating such a machine. When Diefenbaker killed the Arrow project, the team left Canada taking its know-how with it, and 14,000 aircraft workers lost their jobs.

An industry died and Diefenbaker stamped on its grave by personally demanding that the five Arrows in existence be completely destroyed. These magnificent flying machines, which had cost $685 million to develop and build, were towed fifteen miles along the Queen Elizabeth Way to Waxman's junk yard, and melted down to nothing. It was the most extravagant display of vandalism in Canadian history.

The government's excuse for cancelling the Arrow was that the plane was becoming too costly — an eventual seven million apiece instead of the expected two million — and that the threat of attack by manned Soviet bombers, which the Arrow was designed to shoot down, had diminished.

Apart from all that, the Arrow was a Liberal plane, and Diefenbaker was piqued by the shameless lobbying of A. V. Roe's president, Crawford Gordon.

Something had to take the place of the Arrow in NORAD, the joint U.S.-Canadian air defence system which Diefenbaker had joined, rather casually, two years before. He announced that Canada would get 56 Bomarc missiles from the U.S. for a mere $14 million.

This air-breathing descendant of the V1 flying bomb was one of several defence systems which the U.S. had adopted half-heartedly in the hope that they might be of some use and in the certainty that their manufacture kept industry going and men at work. The Bomarc was not a very sophisticated weapon even in 1959. While the Arrows were being stuffed into Waxman's furnace the Bomarc 'A' version was still being tested, not 100 percent successfully, and the nuclear-tipped Bomarc 'B' which Canada was to get had not yet flown. The Pentagon planned to scatter a line of Bomarc sites along the U.S.-Canadian border and over in New England. Two sites inside Canada — at North Bay, Ontario and LaMacaza, Quebec, fitted neatly into the pattern.

The mayor of North Bay, hustling for tourists, thought the Bomarcs would make a splendid attraction as they soared prettily into the sky.

So far, so good. At that time, nobody could accuse Diefenbaker of playing politics with defense. He had taken the politically dangerous step of putting 14,000 men out of work and destroying an industry to fulfil his NORAD commitment. His Defence Minister, the gallant General Pearkes V.C., was convinced, from what the Pentagon had told him, that manned bombers, and thus fighters, were finished. Missiles were the thing. Far from being hidebound by his World War One experience, he had made the jump from horses to rockets without touching down in between. Only later did the Pentagon inform him that there might be some use left for fighters as the Russians still kept their fleet of hundreds of manned bombers. So Canada did, after all, buy a fleet of interceptor fighters for continental defence — 64 American Voodoo jets. They went into service in the spring of 1962, ready to do the job that the Arrow would have done.

To meet its NATO responsibilities in Europe, the Diefenbaker government agreed to adopt the Lockheed Starfighter and build it under licence in Montreal. Despite its name, it was to be used as a short-range atomic bomber.

So Canada acquired a full-range of U.S. weapons — the Bomarc, the Voodoo, the Starfighter bomber and the Honest John, a tactical ground-to-ground missile. In the fullness of time it was revealed that not one of them worked properly without a U.S. nuclear warhead attached. And Diefenbaker refused to accept the warheads because that meant accepting American troops on Canadian soil to keep an eye on them. He had sold out the Canadian birthright in the form of a Canadian defence industry, but damned if he was going to eat any mess of pottage.

So the 56 Bomarcs stood headless in their launch-bays; the Honest Johns' heads were stuffed with sand to fool the Reds; the Starfighters couldn't bomb. Only the Voodoos could play a role, though not the role NORAD prescribed, by carrying non-nuclear Falcon missiles. And when their call to duty came, they stayed on the ground.

On October 22, 1962, President Kennedy confronted Soviet Premier Khruschev with the demand that he get his offensive missiles out of Cuba. He threw all the switches that put the U.S. on the alert for all-out war. The one marked NORAD (Canada) didn't work. It took 42 hours for Canada to agree to put its continental air defense units on the same "ready" status as the American units. The Cabinet spent the time arguing. The new Defence Minister Douglas Harkness assumed that Canada was committed by the NORAD agreement. He had already made catering arrangements for the U.S. aircrews who were to move north and use Canadian bases. External Affairs Minister Howard Green argued passionately that if

Canada blindly followed the Americans "we'll be their vassals forever."

Finally the Voodoos were alerted but the U.S. crews did not move north and U.S. nuclear bombers were not allowed to make as many flights as they wished over Canada.

The crisis had two important results. Kennedy moved Diefenbaker up from the category of irritating nuisance to positive danger, requiring to be dealt with. Liberal Leader Pearson reluctantly decided Canada could no longer afford the luxury of nuclear virginity.

Now the facts had to come out. The first installment came from General Lauris Norstad, just two days after he retired from his post as Supreme Commander of NATO and became free to speak out. He told an Ottawa press conference that Canada was not fulfilling its NATO commitments because it refused to accept atomic bombs for the Starfighters.

Diefenbaker tried one more defence ploy. He invited himself to Nassau in the Bahamas where Kennedy and Britain's Harold Macmillan were holding a pointedly two-powers-only conference. (A photograph of the occasion shows the two of them deep in conversation at one end of a table ignoring Diefenbaker who sits by himself, as if superimposed on the print. Still the picture proved that he was there and lent substance to his version of the conference when it was presented to Parliament on his return.)

There had been, he said, "a change in the philosophy of defence," a change in NATO. Canada had been negotiating to have nuclear warheads "made readily available" and Canada's role would be clarified at the NATO Ministers' conference in May. However, Canada's nuclear role had been "placed in doubt" by the Nassau declaration.

It appeared in Ottawa that Diefenbaker was trying to weasel out of accepting nuclear weapons on the excuse that NATO policy was being changed and perhaps they wouldn't be required. It appeared to Washington that he was messing up the NATO alliance and scaring the other allies by accusing

Kennedy and Macmillan of plotting a secret deal. Washington decided the time had come to deal with Diefenbaker. On January 30, 1963, Canadian correspondents in Washington were handed a State Department press release. Short, vicious and shorn of diplomatic frills, it contradicted the Prime Minister six times and all but called him a liar twice. The State Department's Canadian experts had examined word for word the Hansard account of Diefenbaker's report to Parliament on his Nassau encounter. Practically the only part that they didn't contradict was his opinion that God was guiding the West.

The press release was approved by MacGeorge Bundy, the strategist in charge of the "war room" in the White House basement, but was not shown to the President. It was a blatant move to bring down the shaky Diefenbaker government and it worked. Under other circumstances, such Yankee interference might have saved him, but he was already too far gone.

The release stated flatly that Canada was contributing nothing practical to North American defence. Its Bomarcs were incapable of carrying a non-nuclear warhead, and its Voodoos were less than fully effective without nuclear weapons. The question of changing Canada's nuclear role had not been raised in the Nassau agreements. And there was never any suggestion that Canada would join the "nuclear club." In Canada, as in other allied countries, nuclear weapons would be kept in U.S. custody.

On the Bomarc, the press release was less than frank. It stated that no non-nuclear warhead had ever been designed for Bomarc 'B'. In fact a non-nuclear system, known unofficially as Bomarc 'X' was designed and developed between the fall of 1959 and the spring of 1960. A Canadian aircraft firm did the electronics work under contract to Boeing and the project reached the stage of "breadboard hardware" — meaning that a pre-prototype model was built. Engineers working on it were convinced that a non-nuclear Bomarc 'B' would work — not as effectively as the nuclear type, but well enough to stop manned bombers. Having established this, Boeing proposed to develop it further in the hope of further sales to nuclear-shy nations like Canada, but Bomarcs fell into disfavor at the Pentagon and all work on them stopped in the spring of 1961.

The Bomarc 'X' was classified *confidential* at the time, so the Pentagon and State Department could deny any knowledge of it. The Canadian defence ministry knew about it and Diefenbaker may have had it in mind when he said Bomarc 'B' was not "fully effective" without a nuclear warhead. (The U.S. version was that it was totally useless.)

Secretary of State Dean Rusk later apologized if the press release had given offense, but maintained that the need for "clarification" arose from a situation not of Washington's making. In other words, sorry but we meant it. Having destroyed Diefenbaker with one press handout, the U.S. administration saw no need to use two. It battened down the hatches and prepared for a storm of anti-American abuse from north of the border.

This never really broke. The Prime Minister recalled his Washington ambassador as a mark of displeasure, but he had too much to handle within his own Cabinet to leave time to tackle the world's biggest power. Seven ministers were conspiring to dump him as leader. The three Opposition parties planned to overthrow him by a vote of no-confidence in the House. Social Credit with its thirty M.P.s would settle for a Tory government, but without Diefenbaker. The Socred leader, Robert Thompson, feared an anti-American election campaign. With his great gift for the wrong word, he managed to express the inexpressible Canadian feeling towards its neighbor: "The Americans are our friends, whether we like it or not."

The plot to dump the Chief failed, but the no-confidence motion went ahead, backed by the entire Opposition.

In his last speech to the House as Prime Minister, Diefenbaker invoked Macdonald's rejection of attempts to join Canada to the United States. "That idea comes with almost every generation," he said. "When I hear some saying that the fact that one dares to speak out will endanger Canada's economy, I wonder what the future of this country would be if those who have such fears and those who are of little faith held office in our country. I believe in cooperation (with the U.S.) but not in the absorption of our viewpoint by any other nation."

That night his government was defeated by 142 to 111 — the only administration to fall in the House, apart from Meighen's fly-by-night government of 1926, and the only one to be shot down by a Washington press release.

His Cabinet fell apart and its ministers ran like rabbits. Harkness had already quit on principle over the warheads issue; Trade Minister George Hees and associate Defence Minister Pierre Sevigny left to avoid taking part in an anti-U.S. campaign. Donald Fleming, ex-Finance, now Justice Minister, left for valid personal reasons and Davie Fulton, ex-Justice now Public Works Minister, headed for provincial politics in British Columbia.

The Tories entered the 1963 election as they had entered the 1957 campaign with one man, John Diefenbaker, to decide their fate. Although he was still Prime Minister, he chose to disregard this, and also his record of the past six years. He was once more the loner, the underdog, the martyr to powerful forces. The U.S. magazine *Newsweek* helped him with a critical story and a frontpage picture of a demented-looking Dief. "They make fun of my face," the Chief lamented. "It's the only face I've got."

He threw himself once more on the mercy of the "average Canadian" who, he was sure, knew much better than *they* what was good for the country. The sinister *they* now included the Liberals, the State Department, even the Tory public relations men who had mismanaged his 1962 campaign. The average Canadian gave him a sentimental cheer. For the average Canadian had known failure at some point in his life.

The dark hand of the Yankee appeared twice during the

campaign. First came the story of the Purloined Position Paper, broken by Charles Lynch, chief of Southam News Services, and given an extra fillip by Peter Trueman, Washington correspondent of the Montreal *Star*.

During President Kennedy's 1961 visit to Ottawa when he strained his back and then strained his welcome by suggesting that Canada join the Organization of American States (OAS), his staff left behind a paper entitled "What We Want From the Ottawa Visit." It was found in a wastebasket and Diefenbaker got hold of it. Instead of quietly copying it and then returning it, which would have been standard procedure, he held on to it. Later he threatened the U.S. ambassador that he would use it in the 1962 campaign. The Trueman revelation was that the paper contained marginal notes in Kennedy's bad handwriting that were extremely derogatory to Diefenbaker. The Washington version was that the notes included the phrase: "What shall we tell the SOB about that?" White House officials attempted to explain that the President had actually written "What shall we tell the OAS about that?" but as they didn't have the paper the explanation didn't get much credence. Diefenbaker, who had it, never contradicted the SOB story. Much later a Washington official gave a better answer: "How could the President call him a son-of-a-bitch? We didn't know at the time what a son-of-a-bitch he was."

The second campaign story seemed a godsend to Diefenbaker. On March 29, seven days to polling day, the Pentagon's congressional staff chose, inexplicably, to release some six-weeks-old secret testimony about the Bomarc missile, given by Defence Secretary Robert McNamara before a House of Representatives subcommittee.

Under interrogation by two anti-Bomarc congressmen McNamara had admitted the missile was of very little use. The American Bomarc sites were being kept on because they were cheap to maintain and would at least draw enemy fire. The testimony went on:

Congressman Daniel Flood: "If we scratch Bomarc we have

stuck the Canadians for a whole mess of them and we have another problem on our border."

Congressman Minshall: "All I can say is, these turned out to be very expensive targets."

Secretary McNamara: "They did. I agree with you fully."

Diefenbaker raced off with this juicy bit between his teeth. He accused Pearson, who had changed his mind and now wanted to arm the Bomarcs, of turning Canada into a decoy for Russian missile attacks, a burned sacrifice. Here, he finally strained the credulity of his average Canadian, who did not know about Bomarc 'X'.

It was Diefenbaker who had killed the Arrow and brought in the useless and, it now appeared, dangerous Bomarcs. He should have known that the things didn't work without atomic warheads and that he couldn't get atomic warheads without American sergeants to guard them. It was he who played politics during the Cuban missile crisis.

The Liberals, obsessed with their gimmicky New Frontierish campaign, never brought the Chief down to earth. They allowed him to blame their guiltless leader for World War Three — "The day the strike takes place, eighteen million people in North America will die in the first two hours, four million of them in Canada. Mr. Pearson shouldn't play politics with four million dead Canadians."

The Liberals very nearly achieved defeat. It eluded them only because the weight of evidence against Diefenbaker was so enormous that the twenty million live Canadians could not ignore it. They dispatched Diefenbaker and gave Pearson a minority win — 129 seats to 95 for the Tories, 14 New Democrats and 24 Social Crediters.

The Chief was dead, long live the Chief. As he left the prime ministership, some of his best years were still ahead of him.

**PEARSON**
1963-68

# XIII.  *Unblessed was the Peacemaker*

Lester Pearson described the 1963 campaign as "the most degrading experience of my life." It brought him power at the expense of dignity, responsibility without the latitude to act responsibly. He was elected without popular enthusiasm as the best man available and he seemed to accept the job as the best one available. His instincts, his skills and the experience of his sixty-six years, all fitted him for a different kind of work.

Sooner or later, every effective political leader has to jump on his horse and ride off, forwards, backwards or sideways, shouting "Onward, this is the way!" Pearson's meticulous mind told him there were at all times many ways, each with its merits and drawbacks. Absolute certainty was the plaything of absolute fools. Wisdom lay in the careful balancing of the options, in choosing the least undesirable and leaving the others to hand. As a diplomat he faced huge world problems and learned to skirt around them, knowing they would remain. The trick was to smile, pat them gently and make sure they didn't roll over and crush you. Diplomats and impending catastrophes learn to get along together like cops and robbers, each respecting the other's function. Without the Devil, the preacher would be out of a job.

The Liberal campaign of 1963 offended not only Pearson's good taste but every tenet of the British-Canadian diplomatic tradition in which he was reared. Instead of muddling through, the party promised to solve everything in an apocalyptic "Sixty Days of Decision."

It was a cheap slogan, stolen by Ottawa ad-men from Theodore H. White's book *The Making of the President, 1960,* which described in detail the mechanics of the successful Kennedy campaign. Party hacks and flacks referred to it simply as The Book and all political wisdom was supposed to be contained therein. From it, they gleaned ideas such as releasing flocks of pure white doves to light on their man's platform, thus showing his peaceful intent, setting a "truth squad" on his opponent's tail to shout "liar" at appropriate moments, and offering kids' coloring books to corner the cretin vote.

The Book failed to explain that Americans, though apparently impressed by ghastly sentimentality and outrageous hypocrisy, are by nature much more politically cynical than Canadians. In their longer history they have had much more to be cynical about. They demand a vulgar show, enjoy it, guffaw, and forget it the next morning. When a new U.S. president takes office all bets are off and his campaign platform is dismantled and stored away.

Pearson was not allowed to forget "Sixty Days." By the sixtieth his government had demonstrated ludicrous incompetence, bungled its budget, withdrawn it, and was considering the proferred resignation of its finance minister. It took the Diefenbaker government six years to destroy itself; the Liberals nearly managed it in two months.

Finance Minister Walter Gordon, like his very old and close friend Pearson, was an expert, not a doer. He had started out as a chartered accountant and management consultant, advising businesses how to run themselves. Under a series of Liberal administrations he had graduated to telling governments how to run the country. In 1958, his Royal Commission on Canada's economic prospects produced the most thorough examination of the economy ever seen. Like James Coyne, he worried about the steady take-over of Canada by American interests. He entered politics in 1962 resolved to do something about it. Because of the Sixty Days propaganda for which he was largely responsible, he felt compelled to do it at once. So he rammed together his revolutionary budget in 53 days. In the remaining seven he saw it torn to shreds.

Gordon tried to stop further take-over of still-Canadian firms by sticking a thirty percent penalty tax on the sale of shares in these firms to foreigners or foreign-owned companies. In addition he proposed to make firms of less than twenty-five percent Canadian ownership pay twice as much withholding tax as largely native-owned concerns. The permanent officials of the Finance Department and the Bank of Canada told him, and showed him with figures, that it wouldn't work. He had expected this, so he brought in three bright young consultants from Bay Street to write the bright new budget. They were all members of private firms, and two of them stayed on their company payrolls while working for the government in its most sensitive office. It was time, the Liberals proclaimed in yet another Kennedy-like phrase, to "get the economy moving again."

By the 58th Day of Decision, Walter Gordon had become convinced that the take-over tax probably wouldn't work after all (how do you identify the real owner of a Canadian share traded on a foreign exchange?); and even if it did, it would bring on a stock exchange panic. Eric Kierans, then president of the Montreal exchange told Gordon: "The financial capitals of the world have had just about enough from Canada."

Until the tax was withdrawn, he advised his associates to sell short their stock in Canadian companies. Kierans was a fellow economic nationalist; his warning to Gordon was sincere.

At 2:41 P.M. on Day 59, Walter Gordon announced the withdrawal of the tax. The timing meant that there were nineteen minutes for speculators on eastern stock exchanges to clean up, and more than three hours of trading left for nimble bidders in the west. It was unheard-of for a government to announce a vital financial change during market hours. It became worse when Gordon later and reluctantly revealed that the three bright boys from Bay Street knew of the move in advance.

Promptly on Day 60, Gordon offered his resignation. Pearson would not allow his friend of thirty years to depart under such a cloud but suggested another portfolio. Gordon said Finance or nothing, and stayed. When it was made clear that he would stay the investors showed what they thought of him: the industrial index on the Toronto Stock Exchange dropped four points.

The Pearson government was off and running — for cover. In his opening television address, the Prime Minister had presented the thought (taken, naturally, from the Kennedy campaign via The Book) that it was "not an easy time . . . but a time to excite the daring, to test the strong and give new promise to the timid . . . a time of direction and decision."

Watching this after six years of Diefenbaker indecision and two months of Pearson indirection, the average viewer, daring or timid, might well explode in grateful laughter as the finance company carried away his set. What was a nice guy like Mike Pearson doing in a job like that?

Looking at his frank, unlined face with its ever-boyish grin it was difficult to accept that he was a Victorian — born April 23, 1897. He would be the last prime minister born in that century, and despite his air of perpetual wide-eyed youth, he, as much as Diefenbaker, represented the ancient, homely virtues. He had the added virtue of not prating about them, although he came from lines of Irish Methodist preachers on both sides of his family. The Pearsons were ordained ministers, the Bowleses farmers and lay gospellers. All of them, he remembers, were very jolly and very Irish but very strict and puritan as well. Methodists moved around from parish to parish. Lester was born in the village of Newtonbrook (since swallowed up by Metropolitan Toronto) and spent a happy boyhood in half a dozen small Ontario towns.

At sixteen, he enrolled in Victoria (Methodist) College in the University of Toronto. His dean and cadet company commander was Vincent Massey, later to become Canada's first native-born governor-general. Pearson was to encounter him again and again in the small world of Canadian public service.

One day in 1915, while reading a Latin poet, Pearson said to himself "War can't be *this* bad," and enlisted. In the following years he found out just how bad it could be. War wiped out the best of his generation. Pearson survived thanks to a series of accidents and came home feeling that he had been granted a second life. The one constant theme of his future work was that wars solved nothing and could usually be avoided.

He went overseas as a medical orderly and served in Salonika before volunteering for the infantry and later for the Flying Corps. There he got the name of "Mike" because his flying instructor said Lester didn't sound tough enough for a pilot. He crashed his kite-like Grahame-White machine on his first solo. On his release from hospital he was hit by a London bus in the blackout and invalided home. "I got hurt," he said, "before I got killed. You got to a point where you just went on until you were killed like all your friends were being killed. The only thing that would save you from being killed was being wounded and getting out of it."

After finishing his time at the University of Toronto and spending an unlikely interlude as a sausage-stuffer at a Hamilton meat-packing plant, he went to Oxford on a Massey Fellowship, arranged by Vincent Massey. He played lacrosse and hockey for Oxford and blended gently into the tea-and-crumpets atmosphere of those storied halls. When he returned again to the University of Toronto, took a post as a history lecturer and married one of his students, Maryon Moody from Winnipeg, the adventures of Lester B. Pearson seemed to be over. He showed no burning ambition to change the world; the academic life suited him very comfortably, so long as he could coach hockey and football on the side.

When the Department of External Affairs was formed and its under-secretary, Dr. O. D. Skelton, persuaded him to take the entrance examination, he was only mildly interested. "Even if you pass, you don't have to take the job," Skelton said encouragingly. One of the examiners (Vincent Massey) complained that there was "something curiously loose-jointed and sloppy about his make-up," but he passed, and joined.

Having got in on the ground floor, just as Canada began to make its own foreign policy, Pearson rose rapidly. He had no time to study diplomacy as he was too busy practising it.

In the early years "External" had barely a dozen officials in Ottawa and only four missions abroad — London, Paris, Washington and Tokyo. So everyone knew everyone else. Pearson hopped from Ottawa to London, Washington and Geneva, performing increasingly important chores with light good humor. He worked with Mackenzie King, who gave him his classic piece of advice: "More has been accomplished for the welfare of mankind in preventing bad actions than in doing good ones." He worked with R. B. Bennett, who gave him an OBE.

His worst assignment was to replace the unlucky Dr. W. A. Riddell as Canadian representative at the League of Nations after Riddell had tried to scuttle Mussolini and had been disowned by Lapointe and King. Pearson had to sit tight, say nothing, and suffer the cool stares of the anti-Mussolini delegates who had witnessed the surgical removal of the previous Canadian's backbone.

He spent the years of appeasement in London, remained

there for the first two years of World War Two, then moved, via Ottawa, to Washington. So he saw both the faults of the old world and the misdirected enthusiasms of the new. Sometimes he could contribute positive ideas. At other times he sat, as at Geneva, with his mind officially blank. He could advise and list possible courses of action but, as he told a colleague, "when the essential decisions are made, you're not even in the room."

In 1948 St. Laurent brought him into the room as External Affairs Minister and his years of brilliance began. When he made the leap from the civil service to politics he must have suspected that he had been chosen to be St. Laurent's heir, just as St. Laurent had been picked by King. But he chose to regard the honor as one more step up the diplomatic ladder. Reporters asked him when he had become a Liberal and he replied breezily, "today." The party label went with the job; it meant member of the governing class in what had almost become a one-party state. So as the party remained the government, Pearson saw no need to parade his party affiliation or to take it very seriously.

In his great years as boss of External he ranged far beyond the dismal pettiness of domestic politics to become the best-known and most-admired Canadian in the world. He was chairman of the council of NATO, President of the United Nations General Assembly. He was proposed twice for the job of Secretary-General of the United Nations, only to be vetoed by the Russians on both occasions.

He was an all-round good guy in the world league, a cheerful homely figure in a bow-tie. Anyone could talk to Mike and feel better for it. He took the starch out of diplomacy and also the vitriol. No party in any dispute was to be deeply wounded. If the settlements reached weren't perfect, this was only to be expected, as any settlement was better than war. He was a toiler on the brink and he liked his work. Grant Dexter of the Winnipeg *Free Press* remarked: "Mike is happiest when he's clinging to a precipice and about to fall off."

The world was that way during most of the time when Pearson was creating his individual style of Canadian diplomacy. There was still room for a nation which retained some of its youthful innocence to manoeuvre for the good of all. The scrubbed, hopeful face of Mike Pearson was the face of Canada. It never showed the underlying pessimism acquired in twenty years of negotiating or the underlying fear, revealed only in very private conversations, that civilization was probably doomed anyway and that the pious posturers at the U.N. were strutting on the lip of eternity.

Canada had no direct interest in the Middle East or Korea. Pearson could have steered clear of the Palestinian crisis of 1947–48, the Korean war or the 1956 Suez affair. But he played a leading part in drawing up the partition of Palestine that created the state of Israel, earning an Israeli medal of valor. He persuaded Ottawa to send a brigade of troops to Korea. And after that war ended, the brigade was earmarked for future United Nations peace-keeping operations.

His achievement at Suez when, according to the Nobel Peace Prize committee, he "saved the world," lay not in his suggestion that a U.N. police force should go in to separate the combatants, but in the way he persuaded all sides to accept it. It was a coup admired by the professionals for its technical brilliance — the way Mike kept everybody talking, how he muddied over the details, how he cornered the big fellows, and so on.

The world league applauded. Then some of the fans back home began tearing him and St. Laurent to bits. They didn't appreciate how he played the game; they cared only that he'd been playing for the wrong side. He had won a victory for peace, the United Nations and the United States, but he had defeated Britain and France. Pearson had been brought up in the loyalist tradition of smalltown Ontario but he'd been away from home for so long he could not know how strongly the tradition had survived.

Howard Green's cry that Canada had "knifed its best friends in the back" brought him up short. He had wounded one element he hadn't even thought of — the Empire patriots of Canada. He had been forced into taking a clear stand on one of the oldest of domestic issues. Breezy Mike, who had drunk nineteen toasts with Nikita Khrushchev and survived, who had pirouetted on the nuclear brink and stopped a war, now met the horrors of Canadian politics. For the first time he felt the hot breath of Diefenbaker on his neck.

There followed the disaster of his maiden speech as Liberal leader when he asked the Tories to move over and let him govern, and the years of uncomfortable opposition. He grew to dislike Diefenbaker as he had never disliked an opponent before. The non-partisan party leader needed a weapon to destroy this preposterous prophet of unreason. The only one available was the demoralized run-down wreck of the Liberal party and he began to rebuild it.

He used some strange pieces that never quite fitted together. Like Dr. Frankenstein, he made his monster out of parts taken from various graveyards — two left feet, two right arms, and a secondhand brain from Madison Avenue. Fired up with high-voltage advertising, it lumbered forth with Theodore White's Book in its hand, not to destroy its creator but to embarrass him.

Walter Gordon provided much of the organizational talent behind Pearson Liberalism. He was a crusading economic nationalist. On the other hand Mitchell Sharp, who succeeded him as Finance Minister, was an internationalist and a Grit free-trader. Robert Winters was a Bay Street rightwinger, reactionary as any Tory, and Jean Marchand was an anti-Duplessis Quebec union organizer, as leftwing as a New Democrat.

Pearson surrounded himself with men of diverse ideas and contradictory advice. Rather than allow them to tug him this way and that, he sat in the middle, throwing now a crumb to one side, now to the other. Jack Pickersgill, political operator for King, St. Laurent and Pearson, said Pearson was the least idealistic of the three.

A month after Walter Gordon's ill-starred nationalistic

budget, the Kennedy administration proceeded to do what Gordon had failed to do — limit the flow of American money into Canada. It slapped a fifteen percent "interest equalization tax" on exported American funds to limit the drain on the U.S. balance of payments.

Instead of rejoicing, there was frantic alarm in Ottawa. It was one thing to try to tell the Americans what to do with their money once it crossed the border. But at all costs they had to keep sending it. Panic set in. In a day Canadian foreign reserves dropped by $110 million. And the much-maligned Canadian subsidiaries of American corporations began trundling their spare money back home.

Louis Rasminsky, the new governor of the Bank of Canada, sped to Washington to tell the Americans they couldn't do it. The new tax affected twenty-two countries; but Canada was most seriously harmed as it was most completely in the American pocket. Rasminsky persuaded Washington that to hurt Canada was to hurt that pocket, and obtained a conditional exemption from the tax. But at a cost. Canada had to agree to limit its borrowing in the United States to a limit set by the U.S. President and keep down its exchange reserves.

John Diefenbaker said the arrangement was "not in keeping with the sovereignty of this nation." For once he was guilty of understatement. By giving the U.S. government a veto over borrowing, Canada raised to the official level the American domination of the economy that already existed in the private sector. Canada was already well on the way to becoming an economic satellite of the United States. And the Washington agreement implied that Canada's government recognized and accepted this. It was a sell-out, not of assets this time, but of power.

Just before midnight on New Year's Eve, those other symbols of power, the U.S. nuclear warheads, were trucked across the border and installed on the Bomarc missiles at North Bay. It was a sneaky move, accomplished on the one night of the year when newspaper presses were still and Canadians, nationalist or internationalist alike, would be distracted by revelry or too drunk to care.

The sell-out of assets continued during 1964, when the country was distracted by the stormier revelry of the Great Flag Debate.

Back in 1961, Pearson had promised to establish a "distinctive Canadian flag" within two years of taking office. This he determined to do. He believed in his Maple Leaf flag and he fought for it through six months of debate that aroused again some of the primitive passions stirred by the conscription issue and Suez. The Tories accused him of destroying the oldest symbol of nationhood, the Canadian Red Ensign, under which men had fought and died. Yet in a way he was carrying on the work of their patron saint, Macdonald, who first flew that ensign over the Parliament Buildings because it was more distinctive than the Union Jack. It was the Liberal Laurier government that hauled it down (in 1902) and restored the Jack. From then until the end of World War Two, the British flag was the national flag of Canada, and the Red Ensign had no official status except as a merchant ship's flag. However, Mackenzie King in 1924 had it flown on government buildings abroad to distinguish his foreign missions from British embassies, and in 1945 he passed an order in council authorizing its use until Parliament decided upon a permanent national flag.

During the sporadic flag debates of the twenties and thirties, French-Canadian nationalists would have settled for the Red Ensign or something similar. By 1945 the British loyalists were ready to drop the Jack and cling to the Ensign. But now the French wanted a flag with no "foreign symbols" on it. And by the mid-sixties, when Canada finally adopted the Pearson Maple Leaf, Ontario had taken over a modified Red Ensign as its provincial flag, Newfoundland had kept the Jack and Quebec had acquired its own blue and white fleur-de-lis banner. When France's Charles de Gaulle landed at Wolfe's Cove to attempt a reconquest of Quebec, there was not a

Maple Leaf to be seen: only the lilies of old royalist France.

In retrospect the flag debate becomes boring and trivial. If the new flag was intended to smother Quebec nationalism, it didn't work. But Pearson did tackle an issue that had frightened prime ministers back to Laurier. He provided a flag — his most positive accomplishment as Prime Minister. He left bigger problems not only unsolved but practically untouched.

Even in foreign affairs, Canada's greatest diplomat stumbled ineffectually. It would have taken the wisdom of Solomon and the determination of Ivan the Terrible to divert President Lyndon B. Johnson from his shoot-out in Vietnam, so Pearson cannot be condemned for his failure there. But his forays into the United States and the meaningless pronouncements of his External Affairs Minister Paul Martin were a sad anticlimax to the Nobel Prize days.

The arrival of Pearson and Martin at the LBJ Texas ranch in January, 1965 was slapstick comedy. They came to sign the U.S.-Canadian automobile pact which would permit the Big Three automakers to spread their operations across both sides of the border without the inconvenience of paying duty on car parts. (It would lead to the bizarre situation in which cars built in Canada are sold much cheaper in the United States.)

Pearson and Martin, in their neat dark suits, were whizzed onto the ranch airstrip by jet. The President, in his cowboy outfit, greeted Pearson with a welcoming smile. "Hello, Mr. Wilson," he boomed. In Texas one prime minister looked much like another. The Canadians were then crammed into an electric golf cart. The President took the controls and it lurched the one hundred yards to the ranch house with Paul Martin perched precariously at the back, where the golf clubs go. Then they were whirled aloft by helicopter to look at Texas deer, and raced around the ranch by car. All the while their arms were pumped and their shoulders stroked as the President tried to persuade them to show more enthusiasm for his Vietnam war. (Later, Pearson told a joke on himself. "I can get the President any time I want. I just lift the phone and say 'Hello, Lyndon.' And he replies 'Hello, Mr. Wilson'.")

As Johnson proceeded to launch a major war in South Vietnam and bomb North Vietnam, Pearson and Martin dutifully expressed sympathy over his problems. As a member (with India and Poland) of the International Control Commission in Indo-China, Canada was supposed to help supervise the long-dead truce there. This membership was used as an excuse not to take a stand one way or the other. Canada, it was repeated ad nauseam, hoped to act as a mediator one day. From time to time Paul Martin had visions of a bigger role for the ICC, but this was never defined.

In April, 1965, Pearson made the mild suggestion that the U.S. stop bombing the North for a while to permit possible peace feelers from Hanoi. He made it at Temple University in Philadelphia. As a diplomat he should have known better — heads of government are supposed to confine themselves to platitudes while on friendly foreign soil. Knowing Pearson's reputation for statesmanlike caution and aware that he was about to meet the U.S. President, the Washington diplomatic corps and the watchers from Hanoi, Peking and Moscow could assume that the Pearson suggestion had Johnson's support before it was made. Either the Prime Minister presumed too much upon his pally talks in the golfcart and helicopter or he took a deliberate chance, hoping to jar the U.S. administration into some semblance of sense. Either way, he failed.

Next day Johnson was barely civil to Pearson at Camp David, his Maryland retreat. While Canadian reporters who had not witnessed the meeting were on their way home to Ottawa, assured by Canadian officials that the meeting had been a lovely thing, unmarred by the tiniest friction, American officials in Washington revealed that Pearson had been bawled out for meddling and was now in the presidential doghouse.

However, so long as Vietnam was not mentioned, Canadian-U.S. relations meandered along with the jollity of a loan-sharks' convention. Each year, groups of M.P.s got together with U.S. congressmen and senators on joint parliamentary junkets. They exchanged platitudes, fishing stories and golf scores and forgot their differences, if they had any. You could tell the Canadians because they wore maple leaf name tags and they would admit privately after a few ryes that all was not perfect — there was Vietnam, the take-over question and the American habit of taking Canada for granted. But it was better to be taken for granted than thrust into the dog-house. There was usually a pink tea for the wives at the White House, given by Lady Bird.

Canada and the United States lived by a sweetheart contract best expressed in the joint report of a popular Canadian ambassador to Washington, A. D. Heeney, and a popular American ambassador to Ottawa, Livingston Merchant. The two agreed that "Canadian authorities should have careful regard for the United States government's position in the world context." They should avoid as far as possible "public disagreement, especially upon critical issues." In other words, Canada might whine and wheedle over details but it was to leave big matters to Washington, which knew best. It was a new version of "Ready, aye, ready," instant subservience to a bigger power, but it didn't hit Canadians in their dual vitals the way Meighen's slogan did. They knew, with the cynicism of a nation nearly a century old, that these were the facts of life and that it was unprofitable to fight them.

Pearson declared in February, 1966: "We can maintain our economic sovereignty if we are willing to pay the price, and the price would be nationalistic economic policies which would reduce our standard of living by perhaps twenty-five to thirty percent. Not many Canadians are willing to do that and I don't think Canadians should have to do that."

American ownership of Canadian industry was creeping up past sixty percent. By the end of the Pearson years, nine out of ten of the big plants which employed five thousand workers or more were controlled by parent companies in the States. Nearly three-quarters of natural gas and oil resources were controlled in the United States and every nation-wide, integrated oil company was American.

An economic study commissioned by the federal government and published in January, 1968 warned: "Foreign control means the potential shift outside the country of the locus of some types of decision-making. To the extent decision-making is eroded, national independence — being, in a broad sense, the ability to make decisions in the national interest — is reduced." The post-war Liberal governments, with some help from Diefenbaker, had put Canada so far in hock to the United States it had no choice but to salute the pawnbroker.

The feeling that much was wrong but that nothing could be done about it plugged the ballot boxes of November, 1965 with half-hearted votes. The country had endured the faded spectacle of John Diefenbaker trying to re-ignite the fire of his 1958 campaign with a third carbon-copy and Lester Pearson dismally dousing any enthusiasm his flacks managed to work up. The election resulted in another stalemate — another minority Liberal government. The voters hadn't wanted to vote and the politicians had committed the sin of intruding into private apathy. Walter Gordon, who had urged Pearson to call the election, resigned for giving bad advice. Perhaps the worst evidence of the country's malaise was that there were first-rate scandals in Ottawa, but when the time came to vote, nobody cared.

The Mafia had reached deep into the Pearson government in an attempt to free Lucien Rivard, gangster and dope-smuggler, from the Montreal jail where he was awaiting extradition to the United States. The Montreal lawyer representing the U.S. government was offered $20,000 not to oppose bail for Rivard. When he refused the bribe, pressure was applied on him by the Montreal underworld and by prominent Liberals, including two special assistants to the Minister of Justice, and the Prime Minister's Parliamentary secretary, Guy Rouleau.

Judge Frédéric Dorion, who investigated the case, reported

that the original bribe was offered by Raymond Denis, executive assistant to the Immigration Minister. And in effect he
accused the Minister of Justice Guy Favreau of covering up
the affair by failing to lay charges, although he was innocent
of any connection with Rivard.

Denis was fired and later sentenced to two years in jail.
Rouleau was fired and resigned his seat in the House.
Favreau's two assistants were censured, and Favreau himself
resigned.

Meanwhile Rivard got out of jail by other means. At the
height of the Dorion enquiry he and another prisoner obtained
permission to flood the ice-rink at Montreal's Bordeaux Jail
although the temperature was forty degrees and the rink was
slopping water. They used the hosepipe to climb over the jail
wall. (Rivard was later captured, extradited to Texas, and
given twenty years for master-minding a continent-wide dope
ring.)

More scandals followed. Minister without Portfolio Yvon
Dupuis became the first Canadian Cabinet minister to be dismissed in order to face criminal charges. He was accused of
taking a $10,000 bribe to help obtain a licence for a new race-
track in his Quebec constituency. Favreau testified at his trial,
then walked over to the accused, shook his hand and wished
him "*bonne chance.*" He was fined $5,000 or a year in jail
on three counts of influence-peddling, but the conviction was
quashed on appeal.

Harold Chamberlain Banks, a waterfront terrorist facing a
five-year prison term, slipped out of Canada, leaving behind
the impression that he knew where Liberal bodies were buried.
Despite his impressive jail record in California he had been
imported by the St. Laurent government to clean the Com-
munist-dominated Canadian Seamen's Union out of the Great
Lakes, and he did this thoroughly and violently. For the fifteen
years he remained in Canada, he ruled the lakes through his
Canadian branch on the Seafarers' International Union, using
the same terror tactics and piling away the proceeds of graft

and corruption. All this was well known to the Department of Justice which had RCMP reports on Banks filed during the Diefenbaker and Pearson years. It became public knowledge in 1963 after a Royal Commission inquiry. Banks was convicted of conspiracy to commit common assault and sentenced to five years. But he was granted bail of $25,000 — a tiny sum by SIU standards — and jumped it.

He might have been conveniently forgotten but for Toronto *Star* reporter, Robert Reguly, who found him, surrounded by armed thugs, living on a luxury yacht in Brooklyn harbor. The Conservative government of Ontario tried to extradite him on perjury charges, but in 1968 the U.S. Secretary of State Dean Rusk, rejecting the advice of his own legal department, refused extradition. Later it was revealed that the SIU had paid $100,000 towards the Democratic party's election campaign. Hal Banks had once declared: "I can buy any government." The suspicion remains that he bought more than one.

The idea that the Canadian government had a soft spot for rich thugs was reinforced by the case of Onofrio Minaudo. He was a Sicilian-born Mafia murderer of the old school who had been named by Detroit police as a captain of the Detroit-Windsor Mafia "family" which raked in $200 million a year from killing, extortion, prostitution and bootlegging. This less-than-desirable immigrant moved from Detroit to Windsor, Ontario in 1960 and was ordered deported in 1961.

In 1964, after a complaint from the Ontario Police Commission, the Minaudo case was raised in the House. The Commons learned that Minaudo, who had been convicted of three murders, armed robbery and other crimes, was allowed to remain in Canada for three years after the deportation order was issued. Three M.P.s had interceded on his behalf, among them Paul Martin. Interviewed in Sicily, Minaudo claimed he had been deported to cover up pay-offs he had made to high Ottawa officials. He told Mack Laing of the Toronto *Telegram*: "Whether I paid members of Parliament or government officials, and I'm not saying which, certainly it was somebody powerful enough to push the Immigration Department around." Nothing further was heard about the case in Parliament, possibly because both Conservative and Liberal M.P.s had pleaded for him. And nothing more was heard from Minaudo because soon after the *Telegram* interview he was found dead with a bullet in his heart.

To the ordinary Canadian who had never met a Mafia killer or a bully of the stature of Hal Banks, these cases were remote things he read about in the papers. He was affected more deeply by the sordid little furniture dealings of Immigration Minister René Tremblay and the President of the Privy Council, Maurice Lamontagne. They bought their furniture on remarkably easy terms from two dubious Montreal businessmen who had a habit of going bankrupt, and who finally fled the country. Neither minister was found to have done anything illegal, but their careers were ruined. The average householder, hounded for payments on his furniture, suspected that his well-paid ministers were getting away with "nothing down and nothing a month."

That made a total of five Pearson Cabinet ministers touched, justly or unjustly, by the suspicion of scandal. Pearson's own image as a good man in a bad place was, if anything, enhanced, but it was obviously time he did something to clean up the place. Secretly, he had. He was investigating a Conservative scandal that involved sex, national security and more sex, a combination more appealing than all the alleged goings-on between Liberals and crooks.

Peter Newman, in *The Distemper of Our Times,* prints a rare private letter from Pearson to Diefenbaker, dated December 4, 1964. In it the Prime Minister warned that he had before him the file on the "Munsinger Case" and would ask the RCMP to make further inquiries into it. He wrote: "In 1960–61 a minister who occupied a position of grave responsibility in the government was involved in a liaison which clearly endangered security. I have been greatly disturbed by the lack of attention which, in so far as the file indicates, the matter received. The minister was left in his position of trust."

Pearson wrote that his file told him the matter had been brought to the attention of Diefenbaker, then Prime Minister, but no action had been taken. He went on: "I assure you that all incidents during the last ten years are being thoroughly examined and will be followed up without fear or favor if and when the evidence requires it. If there is further information you can provide about the Munsinger case, I will be grateful if you will let me know."

Diefenbaker did not answer the letter. But he knew the gun was cocked and aimed. If the Tories continued their muckraking it would be fired. As events transpired it went off, more or less by accident, on March 4, 1966.

Lucien Cardin, the quiet, worried-looking man who succeeded Favreau as Minister of Justice, was being badgered by Diefenbaker over his handling of a fairly trivial security case involving a Vancouver postal clerk. Diefenbaker was demanding yet another royal commission inquiry. Cardin loathed Diefenbaker with Gallic passion. He swallowed two tranquilizers, shook his fist, and lashed back. Diefenbaker, he gasped, was the very last person to give advice on security cases. Cheers from the Liberals. "Go on!" they shouted.

"Very well," said Cardin. "I want the Right Hon. Gentleman to tell the House about his participation in the Monseignor case when he was Prime Minister of the country."

The name was out, mispronounced it's true, but privileged against the laws of libel. Reporters recalled old rumors about a beautiful foreign spy called Olga. When the Prime Minister's office corrected Cardin's pronunciation (thereby killing a delicious rumor that a Catholic dignitary was involved) the hunt was on for "Olga" Munsinger. Cardin elaborated at a press conference. Mrs. Munsinger had been a spy before coming to Canada. She had associated with Conservative Cabinet ministers (plural) in a manner "worse than the Profumo case" (in which the British War Minister and a Soviet official had shared the same London prostitute). Mrs. Munsinger had since died of leukemia in East Germany.

A riot of colorful stories blossomed in the press. The morals of Mrs. Munsinger got worse edition by edition since she was conveniently dead and unable to sue. The former Conservative Cabinet ministers arose to demand that Cardin name names or quit. They had all been tarred with one brush-stroke and their wives were restive.

They were still complaining when a Member broke in to ask the Speaker if he was aware that a Toronto newspaper had just interviewed Mrs. Munsinger, alive, in Germany and that she had offered to return to Canada.

Hansard records: "Some Hon. Members: Oh, oh."

Once again reporter Robert Reguly had displayed his talent for uncovering conveniently missing persons at the most inconvenient moments. It was suggested the government get rid of the RCMP which had investigated and declared the lady dead, and hire *Star* reporters instead. The *Star* men had looked up Olga (now Gerda) Munsinger in old Montreal phone books, contacted her former neighbors and quickly discovered that she was working in a bar in Munich. When Reguly knocked on her door and identified himself she said, "I suppose you want to ask about Sévigny."

She was a long slinky blonde, still attractive at 36 as the *Star's* pictures proved and a television interview with Norman DePoe on CBC *Newsmagazine* affirmed. She said she had known Pierre Sévigny when he was Associate Minister of Defence. And she had lunch twice with Trade Minister George Hees.

At the subsequent royal commission inquiry conducted by Mr. Justice W. F. Spence, the RCMP produced evidence to show that Gerda had been a prostitute in Montreal working from bars run by racketeers. As Gerda Heseler, she had been refused admission to Canada in 1952 because of a record of prostitution and petty thefts in her native Germany. There was a report that she was a "self-admitted espionage agent" in Germany but in a minor way. She had had contact with a major in the Russian Intelligence Service.

The Spence report concluded that she had indeed been

Pierre Sévigny's mistress and he, by associating with her, became a security risk, although there was no evidence that he had been disloyal or that she had tried to extract secret information from him. George Hees' lunch dates with her showed "a slight but regrettable" lack of discretion. The villain of the report was Diefenbaker, who had failed to dismiss Sévigny or consult the rest of his Cabinet about him.

When the sniggering died down, the Munsinger affair began to rebound on the Liberals. Tormented by their own scandals and the Tories' obvious enjoyment of them, they had scoured old RCMP files for something to throw back at the Opposition. But when they found it, they held on to it for fifteen months. If "national security" demanded a public inquiry in 1966, why not in 1964, when Pearson first obtained the RCMP report? Was it because the government was using it as a threat to silence Opposition scandalmongering? Former Conservative Justice Minister Davie Fulton said Guy Favreau warned him a week before Cardin's disclosure that the Munsinger affair would be revealed unless his party dropped the matter of the Vancouver postal clerk. Cardin, who later resigned, admitted that he had considered dropping the Munsinger name in debate, although he had not planned his outburst of March 4.

The Spence report left other questions unanswered. If the RCMP knew so much about Gerda why didn't they know she was alive? What kind of minor espionage was she engaged in in Germany, and who said she was? It was established later that the U.S. Intelligence Agency had a file on Gerda, classifying her as a security risk. But at the time she was so listed, the classification was being used indiscriminately to prevent German girls of doubtful moral character from marrying U.S. soldiers and entering the U.S. Gerda, who married a G.I. named Michael Munsinger, was certainly one of these.

When the sex scandal was at its height, providing the world press with a new notion of what went on in cold, old Ottawa, Pearson seemed unable to make up his mind whether this was a good thing or not. He worried about the fearsome precedent of investigating a prime minister's decisions in retrospect and the consequent destruction of club-like goodwill among parliamentarians. At the same time, he was getting his revenge for years of Tory preaching and the endless finger-wagging of John Diefenbaker. He said in the House: "Now those gentlemen who have been so free with their accusations over the last few years are getting a little of it. And they don't like it."

It was a revenge much cheaper than Gerda's favors and sweet at the time. But if previous prime ministers had been in the habit of setting the cops on their predecessors, parliamentary life in Canada would have been too colorful to endure.

The Spence report played only a small part in the final downfall of John Diefenbaker. He had to go soon anyway, and so did Lester Pearson. The two aging Victorians had trumpeted and dodged and waffled until the nation was bored and restless. Both parties needed new leaders.

But first came Centennial year, and the biggest bash ever thrown began in Montreal. Expo '67 was a thing of magic and joy — the greatest fair in world history, admired by millions of visitors from older, more confident countries, who knew they couldn't have created anything like it. More than buildings, art and culture, Expo had atmosphere. Canadian self-doubts vanished at the gates and racial differences evaporated. Fifty million people went there and there was no nastiness among them. It was a happy place. In that glorious summer it seemed that Expo's magic would spread out and engulf the land. Certainly, it spread pride. There was nothing Canadians couldn't do. Their centennial projects ranged from new sewage-plants, canoe races, beard-growing contests and a mass burning of privies to one Windsor lady's sewing of a Paul Martin doll.

Lester Pearson presided over this explosion of goodwill and national togetherness. He welcomed sixty state visitors — kings, presidents, prime ministers and an emperor. All came to admire and congratulate Canada on what had been accomplished in one hundred years. All but one . . .

Charles de Gaulle came to destroy Confederation and retake Quebec. There was never any doubt that his visit would cause trouble. External Affairs had been warned that he would encourage Quebec's separatists in some way. Quebec's Union Nationale Premier Daniel Johnson, planned to use the visit to stage a confrontation with Ottawa over the province's unconstitutional efforts to handle its own foreign relations. Still, if Canada wasn't big enough to deal with an awkward visitor, then it wasn't one hundred years old.

De Gaulle arrived magnificently. He steamed up the St. Lawrence aboard the French cruiser *Colbert* and landed at Wolfe's Cove, where the British had landed to capture Quebec two centuries before. *"Vive le Canada,"* he cried and *"Vive la France."*

Premier Johnson's machine took over. Quebec officials fought with Ottawa officials over the press arrangements. Both camps issued their own press credentials and held simultaneous press conferences at separate sites. Next day, De Gaulle made a majestic progress by car along the old royal route from Quebec City to Montreal. His cavalcade wound through sleepy old villages on the north shore of the St. Lawrence. Johnson's men had decorated them with thousands of banners bearing the crests of the areas in Normandy and Brittany from which the *habitants* were supposed to have sprung. Each village was allocated a different French homeland, and wired for sound. As De Gaulle approached, barkers summoned the villagers through dozens of loudspeakers strung from trees, and when he arrived, amplifiers magnified the cheers. There was something Hitlerian about it.

After a full day of this manufactured nostalgia the old general was primed to go. At Montreal City Hall he declared that the journey had reminded him of his triumphal entry into Paris after its liberation from the Nazis. And he shouted the Quebec separatist slogan, *"Vive le Québec libre."*

The plot was going according to Johnson's plan.

Pearson went on television to say that De Gaulle's statements were "unacceptable to the Canadian people and its government." It was not the "Free Quebec" slogan that irritated him so much as the comparison of Quebec with newly-liberated France. Canadians, he pointed out, had fought the Nazis and prepared the way for that De Gaulle triumph. "Canadians do not need to be liberated," he said. "Indeed many thousands of Canadians gave their lives in two world wars in the liberation of France and other European countries."

The Prime Minister's retort was not only applauded in English Canada, it got a great deal of sympathy in Quebec. For a few days, Canadians of all varieties seemed to agree that they could solve their problems without help from a bumptious outsider. In the euphoric Expo spirit they were even grateful to him for raising the separatist slogan so that the majority could show what they thought of it. There were demands that Canada break off diplomatic relations with France. But this, it was soon realized, was exactly what Daniel Johnson wanted. If the Canadian ambassador left Paris, he would send his own.

Jean Drapeau, the tough little mayor of Montreal who had created Expo, answered De Gaulle in a passionate, unrehearsed speech the following day. For hundreds of years, he said, French Canada had had no connection with France and no feelings of gratitude to successive French governments — only to their motherland for its language and culture.

"We are attached to *this* immense country," he said. "If we serve our country better because we serve it as Canadians of French origin, then we will be of greater service to France and humanity."

De Gaulle cancelled his scheduled visit to Ottawa and flew home. Obviously he couldn't meet Pearson after receiving an official rebuke. Obviously he never intended to meet Pearson. His performance had been carefully planned but the plot failed. Separatist feeling was to grow and threaten everything centennial year and Canada stood for. But it would be separatism without De Gaulle.

Expo closed, the visitors departed and so did the euphoria. The Pearson government went into its final decline. A new fiscal crisis arose. A Gallup poll showed that 47 percent of Canadians wanted Pearson to go.

The Conservatives had finally disposed of Diefenbaker at their September leadership convention — a spectacle like the death of a thousand cuts — and their new leader, Robert Stanfield, brought them a national popularity rating nine percent higher than the Liberals.

At a Cabinet meeting on December 14, the Prime Minister announced casually that he had just sent a letter of resignation to the president of the Liberal Federation. He met the press outside and read them the letter. There were a few questions, then there didn't seem to be anything more to say. After a moment's embarrassed silence, the Prime Minister shrugged, gave his modest Mike Pearson smile and said, "Well, *c'est la vie.*"

**TRUDEAU**
1968-79
1980-

# XIV.  *Philosopher King*

By the light of a burning police car, amid the screams and curses of the wounded, the thud of exploding Molotov cocktails, the clatter of police horses and the crunch of clubs breaking heads, the parade went on. The band of the St. Jean Baptiste Society in their medieval costumes, plumes shining in the firelight, halted briefly before the reviewing stand while police threw demonstrators into a paddy-wagon, then blasted forth a happy tune. Go-go girls squirmed on floats, ignoring the carnage around them. A golden palomino police horse was felled by a crowbar and the rider's legs broken. A demonstrator was dragged backwards, spurting blood, across a carpet of broken glass. Rocks and popbottles flew as the police charged.

While hairy students howled "Trudeau to the gallows!" the Prime Minister leaned forward in his front seat on the reviewing stand, waving at the parade and winking at the girls. It

was election eve, 1968. Montreal was winding up St. Jean
Baptiste Day with its traditional night-time parade and several
thousand separatists had turned it into a scene from the
Inferno, carried live on television.

Beside Pierre Elliott Trudeau sat his bitterest political
enemy, Premier Daniel Johnson of Quebec.

As the cameras watched, a pop bottle whizzed across Sherbrooke Street and into the center of the reviewing stand. Missing Trudeau's head by six feet, it shattered on the marble front
of the Montreal public library.

The VIPs, including Premier Johnson, scattered and ran.
Pierre Trudeau sat on, alone but for his two Mountie body-
guards. When they tried to shield him with a plastic raincoat
he angrily brushed them aside.

At that moment the next day's election was decided.
Trudeau's personal triumph was complete. Reporters on their
stand across the street burst into spontaneous cheers. Even
policemen turned from their savage battle to shout "Bravo."
The Prime Minister stood up and waved both arms limply in
a sort of shrug.

It was his style. He had sidled his way into power with an
air of cool detachment, discovering that there was more magic
in that shrug than in all the pounding and roaring of his
competitors.

The parade and the fighting went on for nearly an hour.
Trudeau remained till the end, rejoined, quickly by the Mayor
of Montreal Jean Drapeau, who had seen his wife to safety,
and later by the pale relic of the Premier of Quebec.

"When you are lucky in politics even your enemies oblige
you," commented the Conservative mastermind Dalton Camp.
He figured that the Liberal guess that the incident was worth
forty thousand extra Toronto votes for Trudeau was probably
an understatement.

Yet more than luck or courage was involved. Trudeau had
stared unblinking into the pit of separatism before. He had
fought the dictatorship of Duplessis and the Quebec national-

ism of Le Chef's successors. As a French-Canadian he wanted equal opportunity for French-Canadians. He rejected special status or "associate statehood" for Quebec. It was one of ten provinces and would fit in with the rest of Canada if its politicians would stop exploiting its peculiar characteristics to grub glory for themselves. When the moment of danger came in Montreal he treated it, like its creators, with contempt.

Like Laurier and St. Laurent he had won acclaim in English Canada. Like St. Laurent he was part-English and mocked by Quebec for his middle name. There the comparisons end. There had never been a prime minister like Trudeau. He didn't look or sound like one. He attained the highest office after two years in Parliament and a year in the Pearson Cabinet. He had very little experience of government and admitted it. "The further we advance into the modern age," he said, "the less important experience will become. It's much more important to have the necessary adaptability with which to face and solve new problems."

Trudeau came to the leadership of the Liberal party like a stone through a stained-glass window. Suddenly he was there. He wasted no time crying in the wilderness like Diefenbaker or in the marble halls like Pearson. He had been wandering around sharpening his mind and body like an ancient Greek athlete for no apparent purpose other than the exercise itself.

As Centennial year dribbled to its end after its displays of brilliance and optimism, and as the old leaders prepared to depart or be kicked out, the nation was suddenly ready for him. The Liberal party, it seemed, was merely the chosen vehicle.

Curiously, the ancient Greek arrived in the garb of a mod youngish swinger who wondered aloud if he were just a passing fancy like a Beatle. He had the profile of a Caesar, a balding head made for laurel, huge marvelling eyes, and the alert shyness of a forest creature. He wore sandals in the House.

There was mystery about him. Tales of his early exploits sounded far-fetched. Even his age was uncertain. The Parliamentary Guide and his campaign literature gave his year of birth as 1921, but his brother thought he was older. *Time* magazine dug into Montreal records to establish that a Joseph Phillipe Pierre Yves Elliote Trudeau was born there on October 18, 1919.

He was born rich. His father, Charles-Emile, known as Charlie, was a lawyer who developed a chain of thirty gas stations on Montreal Island and sold his share of them to Imperial Oil for $1,400,000. Subsequent investments built up a family fortune estimated at five to six million dollars. He died in 1934 and Pierre, as eldest son, later took a hand in managing the estate.

Charlie Trudeau's ancestors came from France early in the seventeenth century. Pierre's mother, Grace Elliott, daughter of a Scots United Empire Loyalist family, spoke English to her children as St. Laurent's mother had done. Young Pierre was driven to school by the family chauffeur and isolated from the poverty of the other Montreal down the hillside. He ran with a crowd of kids known as "Les Snobs." As he never had to fight want or war, he fought authority. He said recently: "I became accustomed very young to rowing against the current, attacking authority and not giving a damn for public opinion." His father insisted that he learn boxing and Pierre enjoyed applying this skill. Tales are told of his fights on Montreal street-cars.

At Jean de Brebeuf, the Jesuit college where he studied classics, he is remembered as a fighter and practical joker as well as an outstanding scholar. He was expelled several times. Later, while attending law school at the University of Montreal, he was thrown out of the Officers' Training Corps for lack of discipline. He wore a black leather jacket and rode a large Harley-Davidson motorbike. During the war his aggressive spirit turned against the conscriptionists in the Mackenzie King government. "Like most Quebeckers," he said, "I had been taught to keep away from imperialistic wars."

He campaigned for Jean Drapeau, then an anti-conscription

candidate, in a 1942 by-election in Outremont. "If we are no longer in a democracy," he shouted, "then let us begin the revolution without delay. The people are being asked to commit suicide. Citizens of Quebec — do not be content to complain. Enough of patchwork solutions — now is the time for cataclysms!"

No cataclysms descended. Drapeau was badly beaten and Trudeau retired from politics for a while. According to his close friend Gérard Pelletier, he was "dying to get involved in the war, but the idea of turning his back on a population betrayed by the Mackenzie King government repelled him more than inaction."

Having mastered law and been called to the bar, Trudeau put law aside and went to Harvard and then on to Paris and London, studying political economy. He never practised as a lawyer; he was a perennial student or teacher, never a tradesman.

He wandered. In 1948 he set off from London with a knapsack, shorts and long beard, drifted through occupied Germany on faked papers, was slung in jail for trying to enter Yugoslavia without a visa, then floated on through Greece and Turkey and into Palestine.

There, he was arrested as a Zionist spy and thrown into a dungeon where Christ is supposed to have been held. After emerging, he was accosted by bandits, whom he scared off by feigning madness and raving in Montreal slang. He moved on to India, where his sampan was attacked by pirates, visited the Khyber Pass during the India-Pakistan conflict, crossed Burma during a civil war and reached Vietnam in time to join a French convoy under attack by the Viet Minh.

He got into China just as Mao's armies were sweeping the Nationalists off the mainland and left Shanghai in a hail of shellfire. The entire unpackaged adventure tour cost him $500, plus a boat ticket home, and brought him much of the war experience he had avoided in World War Two, coupled with a lasting distrust of nationalist movements.

Four years later he was off again in search of further adventure. He was blacklisted by the United States for attending an economic conference in Moscow. He offended the Russians by insisting upon attending mass and throwing snowballs at a statue of Lenin. He toured Communist China in 1956 — long before this was a respectable thing to do — and, in 1961, he attempted to paddle a canoe from Florida to Castro's Cuba.

This last episode revived American suspicions of Trudeau. His name had recently been removed from the list of persons barred from the States. Now it appeared that he was trying to smuggle arms to Castro. Trudeau said he was simply trying to prove that it was possible to cross the treacherous Florida straits by canoe (it wasn't) and the shrimp boat crew who fished him out found no weapons in the canoe. But the suspicions lingered. Eight years later the same wanderer, minus beard, would be welcomed at the front door of the White House.

During the 1950s and early '60s he was mostly, as his friend Jean Marchand put it, "underemployed." He drifted back into politics almost by chance. In 1950, when Gérard Pelletier, then labor reporter for *Le Devoir*, was sent to cover a bloody miners' strike at Asbestos, Quebec, Trudeau went along for the ride and met Marchand, the strike leader. This led to the formation of the trio, Marchand, Pelletier and Trudeau, who were to become the "three wise men" of the Liberal party.

That historic strike exposed the boss-cop-priest conspiracy that was the Duplessis regime and opened the way to its downfall. Trudeau and Pelletier helped by founding the little Montreal magazine *Cité Libre*, whose shrill, small voice brought the case against *Le Chef* to an influential audience.

In 1962 the federal Liberals tried unsuccessfully to lure the trio into the party. They really wanted Marchand, but it was understood that the three came as a package.

Trudeau continued to blast the establishment party in *Cité Libre*: "I am concerned with the anti-democratic reflexes of the spineless Liberal herd . . . I have never seen in all my examination of politics a spectacle so degrading as that of all those Liberals turning their coats in unison with their chief when they saw a chance to take power . . . The head of the troupe having shown the way, the rest followed with the elegance of animals heading for the trough."

That article was not reprinted in *Federalism and the French Canadians*, the collection of *Cité Libre* pieces which is the nearest thing to a Trudeau *Mein Kampf* or *Industry and Humanity*. By the time it was published, the three wise men had turned their coats from the NDP to the Liberals and Trudeau was jockeying for position as head of the troupe.

All three ran for Parliament and were elected. Trudeau had the most difficulty in finding a seat because no French-speaking constituency would have him. He was forcibly "parachuted" down upon the reluctant *anglais* of Mount Royal, then appointed Parliamentary Secretary to the Prime Minister he had derided as "Pope Pearson" two short years before.

He did not shine in his first year in the House. The strange bird from Quebec — swinger, sports-car driver, judo expert, skin-diver and skier — was too exotic for the grey men on the venerable benches. So was his plumage. He would climb out of his Mercedes 300-SL, hang up his green leather coat and shuffle into the House in sandals. When he became Minister of Justice he adopted shoes, but his yellow ascot with polka dots was denounced by an outraged Diefenbaker as not in keeping with the dignity of the green chamber.

Polka dots notwithstanding, his work on the Divorce Bill and reform of the Criminal Code caught public attention. He appeared to solve the problems of abortion and homosexual relations between consenting adults with one throwaway line: "The state has no business in the bedrooms of the nation." And he promised to separate sin from crime: "You may have to ask forgiveness of your sins from God, but not from the Minister of Justice."

However, there would be no forgiveness for the sin of

French Canadian nationalism. "Particular status for Quebec is the biggest intellectual hoax ever foisted on the people of Quebec and the people of Canada," he declared. And English Canada nodded approval.

Particular, or special, status was on everyone's mind that Centennial summer of 1967. The Tories tried an intellectual hoax of their own that resembled Sir Charles Tupper's attempt to get away with saying one thing in Quebec and the exact opposite in Ontario. A party thinkers' conference fabricated the concept of "*deux nations.*"

The French could interpret it as they pleased — it was their language. It could mean an association of two nation-states, a French homeland within Canada, even two warring tribes under one banner. But the Tories translated it into English as "two peoples" — simple recognition of the fact that Canada had been founded by two sorts of people, now blended harmoniously into one. Merely that and nothing more.

Diefenbaker shouted "One Canada" and went down to defeat. Trudeau picked up the same slogan and triumphed. When the Liberals tossed the *deux nations* idea around at *their* thinkers' conference, he and Marchand stood firm for federalism.

It became clear to Pearson that one or the other must try to succeed him. The night he resigned, while a dozen would-be successors clamored to be anointed, he invited to his residence only Trudeau and Marchand. By February, 1968, when the leadership race was under way, they had worked out between them that Trudeau should run. His health was better and so was his English.

He announced the decision in typical offhand manner. He was, he said, an accidental candidate, the result of a press prank that went wrong. He told reporters that they had built him up as a curious alternative to the regular politicians — "and now you're stuck with me."

Trudeau never liked the writing press — few ex-journalists do — but he enjoyed television and knew how to use it. Pierre

Trudeau looks good on TV. This quality has nothing to do with virtue or sincerity, as many people still believe. It lies somewhere in the nature of vidicon tubes and miles and miles of wire. So, in his leadership campaign he avoided probing press interviews and let the passive medium carry his message.

In retrospect the triumph of Trudeau seems natural, a steep thundering ascent like the take-off of his campaign jet. It was not like that to those on the ground at the time. The nation shivered like a 100-year-old virgin faced by what zoologist Dr. Desmond Morris called a man with "certain animal properties." For generations, hoary old men had preached about this *young* country. Now a young man (of nearly 49) was dancing and kissing his way to power, backed not so much by the voteless young but by those who wanted to feel young.

That dizzy spring the Liberal party, the press and the country were ready to take a chance. Trudeaumania was abroad in the land.

He won the Liberal leadership on the fourth ballot, assumed the prime ministership which went with it, then sneaked down the secret Mackenzie staircase to visit the Governor-General and call a snap election.

The kissing began. A 17-year-old girl accosted him outside the East Block and asked for the first kiss. "Why not — it's spring," he said. From then on, kids turned out in their hordes to scream and touch. Matrons left their husbands to peck him at formal luncheons. Twelve thousand people came out to see him in Vancouver, sixteen thousand in Hamilton and more than fifty thousand in Toronto. It wasn't a campaign so much as a happening.

The new Tory leader, Robert Stanfield, was a worthy piece of Canadiana, a man of such natural dignity that he could eat a banana during a TV interview without loss of composure. But he did not look like a man for tomorrow. He looked like a Tory's Tory, unearthed by party engineer Dalton Camp to rescue the party from the excesses of Diefenbaker and set it back on the road to yesterday. Stanfield's lugubrious face reflected generations of Maritime gloom. His lean form seemed built for the unshrinkable long johns the family looms in Nova Scotia had made famous. Few knew that the private Stanfield was a cheerful man with a rich, wry sense of humor.

In the vague generalities of the 1968 campaign there wasn't too much difference between what he said and what Trudeau said, but Trudeau always seemed to say it first. He sizzled around in a DC-9 jet while Stanfield lurched behind in an old prop-driven DC-7. Although the Liberals had been in power for five years, it was the Tory leader who was on the defensive. He was fighting Trudeaumania and the new Canadian confidence that had begun with Expo.

A shocking truth was voiced by Toronto professor Paul Fox: "Beneath his dashing image, Pierre Trudeau is a *conservative*." But so what? Pierre was whatever you imagined him to be and the Just Society he promised could be just anything or just nothing. At least, he was different.

As he cast his ballot in Montreal the day after the St. Jean Baptiste riot, a nun clasped his hand and breathed her thanks that he hadn't been killed. "But my goodness," he grinned, "I was sitting beside the Archbishop!"

That night he won the majority Pearson only dreamed about: 154 seats to 72 for the Conservatives, 23 NDP and 14 Creditiste. "For me," he said, "it was a great adventure of discovery and for all of us a period of self-discovery . . . that which came across most strongly to all Canadians in all parts of the country was the total message of the future of the country."

That was pardonable victory-night nonsense. What had come across was Trudeau. He had demanded a blank cheque and got it. Canada had bought a pig in a poke. "But," wrote Lotta Dempsey in the Toronto *Star*, "What a pig! And what a poke!"

Members of Parliament, Liberal and others, had vague premonitions about the poke they were getting into. Even back in his Justice Minister days, Trudeau had shown his contempt

for some of the ways of the House: "When you howl like animals, I cannot hear very well the questions you are asking."
The Montreal *Star*'s W. A. Wilson described "a Pierre Trudeau
who possessed neither charm nor sensitivity, had thoroughly
bad manners and could exhibit a crushing spitefulness towards
those who irritated him. As time went by [the House] became
better acquainted with this personality, as well as with the one
compounded of grace, charm and a sensitive tact."

The Opposition was to learn exactly what the Prime Minister thought of it one afternoon in February, 1971, when he
told it to f— off. The obscenity was mouthed, rather than
articulated — Trudeau later translated it as "fuddle-duddle"
— but the historic green chamber turned blue.

(Trudeau achieved a similar breakthrough in the other
language when he advised a group of striking Montreal mail
truck drivers: "Mangez de la merde." The private language
of statesmen has never been pure, but Trudeau brought it out
into the open and the newspapers blushingly printed it.)

Walter Stewart, in his book *Shrug: Trudeau in Power*, commented: "Under pressure, the wordly prime minister reverted
to being the Montreal snob and demonstrated not merely that
he doesn't care about the Commons, but that he doesn't understand what parliamentary democracy is all about."

And NDP leader David Lewis remarked that when he looked
across the aisle at the disdainful P.M., he told himself: "There,
but for the grace of Pierre Elliott Trudeau, goes God."

God would never make a good parliamentarian and neither,
it seemed, would Pierre. But the people were behind him and
if Trudeau could not adjust to the ways of Parliament, Parliament must adjust to Trudeau. In his government's first Throne
Speech he had the Governor-General declare: "Canadians feel
that Parliament is too far removed from the people it serves;
its operations are too slow and ponderous; its decisions are too
few and too much delayed."

This was probably true. The dithering of the Diefenbaker-
Pearson years had sapped confidence in the House (there had

never been any confidence in the Senate) and the Trudeau campaign had hinted at a new way of getting things done: participatory democracy.

This catch phrase has since become as meaningless as "fuddle-duddle." It was a suggestion, rather than a promise, that the masses might be able to take part in government decision-making, even commune with the Leader himself, without the bother of writing to their M.P.s.

The instrument of participatory democracy would be the Liberal party, that cowpen of the "spineless herd" which previous prime ministers had used and abused. For 50 years it had represented the Canadian establishment; now it was to represent the people, too.

"The government is not in Quebec, not in Ottawa, but out in the street," Trudeau told an elegant party dinner in Montreal. "We, too, must take to the streets."

The sally into the streets began in a luxury hotel in Harrison Hot Springs, B.C. Experts on every social problem, including a token student radical and some token poor, were flown there to tell the assembled leaders of provincial and riding Liberal associations what was wrong with the country. Each delegate attended dozens of seminars and got 62 background papers to read. Then he was sent home to organize similar discussions in his own bailiwick — not just for Liberals, but for the less privileged and the wrong-headed as well.

It didn't work. Only 25 local parties managed to get the public involved, another 50 tried and failed, and about 200 didn't want outsiders at their policy meetings.

In November, 1970, the results of a year's participatory soul-searching were displayed at a party conference in Ottawa. The delegates wanted a guaranteed income policy, easier marijuana laws, some form of legalized abortion and more Canadian control of the economy.

Trudeau listened but did nothing. "To participate doesn't mean that you're going to make the decision," he explained later. So participatory democracy passed away in its sleep. It was a vaguely sinister idea, with connotations of commissars and the one-party state. And as a phrase it wasn't as telling as "mangez de la merde."

Meanwhile Trudeau was revamping the real instruments of power, which were not on the streets but on the grass of Parliament Hill and in process of being transported from the Centre Block debating chamber to the Prime Minister's Office in the East Block.

Mackenzie King, most secretive of prime ministers and the oddest one until Trudeau, preferred to keep the nation's business in his head. He managed with a handful of aides until the complications of running the war effort forced him to increase the P.M.O. staff to 30. Pearson upped it to 40.

Trudeau, the outsider who had never been a part of the Liberal establishment and had no more reason than Diefenbaker to trust the old guard Liberal civil service mandarins, moved in squads of his own men. The staff jumped to 85, then 92.

According to Walter Stewart, he didn't bypass the bureaucracy; he set up a counter-bureaucracy: "To all intents and purposes, Canada is no longer run by Parliament or the cabinet or even the party in power; it is run by the Prime Minister and his own personal power bloc. The Supergroup is an informal, loosely organized ring of advisers, some in the public service, some elected, some conspicuous holders of high office, some minor officials unknown to the general public. These are the People Who Count, not because of age or experience, rank or title, but because they have the ear and respect of Pierre Elliott Trudeau."

By setting up Cabinet committees he watered down the power of individual ministers who did not belong to his inner circle. He reached decisions after lengthy, academic debates — but the debates were not held in the House, only among his trusted advisers.

As he saw it, he had been elected by the people to rule the nation. Opposition Members had been elected by their con-

stituents to blow off steam at question period. "When they are
50 yards from Parliament Hill they are no longer Honorable
Members," he said, "they are just nobodies." He allowed his
ministers to skip question periods two days a week to get on
with their business.

He was accused of trying to transform the Hill into a U.S.-
style Congress, with himself as President in the East Block.
But at times he behaved more like a king than a president. A
Canadian prime minister with a weak opposition has more
authority than a U.S. president. And he joked privately that if
Canada set up a Congress it would weaken his power.

He welcomed the power that had been thrust upon him or
achieved with little effort. And he was to use it all in the
October Crisis of 1970 — the biggest peacetime upheaval
since the Riel rebellions — an event so staggering and unreal
that it belongs in the pages of cheap fiction.

Canada had escaped the convulsion of riot and confrontation that tore the vitals of American society throughout the
'60s — for the obvious reason that Canada never had a significant color problem or a Vietnam war on her hands. Yet
Trudeau, ever mindful of Quebec, feared that the rioting would
spread over the border.

In November, 1968, he told a student audience in Kingston,
Ontario, that he foresaw "large rebellions and large disturb-
ances of civil order and of social stability in North America.
. . . I am perhaps less worried now by what might happen
over the Berlin Wall than what might happen in Chicago,
New York and perhaps our own great cities in Canada."

This fear of rebellion, translated as "apprehended insurrection," was to be the key phrase used to justify his government's
incredible actions during the FLQ crisis.

The Front de Libération du Québec was a series of small
terrorist groups rather than a continuing terrorist organization.
They appeared, threatened, planted their bombs, then departed
to jail. Although Montreal is the most violent city in Canada

and its police have not succeeded in controlling organized crime, gang killings or labor thuggery, they have been extremely efficient in arresting terrorists.

The first FLQ group, led by a Belgian, planted dynamite in mailboxes and at military installations symbolic of English Canada and may have had a hand in toppling the Wolfe monument on the Plains of Abraham. They were all safely behind bars by late 1963. Another group took over, using the same initials but stealing rifles and cash instead of bombing. They, too, were soon arrested.

The third FLQ, led by a former sergeant in the French Foreign Legion, held up a Montreal gunshop. Two people were killed in a shoot-out and the gang was jailed for life.

Three down and three to go. Then the terrorists acquired a philosopher: Pierre Vallières, author of *White Niggers of America* (his view of the French Canadians). He was an unsuccessful bomber if, in fact, he was a bomber at all. But, singlehanded, he created the illusion of an omnipresent, idealistic, underground threat to capitalist society called the FLQ.

He was a separatist as well as a Marxist but, strangely enough, he had been greatly admired by Trudeau in his *Cité Libre* days. He and Pelletier appointed Vallières co-editor of the magazine in 1963, although he lasted only six months in the job and became a bitter foe of the founders. The intellectual world of Montreal is a small one.

There were about 200 bomb incidents in Quebec between 1963 and 1970. The home of Mayor Jean Drapeau was blown up; so were the Liberal Reform Club, the Stock Exchange and a federal government bookstore that bore the offensive name of Queen's Printer. Two further generations of FLQ bombmakers went to jail.

Vallières spent three and a half years there, first charged with murder, then convicted of manslaughter following an FLQ explosion that killed a girl. He was released on bail in the summer of 1970 and promptly resumed his propaganda.

He told an interviewer: "Today, the FLQ represents a real political force in Canada. . . . the bombs are only like the tip of the iceberg."

When the crunch came, Trudeau, his old admirer, believed him.

On Monday, October 5, four men with revolvers kidnapped the British Trade Commissioner James (Jasper) Cross from his Westmount home. The first ransom note, bearing the FLQ symbol, demanded $500,000 in gold, the name of the police informer who had broken up the last FLQ gang, release of 23 FLQ "political prisoners," publication of an FLQ manifesto, an aircraft to fly the kidnappers to Cuba, and the rehiring of the mail truck drivers Trudeau had insulted.

The kidnapping of a British diplomat was no ordinary police or provincial matter. The Department of External Affairs was responsible for his safety. At a Cabinet meeting the following day, Trudeau faced his first major decision. He would not give in to outrageous demands, as some Latin American governments had done recently, but he would pretend to negotiate in order to keep Cross alive.

First, he could hope that the Montreal police, with their near-perfect record of capturing terrorists, would find the trade commissioner. They didn't.

On October 8, Trudeau backed down so far as to allow the CBC to broadcast the FLQ diatribe (which, among other things, called him a "fairy"). Quebec Justice Minister Jérôme Choquette refused to release the FLQ prisoners but talked of clemency and offered the kidnappers a free ride to Cuba in return for Cross.

It was an awkward situation but not a national crisis — until Saturday, October 10, when hooded men with an automatic rifle grabbed Quebec Labor Minister Pierre Laporte outside his suburban Montreal home and hustled him off in a blue Chevrolet.

Cross was an outsider, a professional pawn in the international power game. Laporte, a 49-year-old former journalist, was part of the small world of Quebec politics that included Trudeau and, for that matter, Pierre Vallières.

Anthony Westell wrote: "When Laporte was kidnapped, it was suddenly civil war within the family."

Who would be next? Premier Robert Bourassa fled to a guarded suite on the twentieth floor of Montreal's Queen Elizabeth Hotel. Panic struck Ottawa. The government called in 500 heavily armed troops to guard buildings and escort Cabinet ministers — even in the corridors of Parliament. This was the ultimate affront to the dignity of the House. It outraged many M.P.s and at least one reporter, the CBC's Tim Ralfe.

Ralfe confronted Trudeau on the Hill and obtained the most revealing interview he had ever given. It was a filmed argument so heated that the CBC edited most of the sense out of it in an attempt to preserve the myth that its reporters had no opinions of their own. But an unedited version was shown by the rival CTV network and on television screens around the world.

Ralfe challenged Trudeau on the need to have soldiers with guns on the streets. He replied: "Well, there's a lot of bleeding hearts around that just don't like to see people with helmets and guns. All I can say is, 'Go on and bleed.' But it's more important to keep law and order in society than be worried about weak-kneed people who don't like the look of an army."

Asked how far he was prepared to go in reducing civil liberties, he said: "Just watch me. . . . I think that society must take every means at its disposal to defend itself against the emergence of a parallel power which defies the elected power in this country and I think that goes to any distance."

Any distance? Yes. Four days later, on October 16, the Governor-General was awakened at 4 A.M. to sign an order imposing the War Measures Act — martial law.

The police could now search homes without a warrant, arrest people without any charge and hold them in prison without bail. Which they did. More than 400 Quebeckers were incarcerated for up to three weeks because they were separatists or friends of separatists or, in some cases, because they happened to be around when separatists were being arrested. None of them was ever linked directly to the FLQ kidnappings. Yet separatism and terrorism seemed inextricably mixed in the minds of government leaders in Ottawa and Quebec.

Trudeau's declared reasons for invoking War Measures were threefold: two important people had been kidnapped; the Quebec government and the Montreal authorities had asked for exceptional measures because "a state of apprehended insurrection" existed.

"The third reason," he told the House, "was our assessment of all the surrounding facts, which are known to the country by now — the state of confusion that existed in the province of Quebec in regard to these matters."

The state of confusion was real enough. Jean Marchand, then Regional Affairs Minister, talked of an organization with thousands of guns, rifles, machine guns and enough dynamite to blow up the core of downtown Montreal.

"These people have infiltrated every strategic place in the province," he said. "Every place where important decisions are taken."

There was a story — obviously believed by Trudeau and his Cabinet — that a group of important Montrealers was plotting to set up a "provisional government" of Quebec. According to Peter Newman's story in the Toronto *Star*, the government believed the plotters intended to oust Bourassa and this "could have ended in the destruction of democracy in Quebec."

It all started with a meeting in the editorial office of *Le Devoir* where ideas, wild and otherwise, are batted around to stimulate thought. The paper's editor, Claude Ryan, suggested that Bourassa might have to open up his Liberal government to other parties — even separatist leader René Lévesque. According to Ron Haggart and Aubrey Golden in their book on the crisis, *Rumours of War*, Ryan put it to Bourassa, then to Lucien Saulnier, chairman of Montreal's city executive committee. Saulnier disagreed with it, and it died.

It was hardly a seditious idea — coalitions are common in times of war — and five days after it was suggested Canada was legally on a war footing, under an Act that had been framed for use only in World Wars One and Two and left around to be handy for Number Three.

The thought that Trudeau and his brilliant Supergroup were stampeded into a rehearsal for World War Three by two amateur kidnappings, an editorial brainstorm and a state of confusion in a traditionally confused province is hard to take.

Walter Stewart's theory is simpler: "Trudeau saw in the October crisis a chance and a duty to meet what he considers to be the separatist menace head-on, and he took it."

If we accept the picture of Trudeau as the cool, courageous thinker who knew just what he was doing, this makes sense. If we remember his 1968 predictions of "large rebellions," it is conceivable that he lost his cool. Now that the facts of the "insurrection" are on the table, it is evident that he overreacted, to say the least.

However, two days after he proclaimed martial law, an event occurred that brought him instant justification and overwhelming support from the country. Laporte's body was found in the trunk of the abandoned blue Chevrolet. He had been strangled with the chain of a religious medal he wore around his neck.

A national poll showed that four out of five Canadians supported Trudeau's actions and a majority would have sent the army into Quebec to prevent the province from separating.

In fact, two tiny bands of weird-o gangsters were holding the nation at gunpoint while the police had a picnic settling scores they couldn't settle under the law.

As the *Globe and Mail* said, it was a time for "hippie-bashing." All the kooks in Montreal could be rounded up without complaint. It was Canada's answer to the Chicago police riot of 1968.

Pierre Laporte spent the last eight days of his life lying hand-

cuffed on a mattress in a small bungalow in the Montreal sub-
urb of St. Hubert. His captors were Paul Rose, a 27-year-old
former schoolteacher, his brother Jacques and girlfriend Lise
Balcer, Francis Simard and 19-year-old Bernard Lortie. The
Roses had been touring the United States by car when they
heard of the Cross kidnapping, raced back to Montreal and
bought two automatic rifles and a shotgun from a pawnshop.

They had no direct connection with the Cross kidnappers,
who belonged to a separate, and possibly rival, FLQ cell. They
said later they considered Cross an unsuitable victim. A
French-Canadian was needed, so they seized Laporte.

Unlike Cross, the Labor Minister knew the kind of people
who were holding him and understood the danger he was in.
He wrote a shaky letter to "*Mon cher Robert*" Bourassa saying, "decide . . . on my life or on my death. I rely on you and
thank you." The letter asked the premier to call off the police
raids and release the "political prisoners."

When he heard by television of the War Measures Act and
the stepped-up raids, Laporte knew that his time had come.

He slipped out of one handcuff and lunged through a window, pushing a pillow before him. He was pulled back, cut in
the wrists and chest. The next day he was found strangled.

Jasper Cross often thought of Laporte, whom he had never
met, as he sat counting the days in a first-floor apartment on
the Avenue des Recollets. He, too, was handcuffed and wore
a hood that allowed him to look only straight ahead. His kidnappers wore masks when in view and he never saw their faces
until the last day of the drama.

They were Jacques Cossette-Trudel and his wife Louise,
Jacques Lanctôt, Marc Carbonneau and Yves Langlois. From
their conversation he concluded that they were typical revolutionaries, prepared to go to any length including violence
and their own deaths. As a diplomat, he tried to keep up a
polite conversation with them in his none-too-fluent French.

But as he listened to the constant television reports of attempts to find him, and suggestions that he was passing code

messages to the police in the letters his kidnappers made him write, he worried.

"There's been a lot of talk about journalistic responsibility," he said afterwards. "But people have a responsibility to the kidnapped, to the chap in there. He's the loneliest man in the world. And speculation about what he's trying to do may cost him his life."

All the military activity and the "hippie-bashing" failed to locate the kidnappers of Cross or Laporte. They were unearthed by normal police methods.

The Roses and Simard hid out on a farm 20 miles southeast of Montreal. They built a tunnel extending out from the basement, and sheltered there when anyone approached. After the murder they had no bargaining counter and could only wait for arrest. It came on December 27. As they were hauled out of the tunnel, Paul Rose said they were part of a lost generation. Simard said it was cold down in that hole.

On December 4, the RCMP moved in on the Avenue des Recollets. They arrested the Trudels on the street, then occupied the second-floor apartment above the other kidnappers.

Negotiations began. At daybreak the area was surrounded by troops. The kidnappers were allowed to drive Cross in their own car to the Canadian pavilion at the former Expo site, which had been proclaimed Cuban soil for the occasion. There the Cuban consul took charge of the hostage while the terrorists were flown to exile in Cuba.

Jasper Cross said later: "It was a case of six kids trying to make a revolution." Considering the panic they caused, the suspension of law and mass jailings, it was a good try.

If Trudeau had any regrets, he shrugged them off. He told an interviewer: "I didn't have to, sort of, weigh back and forth the kind of struggle that goes on between Creon and Antigone in Sophocles' famous play about what is more important, the state or the individual. Democracy must preserve itself."

Anthony Westell points out that Creon thought he was acting in the best interests of the state when he had his niece

Antigone entombed for defying him. But the gods disagreed and the tragedy ends with Creon crying ". . . all that I can touch is falling — falling — round me, and o'erhead. Intolerable destiny descends."

In the election of October 30, 1972, intolerable destiny descended — not because of the way Trudeau handled the crisis but the way he handled the campaign. It didn't quite crush the philosopher-prime minister, but it brought him to his knees.

The campaign, as he planned it, was to have been a lofty dialogue between the Prime Minister and his people — "conversations with Canadians . . . about the integrity of Canada."

The Liberal advertising machine was proclaiming in words and music: "Together — the Land is Strong." But out in the strong land, unemployment was raging at over 7 percent, and inflation, which Trudeau had pronounced cured, was again battering at the surgery door.

His government had accomplished a lot in four years. By recognizing Communist China it could claim to have prepared the way for the subsequent breakthrough in U.S.-China relations. He had made a successful visit to Russia. He had kept relations with the United States on an even keel, despite the problem he described so graphically in a Washington speech: "Living next to you is in some ways like sleeping with an elephant . . . even a friendly nuzzling can sometimes lead to frightening consequences."

Through the Official Languages Act, he had at least established the goal of bilingualism — that both French and English speakers should be able to make their own way in their own tongue.

And an enormous amount of tax money had been dispensed in hand-out programs, which were viewed as the long-overdue rightings of wrongs, pure-minded charity, low bribes or highway robbery, depending on whether the viewer had been blessed as a giver or a receiver.

More than two billion dollars had been taken from the

rich provinces and given to the poor. The Opportunities for Youth schemes gave the young things to do other than rebel (in fact, they didn't rebel); the Local Initiatives grants provided fascinating forms of nonjobs for the jobless. And the aged got New Horizons activities to keep them amused and off the labor market.

All in all, the Liberals might have run on their record and won handily. Instead, they went back to the big-lie advertising techniques that had served Pearson so badly. The land must be portrayed as strong and united, when in fact it had become a weak dependent of the United States and was less united than ever.

Trudeaumania was dead: the pig had come out of his poke and many voters were ready to send him to market.

He was nearly defeated — for a time the television computers showed the Tories two seats ahead — and the final count showed: Liberals, 109; Conservatives, 107; NDP, 31; Socred, 15; Independents, 2.

Once again, a Pearson-style minority Liberal government. Mike Pearson almost lived to see it, but not quite. He died of cancer on December 27, 1972.

Trudeau was humbled, but not about to don sackcloth and ashes. Instead, he appeared in a brilliant new costume of beaded and fringed buckskin, murmuring his favorite quote from *Desiderata*: "Whether or not it is clear to you, no doubt the universe is unfolding as it should."

When the new Parliament opened on January 4, 1973, he was back in parliamentary dress with, apparently, a new respect for that institution.

It was David Lewis's finest hour. His NDP held the balance of power and the government would live or die by the 31 NDP votes. But he didn't really enjoy it, for with the new power came the responsibility for keeping the Liberals in office. The public didn't want an early election and the parties, particularly the NDP, couldn't afford one.

Lewis steered an uneasy course for 18 months, denting a

few NDP principles along the way, then voted against a Liberal budget, bringing on an election and his own personal defeat.

Trudeau made small bows to the NDP for keeping him in power, but if he bent Liberal principles it was hardly noticeable since the party had always been flexible. It was David Lewis who was dubbed the Happy Hooker.

The summer campaign of 1974 began in apathy. Another six long weeks of speeches stretched ahead, followed, no doubt, by another minority government, possibly even a Tory one.

The Liberals said leadership was the issue; the nation needed a strong, liberated Trudeau, without a David Lewis on his back. The Conservatives chose inflation — the consumer price index had gone up by 11 percent in a year — and claimed they could solve the problem by a 90-day freeze on wages and prices, followed by some form of controls.

Stanfield took this bit between his teeth, ran with it, gagged on it, stumbled and finally tried to spit it out. By mid-campaign it was obvious that Canadians, even Tories, didn't want controls and didn't believe they'd work. By the end Stanfield seemed to agree.

It would be easy to freeze wages — every employer would be delighted to cooperate — but prices were something else again. The notion that industry and workers should sacrifice together to save the economy was an idea whose time had not yet come. Inflation was a bad thing but, as the Liberals pointed out, it was a world-wide problem and Europe was in a worse fix than Canada.

It was not a time for blood, toil, tears and sweat, as Stanfield seemed to be saying, while Canadians still had Band-aids, LIP grants, Kleenex and under-arm deodorants.

Trudeau abandoned slogans and low-key conversations with Canadians and tore into the campaign with the verve of an old-style politico. He promised it would be "less rational and . . . more impassioned" than the 1972 effort; and it was.

For the first time he hurled his wife and family onto the hustings.

The transformation of Trudeau from the swinging bachelor who delighted in not-too-secret dates with actresses to the respectably married statesman had taken place at jet speed.

One night in March, 1971, he was dancing with Liberal matrons in Toronto's Royal York Hotel; the next day he was in Vancouver, suddenly and quietly married to 23-year-old Margaret Sinclair, daughter of a former Liberal Cabinet minister. His friend and closest adviser, Marc Lalonde, didn't even know they were engaged. Gone was the aging playboy: enter the ardent newly-wed, bearing on his arm the loveliest leader's bride since Jackie Kennedy. She was shy, girlish and given to well-photographed kisses, hand squeezes and adoring glances at her husband.

Politically, she was perfect, but Trudeau said she would take no part in politics. The marriage became almost supernatural when it was blessed by two boys, both born, miraculously, on different Christmas Days.

Margaret on the stump, backed by two-year-old Justin and Sacha, a bundle of five months, was almost as devastating in her quiet way as the 1968 Trudeau. It was Maggiemania this time.

When she talked of Pierre: "a quite beautiful guy who has taught me a lot about loving," a new, a startling element entered Canadian politics. *Loving!* It had nothing to do with the rapidly rising price of eggs, but it was much more fun than inflation. The opposition was impotent. To attack Margaret would be worse than damning motherhood; it would be an assault on the madonna of the Christmas miracles.

She campaigned like the politician's daughter she was. When it was over, and Trudeau had won a commanding majority, she checked into hospital for psychiatric treatment.

Back home again, she talked bravely before television film cameras about the strain of being a P.M.'s wife. She described herself as a flower child who had prepared herself for marriage to Pierre, but not the Prime Minister. She said she longed for the day when he would retire. But her efforts had helped enable him to stay in power for another five years, years that would see the breakup of their marriage and his government.

Political and marital decline began immediately after the election triumph which restored his comfortable majority in the House. Within two years the Liberals' popularity rating in the polls reached its lowest since the Diefenbaker sweep of 1958. His "impassioned" campaign, with much shouting on the hustings, had raised expectations of exciting new leadership which were not fulfilled. He waited 84 days to call Parliament while reshuffling his war-weary Cabinet and looking for new policies.

Behind the gates of 24 Sussex Drive he dealt with domestic matters such as the increasingly rebellious Margaret and the installation of a $200,000 swimming pool, paid for by very-anonymous businessmen who wanted to do something nice for prime ministers in general or this one in particular. (The next would be a non-swimmer.)

Trudeau promised to "wrestle inflation to the ground" but his finance minister, John Turner, obviously didn't know the stranglehold to use. Turner, a handsome charmer who once danced the evening away with the young and beautiful Princess Margaret, was touted as Trudeau's successor. But in September, 1975, he resigned to become a grey Toronto lawyer, signalling that the wrestling match had been lost.

A month later Trudeau suddenly embraced wage and price controls ("a proven disaster," he had said) the issue on which he had beaten Stanfield. These would be imposed for three years to create "a breathing space to change our social structure and values in some way."

In a soon-famous Christmas interview with Bruce Phillips of CTV he proposed a way. Pure capitalism was dead. The free-market system didn't work. Looking beyond temporary wage and price controls Trudeau foresaw an "interventionist state" which would keep a tight rein on industry, unions and governments. He mused and rambled, horrifying Canadian business. Pure capitalism had been dead for generations but what he proposed sounded like pure socialism. Was Pierre, the parlor pink of *Cité Libre,* reverting to type? Was Castro's admirer, the adventurer on the U.S. blacklist who tried to canoe to Cuba, finally shedding his cover?

His "musings" reverberated in editorials through 1976. He was accused of every sin from fascism to communism. That one interview alarmed Big Money and Big Labor and reminded small money and small labor that they were now chained by the controls they had voted against.

The advent of a new Conservative leader diverted attention from Trudeau's troubles but did not ease them. Joe Clark did not, at first, look like much of a threat. He was 36, with droopy ears, a receding chin and a wife who wouldn't take his name. A high school debating champion and Tory student leader who had served time in the backrooms of a powerless party. The Ottawa pros said Trudeau would eat him for breakfast.

Still, the Conservative convention of February, 1976, showed television viewers the graceful exit of Robert Stanfield and the selection of a bright, curious new face from a line-up representing the best and the worst of the Tory party.

Eye to eye with Trudeau across the Commons carpet, Clark grew in stature. He wasn't eaten, he was barely nibbled. And he bit back, drawing blood over a series of scandals involving a Liberal senator and two cabinet ministers. Trudeau drooped, and knives were tentatively unsheathed in the backrooms of his party. He might have to go. He didn't seem to *care* any more. And Margaret was becoming a national embarrassment.

After the birth of her third boy, Michel, in October, 1975, she embarked on a part-time career as a photographer, using $2,000 worth of camera equipment given her by King Hussein of Jordan and another free camera she collected in Japan on a junket trip paid for by a Hong Kong shipping magnate who happened to do business with the Canadian Wheat Board. *People* magazine in New York gave her an assignment. A *People* editor admitted that who she was, was as important as her skill with a camera. As the prime minister's wife she used free airline passes on assignments. Eyebrows were raised.

In a radio interview she said she and Pierre had an agreement that while their children were young she would look after the home while he went about his important work. She added: "In the future perhaps this will change . . . I'll be the one who'll go out and fulfill myself outside of the family. He'll be the one who'll take responsibility within the home."

On state visits abroad she began to attract more attention than her husband. She got a lifetime supply of 200 cigars a month from an admiring Fidel Castro (she said she smoked the occasional cigar after dinner, although Pierre detested smoking). This brought threats from anti-Castro Cubans when she visited Florida. At an official function in Venezuela she performed a mock salute during the playing of "O Canada." This flippancy was jumped on by the press who had condoned a worse performance by Trudeau: he was photographed pirouetting behind Queen Elizabeth's back at Buckingham Palace.

But at least Pierre didn't sing. At a banquet in Caracas for Venezuelan President and Mrs. Carlos Andres Perez, Margaret stood up and crooned: "Senora Perez I would like to thank you/I would like to sing to you/To sing a song of love/For I have watched you/With learning eyes./You are a mother/And your arms are wide open/For your children/For your people/Mrs. Perez you are working hard."

Mrs. Perez was delighted. Officials cringed. Margaret sang the song again for radio reporters on the plane home and it was broadcast in Canada. The audience cringed.

Margaret told an Ottawa women's group: "It's the first time I've been free to sing. I'm feeling free. I've got a lot of stories to tell and I'm going to tell them."

Later, she would tell the stories, with devastating effect.

By November, 1976, Trudeau was almost ready to stay home and mind the kids. Then, as he put it, the fates cornered him and put him back to work at the task for which he had entered politics — keeping Quebec in Canada.

The separatist Parti Québécois, led by René Lévesque, took 71 of the 110 seats in Quebec's National Assembly, almost obliterating Robert Bourassa's Liberal regime and leaving Bourassa without a seat. As Lévesque admitted, it was not primarily a victory for separatism. The PQ had campaigned against the corruption of the party in power — the issue on which most Quebec elections are fought, regardless of who's in power. But it promised a referendum to decide whether Quebeckers wanted a new relationship with the rest of Canada. Lévesque called this "sovereignty-association," an undefined have-your-cake-and-eat-it arrangement by which the province would become an independent state but still retain the economic advantages of Confederation.

Trudeau the ex-dilettante and Lévesque the ex-foreign correspondent were men of the world who had known each other for years. In the *Cité Libre* days, when Lévesque was a CBC reporter, they enjoyed bull sessions in Gérard Pelletier's kitchen. But when the Prime Minister wrote to the new premier of Quebec, icily acknowledging his victory, the letter began, "Dear Sir."

There was no hint that Lévesque had just rescued his old friend's career. Trudeau, the fervent Quebec federalist, was the one leader who could save Canada from the pit of separatism. Like him or loathe him, most Canadians felt this instinctively. A few noted that if Trudeau's Quebec policies had been more successful there would be no PQ and no René Lévesque — but they were a silent minority.

In his 1976 year-end talk with Bruce Phillips, the Prime Minister agreed that there was now a "distinct possibility" that Quebec might leave Canada. He hinted at the possibility of civil war, although he said he would not be the man to lead it. Later, he said he might have to use "the sword" if necessary.

Gone, for a while, was the shrugging professor. Here was the tough Trudeau who had faced down in 1968 St. Jean Baptiste Day rioters, the scourge of the "bleeding hearts" during the 1970 FLQ crisis. He welcomed the separatist challenge because, he told Phillips, "Canadians were growing soft in their desire to exist as a country."

This was debatable. Canadians had become hardened to the disregard for civil liberties that began when Trudeau suspended the rule of law during the FLQ crisis. Encouraged by this, the RCMP ran wild in their pursuit of supposed subversives. Officers burgled offices, seized Parti Québécois files, opened masses of private mail and burned a barn. These wrongdoings were revealed at a series of public inquiries but no wrongdoers were charged. Editorial writers raged and a series of former Liberal solicitors-general denied, unconvincingly, that they knew what was going on. The public took the side of the Mounties. The government, supported by Joe Clark, said if the Mounties had broken the law, the law ought to be changed.

Even the persecution of Peter Treu, an engineer subjected to a secret trial and forbidden even to talk about it (he was cleared but never compensated for his ordeal) and the hounding of the anti-Trudeau *Toronto Sun,* whose editor and publisher were threatened with fourteen years in jail for printing "secrets" that were already public, failed to cause an outcry.

Trudeau's clarion call for "national unity" covered the failure of his principal policy to maintain it: bilingualism. Rejecting "special status" for Quebec he spent 10 years and billions of dollars trying to make French Canadians feel at home in other parts of Canada through the official use of their language. Aging civil servants were shipped off for a year to try to learn French, although they might never be called upon to use it. Federal offices across the resentful land sprouted French signs which their occupants couldn't read and bulged with paperwork in both languages. Canada became officially bilingual but showed no signs of becoming actually bilingual. The primary schoolchildren who, alone, could create a two-language society, were given bilingual cornflake packets and little else. Education was a provincial responsibility; and bilingualism aroused dark suspicions in Quebec and irritation elsewhere. It was supposed to assuage the French-speaking minorities outside Quebec and encourage French Quebeckers to venture forth from their ancient sanctuary and mingle. They showed little interest in the French minorities and no desire to leave home. Their governments, beginning with Bourassa's Liberals, moved to drive the English language out of the province.

Trudeau tried to make Ottawa the heart of both Canadas and proved it was the heart of neither. After a decade of official bilingualism a jeweller in Hull, Quebec, within sight of the Peace Tower, was threatened with a $1,000 fine if he refused to take a "Merry Christmas" sign out of his window.

Billions of cornflakes had died in vain.

Official bilingualism was at least an honest try, and the opposition parties supported it, while complaining about the way it was handled. The Canada Day circuses of 1977 and '78 were propaganda exercises, designed to out-shout the voices of discontent in Confederation, using the best singers and the loudest sound systems obtainable.

Dominion Day, July 1, had been a fairly quiet family celebration ever since the Union Jacks waved and the guns boomed for Sir John A's national birthday in 1867. Apart from the genuine outburst of joy in Centennial year, it had become just one more day off. Quebec's St. Jean Baptiste day was a louder, jollier party. After the PQ win, Trudeau decreed a show of federal force in the form of bands, fireworks, rock groups and organized enthusiasm for Canada Day, as it would be called. The centerpiece was an outdoor extravaganza in Ottawa on July 1, 1977, greeted by the worst summer thunderstorm in years.

It cost the taxpayer $3.5 million but a good time was had by most. The theme song "Canada, I Want to Shake You by the Hand" (adapted from "America, I Want to Shake You by the Hand") was marginally better than Margaret Trudeau's ode to Senora Perez.

The tide of ad-agency programmed, government-financed patriotism mounted toward a federal election, expected in the spring of 1978. Election fever rose — Trudeau had been in for four years —then receded as the sad facts of economic life surfaced. Far from being wrestled to the ground, inflation was up and dancing around the ring while the printing presses roared, grinding out cheap money. The supply increased by up to 14.5 per cent a year, while government spending rose by 370 per cent over 10 years.

The patriotic circuses could no longer divert attention from the dubious quality of the bread. Trudeau read his disappointing ratings in the polls and postponed a vote until the fall. The fall brought him disaster in nine by-elections and the general election was off until the spring.

He finally called it for May, 1979, about the last deadline available under the existing constitution. He entered the fray boldly, waving the banner of national unity. It was "almost treasonous" to ignore its importance, he declared. It was the only banner he had, for his latest government had accomplished little in foreign policy, energy policy, provincial relations or anything else during nearly five arid years. He was preoccupied by national unity, meaning Quebec, and the voters were sick of lectures on that subject. Canada was weary of trying to shake itself by the hand. And Trudeau was no longer the only French-Canadian who could take on Premier Lévesque. Claude Ryan, the flint-faced former editor of *Le Devoir,* the man unjustly accused of proposing a "provisional government" during the FLQ uproar, was now leader of the Quebec Liberals. He was another intellectual of the Trudeau-Lévesque type as tough and demanding in his own way.

Trudeau was now a single parent minding the kids. Margaret had walked out in 1977, sporting a black eye, and was raising hell in the haunts of the international jet-setters. The marriage broke up after she spent a couple of days in Toronto as a groupie of the drug-racked British rock group, The Rolling Stones. Juicy newspaper stories about her premarital sex exploits, pot-smoking at Sussex Drive and her fondness for garterbelts had made her a world celebrity of sorts.

She had promised to tell all in her autobiography *Beyond Reason,* due to be published during the election campaign.

Previous prime ministers, particularly Macdonald and Mackenzie, had campaigned bravely with domestic tragedies on their minds. None had been so public as this one. Trudeau rode over the Maggie scandals with grace and dignity. They didn't hurt him but he was doomed anyway.

The country voted heavily against him and just happened to elect Joe Clark — with 136 seats to the Liberals' 114. That night Margaret was photographed kicking up her heels in New York's wildest disco.

Six months later Pierre Trudeau announced that he would resign the leadership of the Liberal party. His voice choked with emotion and tears flowed down his cheeks. He drove home to 24 Sussex. Margaret drove there, too, in her Volkswagen Rabbit, wearing a mink coat and carrying a cat.

An Ontario Liberal watched him go and said, "It's like Judy Garland's last performance. She couldn't sing, she couldn't dance and she had to be taken off the stage."

He was all washed up. *Fini. Kaput.*

Or so it seemed at the time.

**CLARK**
1979-80

# XV.   *The Year of the Child*

Prime-Minister-elect Joe Clark delivered his sonorous victory speech at the Spruce Grove, Alberta, ice rink. He flapped his long, awkward hands in the double V-sign made unpopular by disgraced U.S. President Nixon then strode forth to rule. The RCMP had provided a long, black limousine. Unused to large cars he climbed in, missed the back seat and sat down with a bump on the floor. He would fall further and harder in the next seven months.

His was to be the shortest elected government in Canadian history, and one of the least successful. Whether it was unsuccessful because it was short or short because it was unsuccessful is arguable. Tories, but not all Tories, said he should have been given more time to show what he could do. Liberals and NDPers said no, they'd seen enough.

The Clark government expected to have more time, but didn't bargain for it. It self-destructed. It was a minority that ignored all the rules of minority government. It took the Liberals decades of power to grow their impenetrable layers of arrogance. The Tories graduated from cockiness to arrogance in weeks.

Joe Clark suffered from his media image in an era when media, not manners, make the man. In the panoply of prime ministers he was the tail end, the street-cleaner after the parade of the imperious Trudeau. Still, he *was* Prime Minister, but that was something Canadians never quite accepted.

He was ridiculed but not despised, joked about, but never disliked. Much was made of his age and inexperience — he took office just before his fortieth birthday. But he had worked longer and harder in politics than many of his critics and served a far more rigorous apprenticeship than Trudeau.

He was born and raised in the Tory town of High River, Alberta (pop. 3,000). You could tell it was Tory country because the Social Credit government didn't fill the potholes on the highway. High River nestles pleasantly against the dramatic backdrop of the Rockies. Vast cattle ranches — the Bar U, the EP, the Anchor P — spread out on one side of town and grain fields on the other.

Grandfather Charles Clark founded the weekly *High River Times* in 1905 when Alberta became a province. The previous editor in town was the notorious Bob Edwards whose *Eye-Opener* proved too irreverent for the citizens. Edwards moved his paper, his impish humor, and his jugs of rye to nearby Calgary and High River returned to what Grandfather Clark called "orthodox newspapering." The weekly and the large frame family home were later passed down to Joe's father, who hoped that Joe and his brother Peter would one day take over. But by the time dad retired Peter was a successful lawyer and Joe had decided to spread his wings beyond the foothills. The paper was sold to a longtime employee.

At 16 Charles Joseph Clark won a Rotary Club public speaking contest and with it an "Adventure in Citizenship" trip to Ottawa to see how the country was governed. He saw, and was not impressed. It was the year of the pipeline furor, when the St. Laurent Liberals guillotined debate by imposing closure. Young Clark watched the brawl in the House and concluded "that we didn't have democracy in Canada."

Outside, he met then-Opposition Leader George Drew and John Diefenbaker. The high school debater picked up some of the grave Diefenbaker mannerisms. They sat oddly on a 16-year-old and remained slightly odd as his style matured.

As a campus politician at the University of Alberta Joe tangled with another bright young man who would dog him throughout his political career. Jim Coutts, chubby and baby-faced, was Liberal leader in the student parliament. He became prime minister while Joe only made leader of the opposition. Clark's biographer David L. Humphreys quotes Coutts' opinion of his rival: "in this game you have to be a bit of a sonofabitch. Joe doesn't quite have it."

Coutts became Trudeau's principal secretary and election strategist. In this capacity he lost to Joe in 1979 but beat him hands down in 1980.

Clark the journalist struggled with Clark the politician during his early twenties. He became editor of the university paper, promising to "raise hell and attack convention." He spurned the *High River Times* as too parochial, worked for a while on the Calgary *Albertan,* but downed tools whenever politics called. He took an arts degree with one notable failure — French — failed a year in law at Dalhousie, then returned to the University of Alberta to take a graduate course in political science.

Between these courses, he drifted around Europe. He lived with a family in Bordeaux for several weeks in attempt to learn French but found the family uncommunicative in any language. They ate enormously and slept a lot.

Joe was thrown out of the casino at Monte Carlo for not wearing a tie.

The fleshpots of Europe failed to engulf him. His weakness was Coke which he consumed by the case, accompanied by potato chips, peanuts and candies. He was tall and gangly but Diefenbakerish jowls were sprouting.

While at Dalhousie he was elected president of the Progressive Conservative Student Federation, a position which allowed him to travel Canada, meeting important Conservatives. He moved to the University of British Columbia and worked for Diefenbaker's former justice minister E. Davie Fulton who had taken over leadership of the broken-down B.C. Tory party. When Fulton was crushed by the Socreds he returned to student politics to rescue Diefenbaker. The Chief, ousted by Pearson, was in danger of being ousted as party leader. At the Tory national convention in February, 1964, Clark's students gave him a narrow vote of confidence and Joe was chosen to introduce him to the full meeting.

He described the day in 1957 when Dief thundered into High River bearing his Vision. Joe dropped his schoolbooks and rushed to the town hall to hear him and share It. The Chief, he declared, had wrought a revolution in the attitudes and aspirations of Canadians. His decision to face his critics at the convention was that of a "strong, great man."

The Chief was overwhelmed. Like his hero, Churchill, who cried easily, he knew when to be overwhelmed. "If there were no other rewards in public life," he tremolo-ed, "than to have done what was stated by the brilliant Joe Clark, I would have been rewarded more than I could hope for."

It was the first and probably the last time Joe was described as brilliant. In his last weeks of life, Diefenbaker turned on him and knifed him horribly. But such is politics, the career Clark had now chosen.

Playing barker for Dief was a useful introduction to the national stage but a politician needs roots. So he returned to Alberta to work for Peter Lougheed, the provincial Tory leader. He ran as Lougheed's candidate against the Socred speaker of the legislature. It seemed a hopeless cause but he came within 462 votes of victory.

A Clark campaign flyer, designed to introduce him to the voters of Calgary South was headed, "What'sajoeclark?" The question returned to haunt him when, as opposition leader, he was called "Joe Who?"

Calgary South won him a small pair of spurs. In 1967 the phone rang from Ottawa. Stanfield, having succeeded Diefenbaker, was offering a few weeks' work in his office. Clark moved in as a speechwriter and tried to master Stanfield's slow, drab, responsible but boring style. He spent his evenings reading French novels. His long quest for mastery of French was a measure of his devotion to politics. Eventually his French became fluent.

In the Trudeau era, leaders were expected to be athletic as well as bilingual. As a child, Joe had nearly drowned falling into a river and this had left him with a lasting fear of water. He couldn't swim. He took lessons with classes of children at the Ottawa YMCA but soon gave up and tried another French immersion course at Besançon.

During this period in France he wrote in a letter to David Humphreys: "I don't consider Trudeau a representative Canadian; he is much too rationalist to be French, too inflexible to be Anglo-Saxon; when he went to Harvard he followed his true instinct; he belongs to the modern Puritan society where everything is coded and the code is everything. That is most alarming if one is worried about the various implications of 'continentalism' because, if other prime ministers were continentalists by convenience, Trudeau is by conviction; he prefers the American value system more than that of France or Britain, more than that of Quebec or Ontario. And of course he presumes Alberta not to have one."

This assessment of Trudeau, as viewed from France by the 30-year-old Albertan, was an incisive as any made by grizzled heads in Ottawa.

In 1972 Clark tilled the political soil of Rocky Mountain riding, just west of High River and won the Conservative nomination. When older aspirants accused him of inexperience he gibed that they should be running for the Senate. The Tories swept the west that year and Clark comfortably defeated a popular sitting Liberal.

The new Member arrived in Ottawa and hired a research

assistant who had worked for Stanfield: Maureen McTeer. Politically, she was wise beyond her 20 years. Her father John, who
farmed, raised turkeys and bred horses in Eastern Ontario
brought his six children up as bilingual Roman Catholic
Tories — not necessarily in that order. At 16, Maureen was
president of the Prescott-Russell Young Progressive Conservatives. She went on to law school because, she said, many politicians were lawyers and she was training to become a politician.

Joe took his researcher out to dinner in Hull and they talked
about things other than politics. On the drive home he lost his
way, and was followed and stopped by a Mountie. When he
explained that he was a new Alberta M.P., the officer directed
them back across the river to Ottawa. In this wandered way,
romance began.

They married a few months later. Maureen, a feminist,
decided to keep the name McTeer. She said she wanted to see it
on a lawyer's shingle one day, making her family proud. For an
intensely political couple, and a Catholic Tory couple at that,
this made no political sense. Later, when the Trudeau marriage
was raging out of control and it was obvious that even the philosopher king couldn't rule his flower child, Clark was labelled
the leader who couldn't handle his wife. She had too much chin
and he had too little.

The new morality of the seventies permitted Mr. Smiths to
check into hotels with Miss Joneses but international protocol
hadn't caught up. From time immemorial, the Miss Joneses had
been smuggled up the back-stairs of the chancelleries. When the
Clark/McTeers travelled innocently abroad as prime minister
and wife, some of their hosts had trouble introducing them. In
the early Ottawa days it didn't matter, for Clark wasn't well
known and neither was McTeer.

In June, 1974, Trudeau regained his majority. Stanfield had
now lost three campaigns as Conservative leader. Three strikes
and out. Gracious as ever, he bowed, called a party convention,
and a thin blue line of contenders lined up to vie for his job.

The principal candidates were a strange mixture: Brian Mulroney, dynamic young Montrealer with no Commons experience; Flora MacDonald, one-time party secretary fired by Diefenbaker who went on to become M.P. for Kingston (Diefenbaker, at his nasty best called her "one of the finest women ever to walk the streets of Kingston"); Paul Hellyer, who as Liberal defence minister crammed the armed forces into green busdrivers' uniforms then defected, tried to form his own party and wound up a Tory; Jack Horner, the cartoonist's dream of an Alberta cowboy, who would later defect to the Liberals; Claude Wagner, former crewcut justice minister of Quebec who had grown his hair and become a Tory; Sinclair Stevens, a Bay Street financier unpopular among the Bay Street boys.

And there was Joe Clark, one of the minor hopefuls who weren't thought to have a chance. He was only running because Peter Lougheed, now premier of Alberta and the man who could have had the national leadership for the asking, had chosen to stay in his oil sheikdom. Even in Alberta, Clark ran well behind the muscular, well-horsed Horner gang.

Wagner led on the first ballot. Flora MacDonald, a vibrant but vulnerable woman who truly believed in her fellow man, discovered to her shock and dismay that the lines of delegates wearing her buttons couldn't, at the final moment, bring themselves to vote for a woman.

Stevens threw his support to Clark, who was blossoming as a compromise candidate. Mulroney slid downhill but clung on, not wishing to conspire against Wagner, his fellow-Quebecker. Flora walked steadfastly through the carnivorous crowd on the floor and embraced Joe.

That bravely-timed gesture, plus her undoubted ability, would earn her a top cabinet post. Later that night, she wept at her defeat.

Mulroney caved in too late and went back to private life. Clark won on the fourth ballot.

The delegates chanted "Joe, Joe, Joe!" An unfamiliar name, but they learned fast.

Joe watched in his hotel room as his acceptance speech was

replayed on television, mouthing the words as they came on, savoring them. In a formal setting he was good with words. He wrote sparkling private letters, dazzling even Dalton Camp who called them "nearly unique for their light shafts and needles of wit."

When television entered the Commons (in October, 1977) he shone. But he was strangely inept in dealing with voters on the hoof. Trudeau lectured them or snarled at them. Smalltown Joe greeted smalltowners with ponderous, often meaningless remarks and a dry, nervous chuckle. Warner Troyer *(200 Days: Joe Clark in Power)* observed that he seemed smaller than life-sized. A radio reporter walked past him at a shopping-plaza rally without recognizing him. "I thought he was much shorter," she said.

He is over six feet but, Dalton Camp wrote "[he] is a hard, man to find in a crowd . . . he is easily lost . . . Headwaiters from the Chateau Laurier Grill Room to the Louis IX would have been inclined to seat him by the kitchen door."

He had three years in which to grow as leader before Trudeau finally called an election, but the media stunted his growth. The Joe Who? label stuck. As Charles Joseph Clark he might have shaken it off, but that would have sounded pretentious and out of character. If the United States could have a President Jimmy and Canada a Governor-General Ed (later Edward) Schreyer, why not a Prime Minister Joe?

He was elected in May 1979, and the *Toronto Sun* headlined: "Joe — *That's* Who!"

He was modest at first. As Canada's youngest prime minister, just short of his fortieth birthday, he needed time to caress the purple and munch the royal jelly. The voters had acted to kick Trudeau out rather than put him in. Any first-year political science student knew that.

Ontario, where the votes were, had declared itself fed up with Trudeau's national unity issue, perceiving it to be a red herring trailed to distract them from soaring inflation and the plunging dollar. Quebec had gone Liberal as usual but Joe's west had been won.

Clark had toiled harder than most to learn French and woo

THE YEAR OF THE CHILD

Quebec but to no avail. The nation split at the Quebec border. Two years before, in a Commons speech, he had neatly skewered the Liberal Canada Day concept that diversity was pure joy and hands must be extended to Quebec even if they were not grasped. "We must face the fact," he said, "that difference of language and culture tends to divide, not to unite."

This was the story of Canada, to be repeated in the 1979 and 1980 elections.

Clark was in with a workable minority — 136 PCs to 114 Libs with 27 NDP and five Quebec Socreds. It was workable because Canadians don't take kindly to the costly, drawn-out ordeal of the six- to eight-week campaign decreed by horse-and-buggy law. The NDP would settle for four years of holding the balance of power and if the worst came to the worst, Clark could call on the Socreds for support because they had nowhere to go but out.

If Clark had not partaken of the royal jelly his new finance minister John Crosbie had. "We've got a free hand to do exactly what we think is best for the country," he declared.

They hadn't. Crosbie's appointment should have signalled the death of the Clark government but in that crazy summer all signals were crossed. He was a Newfoundlander whose earthy wit tickled the ribs of the Bay Street boys. He was also the sophisticated scion of a millionaire St. John's family, educated at a posh Ontario private school, a Ph.D. from the London School of Economics and an ex-cabinet minister in Joey Smallwood's Liberal government. Normally a silent brooder, he could leap up and turn his squid-jiggin' Newfie accent on or off as required.

Clark dithered. He waited four-and-a-half months before calling Parliament, longer than any prime minister before him. His campaign promises were put to death as most campaign promises are, but they died screaming, unlike previous Liberal ones that quietly passed on. Promised tax cuts died, so did reduction of interest rates. A "stimulative" budget deficit became a reduced deficit, painful and not stimulatory.

One silly promise overshadowed all the rest. Clark made it in

April to attract the 10,000 Jewish voters in Toronto's Spadina riding where Ron Atkey, a former Conservative M.P., was hoping to squeak back in.

He would move the Canadian embassy in Tel Aviv, where it had been since Canada recognized the new state of Israel, to Jerusalem, affirming Israel's permanent possession of the captured Holy City. The other 41,000 Spadina voters, like the great majority of Canadians, had never considered the location of the embassy and didn't give a hoot. But Atkey thought the promise would gain him a few votes; he put the idea to Jeff Lyons, who had tutored Maureen McTeer for her law exams. Maureen mentioned it to Joe and within six weeks the Middle East was aflame.

Ron Atkey squeaked in but was turfed out nine months later.

Honest Joe tried to keep his promise. Votes had been bought and must be paid for. The day after he took office he said the embassy move was "beyond discussion as to [its] appropriateness."

Flora MacDonald, now external affairs minister, put on a brave smile. Nobody had consulted her. The U.S. State Department warned that Canada was in for trouble. (Jimmy Carter had made a similar promise during his campaign, but had conveniently forgotten it.) A few days later, the principal Arab oil states threatened to cut off supplies to Canada and boycott Canadian trade, then running at $85 million a month. Billion-dollar contracts with Canadian firms were in jeopardy. The Arab Monetary Fund announced that it would stop depositing its petro-dollars in Canadian banks, causing a further slump in the Canadian dollar.

Flora's new ministry was blighted before it could flower. She offered to consult with the Arabs, while assuring the Jews that the move would take place. Atkey, now minister of immigration, baited the Arabs by saying their bark was worse than their bite. Yasser Arafat, pistol-toting leader of the Palestine Liberation Organization, said the Canadian "scoundrels" must be taught a lesson. In a week, the new government seemed to have undone all Lester Pearson's peace work in the Middle

East. It was time to hand his Nobel Peace Prize back.

Somebody, not Atkey, had to be thrown to the Arab wolves. The new government looked for a sacrificial lamb and found a loyal old ram: Robert Stanfield. Flora MacDonald brought off her first diplomatic coup by persuading him to pack his tent to go to the Mideast to cool things down. It was the equivalent of a World War II suicide mission — go and don't come back, at least not for a long time. He was told not to report until the autumn of 1980.

Stanfield flew off silently in the night, carrying brochures of every Mideastern country External Affairs could discover on the map. They'd have ordered him to find Dr. Livingstone if he hadn't been found already.

On the well-tested theory that a prophet is best heard outside his own country and a leader looks better from a distance, Clark flew off to Tokyo and Africa to attend international conferences. He did well, but didn't quite erase his image as the innocent abroad.

On a round-the-world foray as opposition leader he had managed to lose his luggage in the Far East and bump into a bayonet while reviewing Canadian troops in the Middle East. There were no such incidents this trip, but the press spent its time looking for them. His remark on arriving at Tokyo airport, "It's obviously a very significant period for Japan," was the verbal equivalent of bumping into a bayonet.

While he dithered, dust gathered in the empty Parliament Buildings and the mess the Liberals left putrefied across the land.

In August he took his entire government up a mountain to Jasper, Alberta, and surveyed the nation below. The view was grand, the piney air heady and the Tories were carried away by the rapture of it all. They decided to *rule* — that was the word — as if they had a majority. Red Tories like Flora, blue ones like Crosbie and grey ones like Atkey agreed: on their mountain, they were unassailable.

Clark agonized over the promises already broken. "If we don't live up to our promises we're dead."

They descended to the plains and entered Parliament at last

in October. Four weeks later their popularity in the polls had dropped to the point of no return and would stay there until their defeat in February. Why? One theory is that the public switched on their TV sets and were startled to find Joe and his team on the wrong side of the House, the government seats worn shiny by generations of Grits. Another was the embassy affair, most conspicuous of broken promises.

Bob Stanfield returned, unexpected and unwelcome, in the third week of the new Parliament, insisting on submitting an interim report. The gist of it was that the Arabs wouldn't discuss anything until the embassy ploy was abandoned. On October 29, Prime Minister Clark told the House: "We do not intend to move the embassy from Tel Aviv to Jerusalem."

Children in grade school were telling Joe Clark jokes. Teachers giggled and so did provincial Tories. Why was there no turkey for Thanksgiving in High River? Because they sent their turkey to Ottawa. Why does Joe carry a turkey under his arm? Because he may need spare parts. Maureen gave Joe a pair of cufflinks, so he went out and had his wrists pierced. Which of the two fellows in the Santa Claus suits is Joe Clark? The one handing out Easter eggs.

There were no Trudeau jokes. No Margaret jokes either. No jokester could top her exploits.

Nineteen-seventy-nine was the International Year of the Child. In his last weeks, Diefenbaker added his joke: "Canada celebrated the Year of the Child by electing Joe Clark."

The Chief chortled over the lad he had called brilliant. On August 15 he met two Ottawa journalists wearing the black T-shirts stamped Election '79, which the CBC had issued to its technicians. "Ah, yes," he said, "May 22. That was the blackest day in Canada's history. You're right to wear them."

It was the Chief's exit line. He died next day, aged 83. Warner Troyer wrote: "His last day had included the elements he'd have wanted in it — a moment to yarn and reminisce and a final feel of the lance in his hand and the swift barb on his tongue."

No previous prime minister had been called a "wimp" and a

"nerd." The words had not been invented and Canadians had more respect for the institution they had created. Mackenzie King and Bennett had been hated, but hatred conveys respect.

Clark had done nothing to deserve this treatment. Not until December, 1979.

Trudeau's resignation speech on November 21 was surprising in its timing, but not a real surprise. His party's fortunes were on the upswing and the Tories were heading for the lowest rating since polling began 40 years before. But there was no doubt that the Liberals needed a new leader, and Trudeau promised a leadership convention for March, 1980.

Press and politicians gushed with praise, tears and relief. Listening to the all-party tributes in the House, Trudeau observed wryly, "People only begin to admit our qualities when we're on our way out." Few noticed that he wore the familiar yellow rose in his lapel for the first time since his defeat in May. His dress was always a clue to his thinking. "The style," he had quoted, "is the man himself."

A month before he had called on all opposition parties to bring down the government. Cynics remembered this warning and wondered if he were staging a Parthian retreat. Clark was not among them. He was sincere in his motion of gratitude and appreciation to his retiring opponent; equally sincere in his belief that he was now home free for six months at least. The Liberals wouldn't force an election until they had a new leader in place. He could call one, but that wouldn't be the gentlemanly thing to do; besides, the voters wouldn't stand for a winter campaign.

So Trudeau lurked, a fresh rose in his buttonhole, while the Clark government blew itself up.

John Crosbie promised "short term pain for long-term gain" — a majority-rule budget, not the kind you offer voters when an election is in the offing. His excuse was that the Liberal mess was worse than he had imagined and the hard Tory times ahead were really hard Liberal times under new management. People must suffer to get the deficit down. There would be plenty of time to offer succor and sweetmeats before the next election. The benefit of banging your head against a brick wall is that it feels so good when you stop.

On December 13 he hurled his thunderbolt.

The House was in an ugly mood. In an attempt to fulfill its one remaining major promise — a tax deduction for mortgage holders — the government had threatened to impose the same closure of debate that had appalled young Joe, the high school debater, in 1956. The NDP were disgruntled; they had kept a Liberal minority government in power for two years and ended up losing seats and looking like pimps; they weren't about to do the same for the Tories. The humble Socreds had begged to be recognized as an official party faction in the House, although they didn't have enough seats. This would have given them much-needed cash to pay staff and acquire dignity. Clark had ignored them, assuming they would vote with him anyway because they knew they'd be wiped out in an election.

Crosbie hit Canadians in their vitals, the automobile gas tank. He raised the excise tax on a gallon of gasoline by 18 cents and promised Alberta a lot more money for its oil at the wellhead. The extra tax money would help reduce the federal deficit but, in real political terms, nobody cared about the deficit. Dearer gas and oil meant dearer everything, for goods had to be transported great distances and most Canadians had to drive to work or play.

Mackenzie King could have steered a tougher budget through without even consulting his mother's ghost. Macdonald, Laurier, even Diefenbaker might have done it. Clark and his green team didn't steer, they drove.

They could have postponed the budget debate until all their troops were in line; instead, they allowed Flora MacDonald to jet off to Paris. The lame-duck Liberal leader had warned that he intended to bring them down but until the last moment they believed that diplomatic sickness would keep enough Liberals at home to enable them to survive. (Genuinely sick Liberals were being carted from their beds and lugged into the House to vote; somebody should have noticed this.)

The NDP, who introduced the no-confidence motion, didn't

expect it to pass. They shared the general contempt for the Socreds, who would bow and scrape to keep their jobs. The Socreds didn't; that afternoon they decided to go down with colors flying and abstain from voting.

Miss MacDonald was summoned back from Paris but missed the flight by ten minutes. It didn't matter. The Clark government was defeated by three votes.

Pearson once weaseled out of defeat on a money bill but there is no escape from a rejected budget.

Clark smiled tightly and called an election for February. Parliament expired with a wheeze and a grumble. The Tory players left the green-carpeted field in a daze, barely comprehending that some of them would not be back. The only noticeably angry man was Crosbie, the noisy architect of disaster.

In its brief span the Clark government had introduced a couple of important measures — a freedom of information bill which would have pried loose needlessly held government secrets and a parliamentary reform to strengthen the hand of MPs in dealing with ministers. But it only passed one bill — a change in pensions.

Pierre Trudeau stayed modestly in the shadows while his party argued who should lead them into the apparently unwanted election. There was never much doubt. There was no time to find a new leader, mount him on his horse, and send him into battle.

The call came three weeks after he resigned. "My duty is to accept the draft of my party," he said. "That duty was even stronger than my desire to re-enter private life." If elected he would serve as prime minister but turn the job over to a successor well before the next election. This would be his last campaign.

Tories greeted this as the least credible promise of the 1980 election. There were suspicions that the aging Machiavelli had orchestrated the whole thing. By resigning he had encouraged young Joe to plunge over the brink, knowing that his disaffected Liberals had no one else to turn to.

Another theory is that he read his own obituaries — a privilege granted to few, if any — and didn't like what he read. Even his approving biographer George Radwanski had said he was "unfulfilled." Perhaps he just looked through hooded eyes at the incredible events of December and decided that the universe was unfolding as it should.

A new, new Trudeau emerged, a leader shy, cold and remote, shaking few hands, offering nothing new and sleep-walking from coast to coast. His handlers Coutts and Keith Davey, concluding correctly that their leader had lost the last election single-handed, resolved to keep him under wraps as far as decency allowed in a democracy.

He was part of the Liberal "team," which barely existed, for the best men had either left or decided not to return when Pierre raised himself from the dead. Faceless candidates were propped up behind him while he went through a standard, passionless, speech, then dodged out through the wings, avoiding the press. He gave no interviews. He had nothing to say; he was just doing his bit for the party and if elected, he'd quit. This dubious promise was more appealing than the Conservative call for dearer gasoline, cigarettes, alcohol; higher taxes and pain for all.

It was the strangest election ever. No party had ever run under the banner of higher taxes and no leader had promised that someone else would lead.

On the surface, the issue was the price of fuel, a vital issue in a Canadian winter. The Liberals offered cheaper gas and oil but wouldn't name a price. The Conservatives, carrying the premier of Alberta around their necks, named their price. But the price of everything was rising by the month, so neither promise was taken seriously.

The real issue was incompetence (Clark) versus trickery (Trudeau). Given the choice between a fool and a villain, the public will always choose the villain. By the time the vicious TV commercials launched by both sides had taken effect, that seemed to be the choice.

The Conservative commercials showed Trudeau, the man to vote against, while hiding Clark. The Liberals featured a leading

Conservative, Premier William Davis of Ontario. Both approaches were nasty, but the Liberal nastiness struck home.

Davis was shown criticizing Clark before the election. He had good reason to. As master of the Big Blue political machine which had powered Ontario since the 1930s he put it to work for Clark in the 1979 election. In return, he wanted a strong Ontario presence in the Clark cabinet and cheap oil for the lamps of Toronto. He got neither. At the Jasper summit, Clark convinced himself that he didn't need Davis. He offered Lougheed a better price for his province's oil than Trudeau was prepared to give. So the Big Blue Machine worked at half speed in the 1980 campaign.

The Liberal way of keeping Canada together was to maintain strict control of the provinces from Ottawa, while offering judicious bribes. Clark wanted to relax this control. "The way to build a whole nation is to respect our indivisible parts," said his throne speech.

These respected parts were not indivisible. Quebec separatism was barely mentioned during the campaign because Trudeau, who had harped on it for so long, was keeping a low profile and Clark thought the separatists had had far too much free publicity already. The east-west conflict was warming up. Alberta was holding the rest of the country up to ransom for its oil, and Clark was seen to be on the side of his native province. Western alienation was rivalling separatism as the national worry. Ontarians remembered the bumper stickers pictured in Alberta a few years before: "Let the Eastern Bastards Freeze in the Dark." They were slowly beginning to resent the western bastards.

In mid-campaign, Clark had a sudden stroke of luck. Muslim fanatics were holding 50 Americans hostage in the U.S. Embassy in Iran. A further six who had been outside the compound when it was captured took refuge in the Canadian embassy and were hidden there for two months until smuggled out to freedom, disguised as Canadians. This feat, engineered by the Canadian ambassador Kenneth Taylor, caused an instant outpouring of

American enthusiasm for Canada and Canadians. Taylor got a Congressional medal and Canadians visiting the States found themselves acclaimed as vicarious heroes, feasted, toasted and *loved* for helping the U.S. in its time of helpless frustration.

The grey External Affairs Department of the Pearson years suddenly became a band of adventurers, led by Flora, the dashing lady buccaneer. She and Clark handled the flood of American tributes with just the right degree of modesty and regret that the affair had come to light. Trudeau was ungracious. He offered half-hearted congratulations to External "if" the story was true.

Miss MacDonald lost no time in telling the country that he knew it was true. He had been informed from the start that Canada was hiding the Americans, but had insisted on attacking the government for not doing enough in Iran and had almost provoked her into revealing the existence of the hidden six.

The "Canadian Caper" as it was called, rallied some support for Clark, but not enough. Trudeau was still promising cheaper oil. PetroCanada, the crown oil company created by the Liberals at the insistence of the NDP, was a side issue. Clark had promised to turn it over to private enterprise, then backtracked and promised to keep most of it. PetroCan had little to do with the price of oil but the government's handling of it indicated indecision, coupled with a desire to sell out to the Albertans and the oil companies.

On election night Joe Clark was back in the Spruce Grove arena watching the hopes of nine short months ago crumble all around him. Maureen stood beside him, tears welling in her eyes as the inevitable results flowed in. The polls had been right. They had scarcely changed since November. Trudeau was back with a bulletproof majority — 146 Libs, 103 PCs, 32 NDP. As expected, the Socreds were wiped out.

Clark had blamed "the wimp factor," the image of stumbling incompetence built up by the media since he lost his baggage at an airport. He said he should have paid more attention to public relations and less to governing.

On election night he admitted his crucial mistake. "Me of all people, I forgot about politics." He had forgotten the politician's duty to pay his political debts, the minority leader's need to keep Parliament happy, and the ancient rule that you don't win elections by promising to dun the electorate for more money.

The *Canmore Miner,* an Alberta weekly, once advised him: "As long as you continue to remain an ordinary Joe and don't forget to consider the hopes and dreams of the other Joes across the country you'll do all right." But, as Val Sears of the *Toronto Star* pointed out, Canadians did not want an ordinary Joe.

They never did. The last ordinary Joe was Mackenzie Bowell, betrayed by his "nest of traitors," and before him Sandy Mackenzie who failed, he complained, because he couldn't qualify as a horse thief or a chiseller.

Pierre Trudeau sauntered back to power. "Well, welcome to the 1980s," he grinned. "I have promises to keep," quoth he. "And miles to go before I sleep." There was no immediate mention of his promise to quit. With no obvious successor in his cabinet or on the horizon, he could rack up as much mileage as he wished.

The Year of the Child was over and forgotten. By the time Parliament reopened with Trudeau in his familiar seat it seemed that it had never happened. The clock had been turned back and the Clark interlude erased from memory like an old video tape. Quebec separatism was again the vital issue, and this time the threat was imminent.

Réne Lévesque called his referendum vote for May 20. He asked for a mandate from Quebeckers to negotiate with the rest of Canada as leader of a Quebec "nation," equal in status to Canada. By agreement with Canada, Quebec would "acquire the power to make its laws, levy its taxes and establish relations abroad — in other words, sovereignty — and at the same time to maintain with Canada an economic association including a common currency." The result of these negotiations would have to be approved through a second referendum. The voters — all adult residents of the province including those residing reluctantly in jail — were asked to record a simple *Yes* or *No* to the proposal.

In labor terms it fell short of a regular strike vote. The union leader was demanding the authority to arrange a walk-out, but would come back to the membership before ordering the workers to hit the bricks. So voters could register a protest against the rest of Canada without real inconvenience. Early polls indicated that they would; the *Yes* side was in the lead.

Claude Ryan, leader of the *No*s, showed little of Lévesque's fire and TV professionalism but repeated grimly and convincingly that he could get more out of Ottawa from within Confederation than any separatist balancing on its walls. Ottawa and the English provincial premiers hailed and supported him while realizing, with a sinking feeling, that he could be just as hard to deal with as Lévesque.

Trudeau was at his best. He declared firmly that sovereignty-association wouldn't wash. If Quebeckers voted to negotiate it they were wasting their time, for there would be nobody to negotiate with. A *Yes* vote meant a dead end; a *No* vote would bring change. If the *No*s won, he promised a new constitution for Canada and a new deal with Quebec. Therefore a *Yes* meant *No* to progress and vice versa.

This ingenious argument probably had less effect than his emotional pleading at rallies in Quebec, but between them he and Ryan put across the message that Quebec's battle had been won before the vote was taken. The union's demands would be met without a strike.

It was a victory for Canada but not a decisive one. The *No*s won by 59.5 to 40.5 per cent in a massive turnout of 85 per cent of eligible voters. But by the time the solidly *No* non-Francophone vote was deducted, French Quebec had split almost down the middle, with a tiny margin to the *No*s. (The prison population voted overwhelmingly *Yes*.)

As Lévesque brushed the mist of defeat from his eyes he muttered "Next time."

Canadian unity had been saved, but it could not be the same kind of unity. Trudeau had promised sudden and dramatic changes which meant, in effect, more power to the provinces. A new deal for Quebec meant either "special status" which Trudeau had opposed throughout his career, or new deals for everyone else too.

Canada's constitution, the British North America Act, still lay mouldering in its pigeon-hole in London because a decade of dreary federal-provincial conferences had produced no agreement on how to "patriate" it (bring it under Canadian jurisdiction) and what to do with it if it were "patriated." ("Patriate" is a Canadian buzz-word that appears in no standard dictionary because only Canadians need to use it.)

The federalist victory in Quebec settled nothing; it only spurred the age-old search for a settlement which had eluded Pierre Trudeau as it had eluded prime ministers before him.

He once said that being prime minister was a lot of fun. Joe Clark, who barely had time to savor it, called it a marvellous job.

It is a peculiar job. Canadian prime ministers are more like field surgeons than warrior kings, forever staunching the nation's wounds rather than slaying the enemy. The national jigsaw is always threatening to fall apart. The threat was as real in Macdonald's 1860s as it is in Trudeau's 1980s.

Yet somehow the puzzle holds together.

# Selected Books on the Subject

Aitken, William Maxwell (Lord Beaverbrook). *Friends, Sixty Years of Intimate Personal Relations with Richard Bedford Bennett.* Toronto: Heinemann, 1959.

Allen, Ralph. *Ordeal By Fire.* Toronto: Doubleday, 1961.

Biggar, E. B. *Anecdotal Life of Sir John A. Macdonald.* Montreal: John Lovell and Son, 1891.

Beal, John R. *The Pearson Phenomenon.* Toronto: Longmans, 1964.

Borden, Robert Laird. *Memoirs* (two volumes). Toronto: Macmillan, 1938.

Creighton, Donald G. *John A. Macdonald: The Young Politician.* Toronto: Macmillan, 1952.

—— *John A. Macdonald: The Old Chieftain.* Toronto: Macmillan, 1955.

—— *Dominion of the North.* Toronto: Macmillan, 1957.

Dafoe, J. W. *Laurier: A Study in Canadian Politics.* Toronto: Thomas Allen, 1922.

Dawson, Robert MacGregor. *William Lyon Mackenzie King: A Political Biography.* Toronto: University of Toronto Press, 1958.

Ferns, H. S. and B. Ostrey. *The Age of Mackenzie King.* Toronto: Heinemann, 1955.

Fox, Paul. *Politics: Canada.* Toronto: McGraw-Hill, 1962.

Fraser, Blair. *The Search for Identity.* Toronto: Doubleday, 1967.

Graham, Roger. *Arthur Meighen* (three volumes). Toronto: Clarke Irwin, 1960. 1963, 1965.

Haggart, Ron, and Aubrey Golden. *Rumours of War.* Toronto: New Press, 1971.

Hardy, W. G. *From Sea Unto Sea.* New York: Doubleday, 1960.

Hogan, George. *The Conservative in Canada.* Toronto: McClelland and Stewart, 1963.

Hutchison, Bruce. *The Incredible Canadian.* Toronto: Longman, Green, 1952.

―― *Mr. Prime Minister.* Toronto: Longmans, 1964.

Lower, Arthur. *Colony to Nation.* Toronto: Longmans, 1964.

Maclean, Andrew D. *R. B. Bennett, Prime Minister of Canada.* Toronto: Excelsior Publishing Co., 1935.

Massey, Vincent. *On Being Canadian.* Toronto: J. M. Dent, 1948.

Meighen, Arthur. *Overseas Addresses.* Toronto: Musson Book Co., 1921.

Merchant, Livingston T. (editor). *Neighbors Taken For Granted.* Toronto: Burns and MacEachern, 1966.

Minifie, James M. *Peacemaker or Powdermonkey: Canada's Role in a Revolutionary World.* Toronto: McClelland and Stewart, 1960.

Newman, Peter C. *Renegade in Power: The Diefenbaker Years.* Toronto: McClelland and Stewart, 1963.

―― *The Distemper of Our Times.* Toronto: McClelland and Stewart, 1968.

Peacock, Don. *Journey into Power.* Toronto: Ryerson, 1968.

Pickersgill, J. W. *The Mackenzie King Record.* Toronto: University of Toronto Press, 1960.

Pope, Sir Joseph. *Memoirs of the Rt. Hon. Sir John A. Macdonald.* London: Oxford University Press, 1930.

Reid, J. H. S., Kenneth McNaught and Harry Crowe. *A Source-book of Canadian History.* Toronto: Longmans, 1959.

Roberts, Leslie. *The Life and Times of Clarence Decatur Howe.* Toronto: Clarke Irwin, 1957.

Schull, Joseph. *Laurier.* Toronto: Macmillan, 1965.

Skelton, O. D. *Life and Letters of Sir Wilfrid Laurier* (two volumes). Toronto: McClelland and Stewart, 1965.

Stewart, Walter. *Shrug: Trudeau in Power.* Toronto: New Press, 1971.

―― *Divide and Con.* Toronto: New Press, 1973.

Stuebing, Douglas with John Marshall and Gary Oakes. *Trudeau: A Man for Tomorrow.* Toronto: Clarke Irwin, 1968.

Sullivan, Martin. *Mandate '68*. Toronto: Doubleday, 1968.

Thomson, Dale C. *Alexander Mackenzie: Clear Grit*. Toronto: Macmillan, 1961.

—— *Louis St. Laurent Canadian*. Toronto: Macmillan, 1967.

Van Dusen, Tom. *The Chief*. Toronto: McGraw-Hill, 1968.

Westell, Anthony. *Paradox, Trudeau as Prime Minister*. Toronto: Prentice-Hall of Canada, 1972.

Wilson, W. A. *The Trudeau Question*. Montreal: Montreal Star, 1972.

## For Sixteen Men

Butler, Rick and Carrier, Jean-Guy. *The Trudeau Decade*. Toronto: Doubleday, 1979.

Camp, Dalton. *Points of Departure*. Toronto: Deneau and Greenberg, 1979.

Humphreys, David L. *Joe Clark*. Toronto: Deneau and Greenberg, 1978.

Nolan, Michael. *Joe Clark: The Emerging Leader*. Toronto: Fitzhenry and Whiteside, 1978.

Radwanski, George. *Trudeau*. Toronto: Macmillan, 1978

Troyer, Warner. *200 Days. Joe Clark in Power*. Toronto: Personal Library, 1980.

Trudeau, Margaret. *Beyond Reason*. New York: Paddington Press, 1979.

# Index